My Life Becoming A Minister

Jerome Meriweather

Copyright © 2019 by Jerome Meriweather

All rights reserved. No part of this publication may be reproduced by any means, graphics, electronic, or mechanical, including photocopying, recording, taping, or by any information storage retrieval system without the written permission of the publisher except in the case of brief quotations embodied in critical articles and reviews.

Jerome Meriweather/Rejoice Essential Publishing
PO BOX 512
Effingham, SC 29541

www.republishing.org

Unless otherwise indicated, scripture is taken from the King James Version.

Scripture quotations marked (ESV) are taken from the Holy Bible, English Standard Version (ESV) is adapted from the Revised Standard Version of the Bible, copyright Division of Christian Education of the National Council of the Churches of Christ in the U.S.A. All rights reserved.

Scripture quotations marked JUB (or JBS) are taken from the Jubilee Bible (or Biblia del Jubileo), copyright © 2000, 2001, 2010, 2013 by Russell M. Stendal. Used by permission of Russell M. Stendal, Bogota, Colombia. All rights reserved.

Scripture quotations marked (NASB) are taken from the New American Standard Bible® (NASB), Copyright © 1960, 1962, 1963, 1968, 1971, 1972, 1973, 1975, 1977, 1995 by The Lockman Foundation Used by permission. www.Lockman.org

Scripture quotations marked (BLB) are taken from the Holy Bible, Berean Literal Bible, (BLB) Copyright ©2016 by Bible Hub

Used by Permission. All Rights Reserved Worldwide. http://literalbible.com/

Scripture quotations marked (NIV) are taken from the Holy Bible, New International Version®, NIV®. Copyright © 1973, 1978, 1984, 2011 by Biblica, Inc.™ Used by permission of Zondervan. All rights reserved worldwide. www.zondervan.com The "NIV" and "New International Version" are trademarks registered in the United States Patent and Trademark Office by Biblica, Inc.™

My Life Becoming A Minister/ Jerome Meriweather

ISBN-13: 978-1-946756-88-6
LCCN: 2019919961

Dedication

This book is dedicated to Jesus Christ, my wife, Ramona Ellis Meriweather; my mother, Anna Louise Slaughter-Meriweather; my dad, Reverend Judge Lent Meriweather; my children, Jerome Jr. and Katelyn; my granddaughter, Joy; my family, Judge Jr., Christine, Geraldine, Doris, Robert, Gary, Kathy, Greg, Timothy; Jerome Jr. and Lynn; my grand daughters, Joy and E'morej. my grandson, Jerome lll and my friends, Keith Hodge, Cortez Collins, Barry Paddock Sr., Barry Paddock Jr., David Barclay, Mrs. Lawrence, Ron Scoon, Ted MCcreary, Mike Kough, Mike Ballard, Norma Bailey-Payne, and Ernest Payne.

Endorsements

Minister Jerome Meriweather's story of his journey to answering the call to ministry is both insightful and inspiring. His transparency and honesty relating to life's challenges and victories is an encouragement to all those that may doubt their worth and insufficiency to God's service. It is a reminder that God's grace covers us all and His divine purpose will always be accomplished.

Pastor Bishop Rice
New Jerusalem Worship Center
122-05 Smith Street; Jamaica, NY 11434

***

Minister Jerome Meriweather has an extraordinary story about many hardships and how he found the Lord Jesus Christ. People who turn to sex, drugs, and a lifestyle of darkness need to hear his testimony to encourage them to turn to Jesus. As you read the pages inside, you will encounter God's grace and appreciate Minister Jerome Meriweather's transformation.

Kimberly Moses
Creator at Rejoice Essential Magazine
Publisher at Rejoice Essential Publishing
Kimberly Moses Ministries

***

TABLE OF CONTENTS

DEDICATION'..v

INTRODUCTION...1

CHAPTER 1:   Childhood.....................3

CHAPTER 2:   Adolescence................16

CHAPTER 3:   Adulthood...................43

CHAPTER 4:   My King Passed Away................68

CHAPTER 5:   My Queen Passed Away.............95

CHAPTER 6:   Jesus Christ Ministries/
                  Ohio..121

CHAPTER 7:   Jesus Christ Ministries/
                  Missouri...................................133

CHAPTER 8:   Jesus Christ Ministries/
                  St. Louis..................................158

CHAPTER 9   Jesus Christ Ministries/
                  Jacksonville...........................173

CHAPTER 10:	Jesus Christ Ministries/ California	193
CHAPTER 11:	Jesus Christ Ministries/ Atlanta, GA	233
CHAPTER 12:	Jesus Christ Ministries/ New York City	247
CHAPTER 13:	Jesus Christ Ministries/ Dallas, Texas	263
CHAPTER 14:	Jesus Christ Ministries/ Houston, Texas	273
CHAPTER 15:	J-C Rehab/Jamaica, New York	284
CHAPTER 16:	My New Home	298
CHAPTER 17:	My Initial Sermon - Prodigal Son	304
CHAPTER 18:	The Wedding	313
CHAPTER 19:	Honeymoon	320
CHAPTER 20:	My Back Surgery	331
CHAPTER 21:	Relationships	343

CHAPTER 22:	Basketball Hall of Fame	374
CHAPTER 23:	Grandson	390
CHAPTER 24:	New York Seminary	402
CHAPTER 25:	Fire Safety Director	419
CHAPTER 26:	Merry Christmas	433
CHAPTER 27:	Happy Birthday	449
CHAPTER 28:	Happy New Years	465
CONCLUSION		470
ABOUT THE AUTHOR		473

Introduction

This book is about my childhood, adolescence, and adult life. I grew up in Evansville, Indiana. During my childhood, I had some very good and sad times. Somehow God was with me all the time. I fondly recall my first day in preschool. I was scared and lost. I didn't know what I was getting myself into. When I went to the first-grade, my teacher, Mrs. Lawrence, was so nice to me. She would always talk to me. She was very positive. I loved school when I was a kid. I had a lot of friends. I liked to go to recess and played basketball every day. We had competition for a few minutes before recess. I remember coming to class sweaty. I would wake up early in the morning and go to my neighborhood community center to play sports every Saturday. My first girlfriend lived down the alley. I met her when I was about nine years old. It's funny because I still remember my old address and phone number when I was a kid.

I was in a car accident where someone was killed. I was in so much pain. I turned to drugs and alcohol to cope with the fact that I lost a close friend. He was my best friend and I didn't want to live. I didn't get the chance to say goodbye because the funeral was held when I was in the hospital. We had a lot of things in common. We had much respect for one another. After these bad things happened to me, I asked God, "Why do bad things happen to good people? Why did it happen to me?" I had goals and dreams. There are things in my life that I didn't understand. I reflected when I was four years old. I went to church with my parents. My father was a minister, and my entire family attended church every Sunday. However, one day, my life was turned upside down. It felt like a roller coaster ride. By the time I entered high school, I was a full-blown alcoholic and addict. My mind and body were different. I was contemplating suicide. I was in numerous bad relationships.

Today, Jesus gets all the credit. I'm a minister in New York City.

CHAPTER 1

Childhood

Proverbs 22:6 (ESV) says, "Train up a child in the way he should go; even when he is old, he will not depart from it."

I was born on December 28, 1967. I was the eighth child out of nine siblings. My parents were Rev. Judge L. Meriweather and Anna L. Meriweather. I grew up in a small town in Evansville, Indiana. We were poor and didn't have much, but we were happy with what we had. We went to church every Sunday. When I was five years old, my Grandma Alma and my parents attended Ebenezer Baptist Church. My grandma played a significant role in the church. Jesus Christ was all she knew. Therefore, my father became a minister.

My brothers and sisters got along with one another. We had our neighborhood friends come over on Saturday mornings. We played in the dirt, sang songs, laughed, and cried. My brothers Gary and Greg were close to me. They were strong and courageous. My oldest brother Robert was in the military and was stationed in Fort Hood, Texas. I remembered when he came back from Korea on leave, he brought me a nice sweat suit.

We lived at 513 East Division Street near railroad tracks, locomotives, and train stations. They blow their horns and whistles every night while we were asleep. My brothers and I stayed up all night playing even though we had to wake up early the next morning to attend Lincoln School.

My father didn't play. One time he warned us once to go to bed. He was upset. One late night, my brother dared someone to be dumb enough to get some snacks. We tried to sneak downstairs, and fire came from the gun that my father shot in the air to scare us. That put fear in my heart, which stayed with me about my dad.

My mother was sweet until you made her mad. She was nice, smart, and played the piano at our church. She worked several jobs and provided the best she could for us. Jesus Christ was the number one priority in my parent's lives. They believed that God and family were everything that they needed. I was fortunate to have both of my parents in my life. It was a luxury. I could talk to both even if the other wasn't around.

There was an old Caucasian lady that lived next door named Mrs. Jordan. On the other side of her was an open lot. She would watch us play with our friends. She would peek out her window often. She dressed old fashioned: black reading glasses, and old mother Hubbard shoes. She stood out because she was original. She lived on the left side of us. The Corbett family lived on the right side, and they were African American. Their names were Beckey, Tilley, Chris, Eleanor, and Alfred. They were nice, and our family would talk to them all the time. We had fun together and attended BBQs in our backyards. Gary and Greg helped our father to help prepare for cookouts.

Psalm 34:18 (ESV) says, "The Lord is near to the brokenhearted and saves the crushed in spirit."

When I was five years old, I attended Lincoln School for Kindergarten. Lincoln School was an African American school from K-8 grades. When I was six and seven years old, my siblings and I had to ride a bus to Harwood Elementary. I was confused and didn't understand why we had to ride the bus five to ten miles away from our home. Harwood Elementary was predominantly white or about 75% white. It was different from what I was used to. Every morning, my brother Timothy and I would stand at the bus stop and anticipated the long bus ride to the north side of town. It would take about twenty to thirty minutes because the bus had to pick up the rest of the students along the way.

The grade school that I attended was very special because I met a teacher named Mrs. Lawrence. She was nice and we clicked immediately. She was my first-grade teacher. She was classy and respected others. This was the first time in my life where I saw eye-to-eye with a woman of the opposite color.

Unlike my next-door neighbor, Mrs. Jordan, Mrs. Lawrence was articulate, funny, young, and nice looking. She had style and charisma. She was educated and treated me like her son. She didn't care what others thought, and she was authentic. She was kind to everybody.

One day as I walked down the hall to History class, I met Mr. Barclay. He was a very nice person and helped change my life as a young boy. He cared for me. I tried out for the basketball team at school and made it. Mr. Barclay would give me rides home after school after practice. He would also take me out to eat after a game and treated me like his son. We played games on Friday evenings and won most of them. At eight years old, I remember playing a game where I scored 51 points! On Saturdays, I would go to the community center to play sports and then go to the girls and boys club. On Sundays, it was church for me. I had a regular routine. At the community center, kids from the south side of Evansville were there.

My entire family was tight, and we had each other's backs. My sisters and I had a good relationship. One of my sisters, Doris, was my favorite. We got along very well because we clicked and had fun all the time. She was witty and fun to be around. She was daring and the type of person I didn't have to worry about. She managed to hold her own. My youngest sister Kathy was daddy's and grandma's girl. She was protected and well-loved. She still believes in God. Geraldine is the quiet sister and the second to my oldest sister. She is kind and charming. My oldest sister Christine is like the mother figure of all my sisters. I remember when I was eight years old, she would ask things such as, "What are you doing today?" or "How are you?" She would always ask questions.

My mother raised my sisters to be very intelligent and beautiful women. I watched my mother teach them how to cook, clean, wash clothes, and wash dishes. In the late 70s, dishwashers did not exist. All the children helped. My childhood wasn't dull. I had good relationships with most of my family members. We went to Amusements Parks in Kentucky. We went to State Parks. We had picnics, family reunions, and family outings. I had friends from all over. My family was well known throughout the city.

Even though we did things as a family, I thought about how it would be like if I did things alone. I wanted to see how it would be like if I played and ate by myself. I wanted to feel some independence. When my family wasn't around, I tried to create my surroundings. I wanted to play sports. I played basketball everyday whether or not it was snow, rain, and sleet. I thought basketball was going to be my first love. I realized that Jesus Christ was always my first love because I was innocent, and I didn't know any better or about what I wanted to do with my life. I was so fragile and helpless. I just went with the flow. Most of my aspirations were what my parents did. It wasn't about us but Jesus and the family.

It is difficult being an eight-year-old African American kid. There wasn't much for me to do other than play basketball. I would run up and down the basketball court for hours. There were times that we played pickup games. We would play two and three games. One day we played seven games. I imagined that we were in the NBA. I remember talking to a cheerleader after some of those games. She was from Arkansas, and her name was Monica. She was very nice to me, but I was shy. She looked me in the eyes. She lived several blocks from me. As young as I was, it wasn't unusual for me to talk or play with girls because I would play with some of my sister's friends. I saw how these girls acted and saw which one I was interested in. Growing up in Southern Indiana is like giving you a chance to choose what you want to do in life. I felt like I had all the time in the world to make up my mind. However, in truth, I was young and dumb while my life was passing me by. I thought that I had all the time in the world to get my life in order.

My parents kept my sisters, brothers, and me together. It was amazing to have a house, and we were like our own little army. I had five older brothers telling me what to do all the time. It got on my nerves. It changed my perspective about how much I could get away with. My oldest sister always got on me. She was very protective of me and would correct me when I was wrong. I respected her because I felt comfortable with her. By the age of nine, I had been through a rough course of basic home training from being told what was right from wrong while getting a steady dose of Jesus. That was the foundation that my parents set that helped me to fulfill my dreams. My whole life changed once I realized how powerful God is. He has done great things for me. By the time I was ready to go out and let loose, people knew me around town by my nickname, "Deke." It was short for deacon from church. I always like that name and never denied it. It fit my description and personality. I didn't know that God was setting me up to be a minister. I didn't realize that He had a plan for me.

Jeremiah 29:11 (NIV) says, "For I know the plans I have for you, declares the Lord, plans to prosper you and not to harm you, plans to give you a hope and future."

Philippians 4:13 (JUB) says, "I can do all things through Christ who strengthens me."

I remember my grandmother Alma telling my father never to stop believing in Jesus Christ when I was nine years old. I would go to my grandmother's house to get anything that she had for my father. She would give me food and other items. I would run down the alley for three blocks. There were three different ways to get to her house: Division Street, John Street, and through the alley. The alley was the fastest route because it led to my grandma's backyard. John Street was the scenic route but the longest way. My grandma always fed me with something different. She was a giving person, and I loved her. She was part Native American and was always cooking or going to church. She fed many people, regardless of their ethnicity.

Acts 20:35 (NIV) says, "In everything I did, I showed you that by this kind of hard work we must help weak remembering the words the Lord Jesus Himself said: It is more blessed to give than to receive."

Giving was a normal thing in our family. We just had to be taught that it is better to give someone food, clothing, shelter to help the community. My mother, Anna, was a loving mother. She would feed my friends that came over to our house frequently. She would also feed my brothers' and sister's friends as well. I thank God for His Mercy and Grace. Our family was close because of God and our parents believing in Jesus Christ, the Son of Man.

Our community was close-knit because everybody knew one another. Some of our friends didn't have fathers in their home. This allowed my friends to come and go as they pleased. My life would be different if I were in that predicament. Living in a single-parent home can be devastating to a child. My friends talked about their parents, and I encouraged them. I would ask questions such as, "Are you parent's still together?" and "Do they love one another?" I tried to put myself in other's shoes. I tried to show some sympathy and empathy for them. Some of my friends turned out to be okay while others went to jail, drank alcohol, and did drugs. My siblings and I saw them do things that made us shake our heads. I had to judge whether what I witnessed was right or wrong.

I was only ten years old and still didn't understand a lot of things. My brother Robert had a girlfriend and drank beer. My sisters Christine and Geraldine had boyfriends. They all were in high school. I looked up to everyone in my family because they taught me a lot. I didn't know if my parents approved of it.

In the summer of 1977, I met Barry Paddock Sr. at a Lakeview Optimist Basketball League for young boys. He asked me if I wanted to play, and I said yes but I had to ask my parents first.

My parents told me yes. I was happy because now after school and in the summer, I had something to do. I had some extracurricular activities. Three weeks later, it was the first day of practice. I was shocked because our practice facility was five blocks away from my house. The basketball league tried to get the whole neighborhood to sign up. You had to be ten or eleven to play. During practice, Barry Paddock Jr. and three other teammates were there with me. We had to have at least five starters and five practice players. We had to get substitutes in case one of us got into foul trouble. We would run up and down the court all day until we got our plays and free throws together.

One day during practice, Coach Paddock asked if I wanted to come to his house to meet his family. I said yes, and I met his wife and two daughters. This was the first time that I met a white family outside of my usual setting, which was the hood. I ate dinner with them. Coach Paddock lived about two miles from me on the east side. While I lived on the southeast side. His son, Barry Paddock Jr., and I became good friends. We protected each other in games. We still have a great friendship today. Coach Paddock was just my coach in those days. However, years later, he became a Pentecostal pastor at his church. I was proud of him when I heard that he became a pastor because God was using him to help people.

The Paddock's would call me all the time and ask me how I was doing because we became close. They came over to meet my parents and got along quite well. I was amazed by their friendships. I looked up to Barry because he was a father figure to me. He taught me right from wrong, even though my father was still alive. Barry knew that we had a lot of children in our household. I was open to Barry because he was always concerned about me and others. Barry taught me how to treat people even though we might not always agree. He taught me how to listen to people when someone was trying to get their point across. He taught me to speak the truth in love and power in whatever relationship you are involved in. I could always count on him for advice on certain situations. I wondered why Barry had me over for dinners because I felt like I didn't deserve it. His house was nice and clean. Barry was a great role model for the community and me.

After Coach Barry Paddock got saved, he eventually founded "The Light of Faith Free Pentecostal Church" in Evansville, Indiana. He started a small church with 70 to 100 people and was always helping others. Coach Paddock gave his all to many people. I saw him buy people food and clothing as he ministered to them. I could call him at night, and he was always there for me like a father would be there for his son. He was always meeting people's needs. Many times, we can't always come with scripture with people. I pray for people, but when people are struggling through hard times, it's good to ask: "How are you doing?" instead of going straight to the Bible. He taught me how to love people for who they are and not pass judgment on people. He always took me to his house to visit his family. His wife treated me with respect. His son and his two daughters were just like family to me. They called me and asked me how I was doing from time to time well after he had stopped coaching basketball. Coach Paddock was a real man of God. Some people make impacts on our lives, and some people can impact your life. There is a difference. He was a role model like my father.

I can honestly say that I had some great men in my life. I had Rev. Judge L. Meriweather, Barry Paddock, David Barclay, Keith Hodge, and, currently, Bishop Calvin Rice. I'm glad to be where I am today. These men are family men. I always wanted to be a family man. It is a wonderful thing to see husband, wife, children, and grandchildren around them. I see God in all these men. I knew that the Lord was getting me ready for something special. They made me feel a part of something. That something is family.

I believe in being a team player and giving yourself to something positive, and then giving it away to help someone else serve God. Help other people learn how to trust in the Lord for guidance, peace, and love. Some of them don't know how to love. They haven't been taught. Some people can't get peace because they are around drama all the time. I want to applaud my son Jerome Meriweather Jr. for being the father that he is to my grandchildren. I know that he will continue to do the right thing for his family. I always tried to work hard at everything I did.

My brother-in-law Keith and I were always talking, and we had gotten close. He would come by to ask me if I wanted to help him wash his car on many occasions. We would talk about life and guy stuff. I was only about 11 years old, and he was 22. He spoke to me about the birds and bees and about what I wanted to be when I grew up. After we were done washing his car, he would take me for a long spin up and down the popular streets. I guess it was where we could be seen. Before he dropped me off, he would always stop by to grab a burger and fries and then give me $20. He always told me that he would call me to help assist him if he had some housework, gardening, cars, and the paper route to do.

Sure enough, a couple of weeks later, he called me to help him for an overnight paper route late Saturday night, so the job would be completed early Sunday morning. He called me to tell me the details and explained to me what we had to do — the job required hard work. I would also be making more money. It was my first real job outside of doing the summer youth program jobs. I realized that he cared about me. He told me that this job needed at least three people, and we had to start loading up around 11 PM and get to Kentucky by 11:30 PM to unload the truck. I learned the work ethic, and I was glad to have a man in my life, showing me the proper way to work a job. He was my supervisor, and I learned quickly to do the job the right way.

I miss all the men in my life who had something to do with all the blessings I have today. They have passed on to be with the Lord. I have long-lasting memories that I will cherish forever. God has always blessed me with a "Ram in the Bush." I'm grateful, and I want to thank everyone for helping me get to a place where I needed God. He has given me a new life because of these men. There are boys. Then there are men. Today, I'm a man of God.

Jerome Meriweather at Harwood middle school in 1977. He was in the 4th grade and 9 years old in this photo.

CHAPTER 2

Adolescence

Early one morning in October 1979, my brother-in-law Keith called me, and asked me if I wanted to go on a paper route with him. I asked my parents and they said yes. Then I asked my Keith what time he was coming by to pick me up. He replied 10:30 p.m. I was so happy because I knew the money that I was going to make would help me get the things I wanted. Even though my dad gave me an allowance, the extra money that I would make from the paper route would allow me to buy shoes so I could play basketball with my friends on the weekends. Also, it enabled me to have nice clothes to wear to school.

My nephew Carl and I were talking to each other earlier that day at about 1:00 p.m. He asked me if he could go with us and I told him that I would ask Keith. I called up Keith and asked him. It turned out that we would need a helping hand. We were so glad that our parents allowed us to go.

Late in the evening, I was getting restless. I felt that I had to get some rest soon. So, I told my nephew that I was going to go lay down before we got ready for our assignment early in the morning. I did not know that was going to be the last time I was going to see Keith alive. When I laid down, all I thought about were the clothes and shoes that I was going to purchase. I took a nap for about four hours. When I woke up, I was energized and ready to go.

When I got up, I felt a bad feeling in my mind and body. I can only describe this feeling as euphoric and anticipation. It was a feeling I never felt before. It was a warm and fuzzy feeling, but I went on about my evening as though nothing was wrong. At about 7:00 p.m., I decided to take a shower and prepare to go to work. I was so happy to go to work that night. My nephew called me around 8:00 p.m. to ask me what time Keith was picking us up. I told Carl that I would call Keith and find out. I called him and asked him. He said 10:30 p.m. because there was a Fall Festival that weekend and it was the last night. He told me that we were going to the festival before we do the paper route. We started laughing and said, "Wow," because we did not have any money. Keith was going to pay for Carl and me to get in. I called Carl and told him to come to my house so we can be together once Keith picked us up.

Meanwhile, I was smiling from ear to ear, knowing that we are going to have fun by getting on rides and eating candy apples and cotton candy all night. My brother-in-law finally got to my house on time, and we thanked him for allowing us to help that night. I noticed that he picked us up in a greenish-white work truck. I sat in the middle. My nephew sat on the right passenger side. We went to the festival. It was hard trying to find a parking space, but we were destined to get there as soon as possible. We walked around and were glad to be there that Saturday night. There were thousands of people there that night. Parents, kids, families, and friends were walking, eating corn dogs, popcorn, cotton candy, Ice cream, and funnel cakes. We all ate some of everything. My favorite was the funnel cake. Then we got on some rides. I got on the merry go round and the roller coaster. I was screaming and hollering. It was a blast and we did not have that much time left. After all the activities, we had to prepare to go to our job site. We stayed until it was time to go. We got in the truck around 12:30 a.m. and the paper route company. I had been there before, but it was my nephew's first time.

Once we arrived on the job site, Keith gave us instructions on how he wanted to stack the bundles of newspapers in his truck. He wanted everything to be neat. We backed up to the paper route dispensers, and we put gloves on. The first ones that came on the truck were always heavy. We were sweating and organizing. It took one hour to load 100 bundles of plastic sealed packages of newspapers on his vehicle.

We looked at the truck. It was loaded down to the wheels. The back end of it was relatively low to the ground. I was 11 years old at the time. I didn't know what hard work was until I worked this route. My arms were sore, and I was sweating like crazy. Once we finished, I just wanted a drink of water and to start our journey. We took a break and started talking about the job. I knew we had a long night ahead of us because we had to go to Kentucky to deliver bundles of newspapers.

We started on the road around 1:45 a.m., and all of us were exhausted. We headed to small counties in Kentucky to deliver newspapers in the area. By the time we got from the newspaper company to Highway 41, it was about 2:00 a.m. We all looked at each other and made our way to the first drop off. Some places got one or two bundles. Some businesses got three.

My brother-in-law was driving at about 55 mph on an early cold morning. We were in Henderson County and was approaching a drop off location. He looked at the route sheet and stopped. My nephew took care of that and dropped off one bundle. He got back in the truck, and we went to another business. We dropped off two more bundles. I thought to myself that it was going to be a long night because I was looking at the time. I thought that after making several stops, we were not going to finish until 4:00 a.m.

What I realized was by the time we unloaded about 30 bundles; it was about 3:00 a.m. We were in Henderson, Union, and Webster Counties. We were exhausted at the time. It was getting colder that night, so my brother-in-law turned the heat up in the truck. He cracked the window so we could get air and not fall asleep. Up to this point we had done about 75 bundles. The job was close to completion and there were only 20 bundles left. We were right on target. We noticed a little daylight although it was still dark outside. We pulled over and took a break. We had a little bite to eat and some drinks. I said, "We are almost done." They said, "About time. Yes, we are!" So, we started on our way to drop off the remaining newspaper bundles. It seemed like once we got back into the truck and got closer to our finish line, finishing our job got harder. We found ourselves going up and down steep hills and curves. A couple of deer would run out in front of us. Then at approximately 4:30 a.m., we were going down this curvy road. The heat was blasting, and we all had fallen asleep.

The next thing I remember is that we had hit a guardrail and went airborne into a creek bed. As we were upside down in the truck, the wheels were still spinning. The vehicle was demolished. I thought I was dreaming, but it was a reality. I was in and out of consciousness. I tried to scream for help alongside my nephew and brother-in-law. I could see my nephew but not my brother-in-law due to hitting my head on the dashboard several times. I had severe hemorrhaging in my brain and was paralyzed from head to toe. As we were laying upside down stuck in the truck, we were moaning and groaning. We asked God for help. I heard some strange gurgling and wheel sounds. It was my brother-in-law dying from blunt force trauma. The steering wheel was crushing his chest. My nephew had suffered two broken legs and contusions to his face. Meanwhile, it seemed like we were in the truck forever. We all were in the upside-down position for at least 30 minutes before someone came to rescue us.

I heard a couple come down the creek bed to help us. They tried to open the doors, but the doors were jammed. The next thing I heard were firefighters and fire trucks coming down the creek bed to free us from this terrible accident. It was the first time that I felt hopeless and lost. The firemen used what they called "the jaws of life" to free us from being trapped in the truck. They cut the doors off both sides and freed us. They got my nephew, Carl, out first. I was second, and my brother-in-law was last because he died on the scene. I was so hurt and in pain from this tragedy. I wanted to give up, but God had a better plan. I remember being brought up on a gurney and I couldn't feel anything in my legs, head, or feet. My nephew and I were put in an ambulance and taken to Welborn Hospital in Evansville, Indiana where we lived. It was a long ride back from Kentucky to Indiana. Nobody told me anything about my brother-in-law for days. I just wanted to know if he survived or not. It was about 7:00 a.m. and our parents were notified of the accident.

I didn't know if we were going to live or die that day. It was early Sunday morning. I was in a state of shock when this happened. I went through all of this hurt, pain, and anguish. Nothing was the same. I remember laying there wishing that God would end it all, but I knew that He had a better plan than I did. Every day that I was in the hospital, I felt sorry for myself saying, "Why me?" It just wasn't my time to go. I would cry every day. Tears were running down my eyes uncontrollably.

I found out that I had been in a coma for months. I could see and hear, but I couldn't walk or talk. The nurses were all around me telling me that everything will be okay. I was fed with a feeding tube. I received pain medicine, and all kinds of things were done to me daily. At times I was wondering if I would ever get out of the hospital. I met my doctor for the first time after being in the hospital for several days. He told me I had suffered head trauma and said it is going to take a while for the swelling to go down. He told me that it would take some time for me to heal from all the nerve damage I had in my body. He said that I was going to need physical therapy at some point in time. I knew that I was on a long road to recovery. There are no accidents with the Lord Jesus Christ.

Isaiah 46:9-10 (ESV) says, "Remember the former things of old; For I am God, and there is no other: I am God, And there is none like me, declaring the end from the beginning and from ancient times' Things not yet done, saying, My counsel shall Stand, and I will accomplish all my purpose."

I knew that it was time for me to go through this storm. I knew God was with me because I was powerless. The only one who was going to get me through this was Jesus Christ. My entire family was there for me as I was recovering from my injuries from the accident. My mom and dad came to see me very often. I had a speech impairment, so I could only nod yes or shake my head no. I wanted to tell them everything that happened, but I just wasn't able. My brothers Robert, Gary, Greg, and Tim came to see me. They couldn't believe what had happened to me. They looked at me as though I was an alien. My sisters Doris, Kathy, Geraldine, and Christine were there as well. All of them knew that I was in bad shape at this point. I knew that we were a God-fearing family because My grandmother Alma was a God-fearing woman. My father was already a Minister at Ebenezer

Baptist Church. My mother Anna played the piano and organ with no lessons. She was very gifted. There was never a dull moment with them. We were very close.

As I was recovering, I never made it home. The doctor came to my room the next day to tell me that I was going to another hospital for treatment. I didn't understand why I was being transitions instead of discharged. Welborn Hospital didn't have the best therapy for brain treatment during my progress, so I had to prepare myself to be transferred to another facility. At this point, I felt that I was going somewhere better. A few days later after I said my goodbyes to the nurses and all the staff, I realized that I was being ministered to by them. I was encouraged and felt the love they gave me. I was wheeled out to the ambulatory on February 15, 1980. I headed to Deaconess for physical therapy. I had body scans periodically. I had to do some stretching and speech therapy as well. I was still in a lot of pain all over my body. Once I arrived at Deaconess, they put me in a large room. The room was clean and huge. I felt comfortable for the first time.

Sometimes when we go through something, we must pray. We must ask God for His healing and blessings. He will deliver on His word. We must act on His word and be obedient to Him. There were times where I felt lost and was never going to be the same. There were times where I wanted to give up. The hope that I had was from God because I knew without a shadow of a doubt that He never gave up on me. Everything that I had done up until this point made me realize that God was in total control of my life. It was hard for me to get out of bed some days. I didn't want to eat because I was depressed. The feeling of guilt came over me. I blamed myself and thought that it was all my fault. I knew deep down that it wasn't my fault, but I just felt that way. The hardest times were when everyone was gone, and I was in the room by myself. I knew that God was with me before bedtime.

One morning my mother and father came to see me. It was as if I had come out of a deep sleep because they were staring at me when I woke up. I was so happy to see them, and I was able to tell them what happened during the accident. God is so great because even though I thought it was all over, I was regaining my strength. My mind was healed by the mercy and grace of the Lord Jesus Christ. We talked about what happened, my recovery, and what I was eating daily. I asked them what everyone was saying about the investigation of the accident. Until this day, I never got a preliminary report or anything. I was on target for trying to prepare myself to come home someday. That was all I thought about every day. I talked to God, my family, and friends. I didn't understand what was going on because I couldn't go to school for almost a year. I knew one thing for certain is that I loved God.

1 Corinthians 2:9 says, "But as it is written, eye hath not seen, nor ear heard, neither have entered into the heart of man, the things which God hath entered into the heart Of Man, the things which God hath prepared for them that love him."

God is love, and His love is unfailing. His love does not hurt or boast. Until I decided to allow God to help me in my recovery,

I didn't feel about my recovery progress. I allowed Him to love me His way.

On March 14, I still was in the hospital and I started getting calls from cousins, aunties, uncles, nephews, nieces, and friends. I got cards and flowers. My friend James called me and asked what was going on. I told him that I was feeling much better and couldn't wait to throw rocks at cars with him again. I felt like God was preparing me for some better things because I heard my doctor talking to my parents. They asked him what my time table for a full recovery was and the length of outpatient rehabilitation. He told them about the first week or the second week of May. I was very weak at that time but able to stand on my feet.

The nurse came in while my parents were there. She asked, "Are you ready for some rehab today?" I told her I was because I was ready to go home and be with my family and friends. The nurse's name was Sherry, and she helped me get in a pool for my muscles. She helped my strength and conditioning which I had to do every day for one hour. Also, she drew my blood and took my blood pressure every day. I loved it when they brought me the menu to order hospital food. It wasn't that good, but I had gotten used to eating it after four or five months. What I couldn't understand was after I came to my senses through recovery, I saw stars, mazes, lots of horizontal, rectangles, and triangles. Until this day I don't understand God's plan, but He does. I love Him.

In the middle of March, I received some bad news about my motor skills and brain activities. I asked my nurse what was going on. She told me briefly. My doctor sat by my bedside to tell me that I needed to go to St. Mary's Hospital for a full checkup and recovery because of my internal problems. I was somewhat devastated because I was anticipating going home. I was able to walk around, pack my clothes, and get my belongings together. I was disappointed that I had already been to two different hospitals and going to another one. When things don't go our way, we get beside ourselves. I managed to stay calm through all my problems. I kept praying and asking God for His wisdom, knowledge, and understanding. I was becoming more skeptical after going through several doctors, nurse practitioners, and several different teams of staff. I got my things together and moved again for the third time in five months.

    The hospital was across town, so I had some time to think. I looked at the transport team, and they looked back at me as if they were asking, "You thought you were going home, didn't you?" I wanted to say yes, but we all knew that it wasn't time yet. We arrived there at about 11 a.m. I questioned some of the things I saw in the hospitals that I was treated or stayed in since my accident. I saw other people who were in accidents. They put the black people in rooms that were not so clean or nice. It seemed like my doctors were very young. They acted like they didn't know what they were doing. I later found out that the reason why they moved me to three different hospitals was that the equipment I needed for my injuries wasn't in one hospital. It was in several places. I found myself going to clinics and rehabs while I was there. I went to rehab for my neck, back, and legs. My injuries turned out to be more internal than external. They ran tests on my brain. I had a right frontal contusion on the inside of my brain.

I found out that my brain was still swollen. I was still stiff from not being able to balance my body as I wanted too. I was making some progress. I felt very different when I would see My family and friends. I just wanted to believe that I was going to make a full recovery. I did, but I wasn't healed all the way. There is a big difference. I was evaluated multiple times on many occasions at this point. My days and nights were getting better. It seemed like I was going through the motions. Never getting ahead of myself except for thinking about life in general. I tried to get out of there. I was seeing if the nurse would do me favors like get me snacks. I was getting very, very bored with hospitals. Just being there was not good for me. I realized that I needed more patience and asked God to give it to me. I realized that I had to rely and wait on God.

2 Thessalonians 1:4-5 (NIV) says, "Therefore, among God's churches we boast about Your perseverance and faith in all the persecutions and trials you are enduring. All this is evidence that God's judgment is right, and as a result you will be counted worthy of the Kingdom God, for which you are suffering."

We go through many ups and downs. Trouble doesn't last always. You must pray and seek God's face. Don't ever give up on God because He will never give up on you. When we are at our weakest moments in life, we must stay focused and wait on God Almighty so we can get our healing and blessings. He heals us inside and out.

The days from being released from the hospital were numbered from days to months. I knew that I was doing much better because I started to heal properly. I was resting and eating right. I was more positive than ever before. It was in late April, going into May of 1980. It was time to get ready to go home, and I was happy. I was thinking about those thoughts because it was indeed the first time in my life that I could see real progress. Everything else until this point was in God's hands. I realized that He makes the choices where we can heal, live, or die.

I was never the same. I felt powerless still because a feeling of being lost and empty came over me. When you are feeling this way, it's like a person filled with lots of joy but somehow cannot express his feelings. I just had to go with the flow. Finally, after going through extensive rehabs, several procedures, several hospitals, numerous doctors, and staff, I was released on May 7, 1980, from St. Mary's Hospital.

The nurse woke me that morning and told me that I was going home that day. I was happy and sad because I felt a piece of me was left behind and that parts of me are going home broken. The doctor came in and asked, "Jerome, you ready to go?" I said, "Yes!" but I felt cheated and robbed because I felt ashamed to go home when my brother-in-law didn't make it and my nephew was already home. I just knew that it was going to be an uphill battle to be functional again. I also knew that I was going to be asked more questions from people who wanted the truth or from people who want to believe what they wanted to believe. I had to trust in the Lord.

My mother and father were there to pick me up from the hospital. My doctor explained to them my rehab dates and regular times to exercise my entire body. My paperwork was thick, and it felt like I had to sign off on my life. We said our goodbyes and thanked everyone for taking care of me. The nurse rolled me in a wheelchair out to my father's car. They let me inside, and I sat down in the seat. They got in, and we drove away. My dad asked me if I was okay. I said, yes. My mother said, "I see your face, and you look better than what you did." We were about thirty minutes away from home, and my dad asked if I wanted something to eat. I said yes. We stopped at McDonald's, and I got two fish sandwiches, fries, and a milkshake. They didn't get anything but drinks.

As we were approaching the house, I saw my family standing outside. My brothers, sisters, family, and friends wished me well as they helped me get out of the car. I was so happy to see some of my friends from the neighborhood. Some kids from my school were there. I didn't realize how popular I was until this happened to me. Everybody was giving hugs and crying because we were so happy to see one another. All I was thinking up until this point was love one another no matter what because you may never know what is going to happen from day to day. From that day forward, I tell people that I love them. A day will come where you will never see them again. I couldn't tell my brother-in-law that I loved him, but today is the day. I love you, Keith. Rest in God.

John 13:34 (NIV) says, "A new command I give you: Love one another. As I have Loved you, so you must love one another."

To my nephew Carl, I love you too. God has blessed you with the gift of boxing. You are doing very well today by the Mercy and Grace of God. I knew that you were going to be just fine. As I was eating the food that my dad bought me, I was delighted to be home. I just felt strange in the hospital because I thought that I might never be released.

To my sister, Doris who lost her husband many years ago, you both are resting until Judgement Day. I want to say thank you both because I would have probably been doing something wrong that day that I shouldn't have been doing. I had too much time on my hands on the weekends. Honestly, if I wouldn't have gone on the paper route that night, I was going to play my favorite sport all day long.

Basketball was my sport. I was desperately trying to get better by rehabbing and building myself up. I knew it was going to take a while, so I decided to set goals for myself. I said to myself, "By next year, I'm going to try to get back on the basketball team at school." Well, it takes a long time to rehab. My school was out for summer in May, so I had to spend the summer and fall rehabbing. It was difficult. Sometimes I was so stiff and could barely walk. I started to think that they let me go home too soon. I just wasn't healed yet, and my bones were broken. Trauma was all in my head and body. I was mad as hell at the world. I put my energy into getting physically fit. I convinced myself that I was going to make it in basketball. I didn't realize that God had another plan.

My brothers would pick me up and sit me down. Tim was my youngest brother. At the time, he was helping me a lot. We were close because we shared the same interest. My other brothers Greg, Gary, and Robert were helping me as well. They helped me get around on different days and times. My sister Kathy, Geraldine, and Christine helped me. The funny part about this is my sisters had moved out already. They had their own families to attend to. They still came by to help me which told me that my family was a loving and caring family. We developed love, morals, and values from our parents. To this day it has done us all some good. You see with all the things that were going on in my life at the time, I realized that I was being ministered too and through most of my life which resulted in "My Life as A Minister". I'm ministering to people in all walks of life. It's about God and the 'Love of The Kingdom of God.'

I found myself going to nursing homes, funeral homes, churches, jails, you name it. Ages 11 to 13 were very crucial for me because I felt crippled and afflicted. I didn't know if I was going to get back to my old self. I lost hope at times. Throughout those days, times, and years I just wanted normalcy. I remember trying to be slick one day. I waited until everybody went into the house one evening at about 6:00 p.m. A friend and I drank a can of beer that he had gotten from someone earlier that day. Drinking was my excuse for being in pain. It led me down a road that only God could take His hand and wash away all my tears. He can make anyone a new creature in Jesus Christ.

2 Corinthians 5:17 says, "Therefore if any man be in Christ, he is a new creature: old things are passed away: behold, all things are new."

I did the old saying: everybody else is doing it, why not try it? It was the biggest mistake of my life. I was fragile and afflicted. I started taking my medication and secretly smoking cigarettes at the age of 13. You couldn't tell me anything. I deserved it because of my condition. "Nobody understood me, and nobody cares," I thought. Satan will lie to you in many ways.

I kept one of my favorite scriptures in my heart for years, and it is so powerful. I was not doing well because I had started something, and I didn't know what I was getting into. By the grace of God, it took me a long time to get my life together because what I started doing was recreational which ended up costing me more trouble than I bargained for. I remember the summer of 1981. I was getting ready for my 8th-grade year. I needed to get myself under control. I started hanging around characters around my neighborhood and girls that I knew that were no good for me. We were going over to people's houses that were just not good people. I saw marijuana, cigarettes, pills, and alcoholic beverages. It was very easy to get hooked because it was free.

This girl came up to me one day and said, "You want to smoke with me?" I just said, "Okay." Afterward, we had consensual sex, but it wasn't love. Right then and there I knew it, but it felt innocent and good. I just wanted to do it and was thinking about the experience. Every time I saw her, it was on until I saw the next best thing. All we had in common was having a good time. It was so sad being around someone like that knowing you will not be happy in a bad relationship. I felt like it was all my fault because I could have said no. I genuinely believe that a man of God knows better, but my desire for God at that time weren't where they should have been. Just because someone gives you the right to have sex with them doesn't make it right. We must choose to do the right thing. I was only 13 years old at the time and about to become a freshman in high school that next fall.

After going through physical therapy every day, I was tired of it. I had to do what I had to do which was to get strength from the Lord. I asked my father to pray for me because I was in pain from that day on. All I did was try to confide in the people that loved me which was God and my family. I went through days and nights asking God to end it all. I was going through the motions at this point, trying to find my way to God. Because I didn't understand what I was going through, I felt self-pity most of the time and was crying and masking pain. I was so far gone because I felt cheated out of a career in sports. I was punished for some reason or another. I kept saying, "Why? God Why?" I talked to this lady, and she told me that she didn't believe in God. She said that God took her older sister and younger brother. I asked her, " Have you ever thought that God used their death to could get your attention?" She looked at me quite amused. I truly believe that God uses tragedies to get our attention. I needed to be more focused on God than being more focused on myself. I was hurt by what happened to me. I used to have bad dreams and sleepless nights.

I fought through and overcame lots of problems that would make the average person throw in the towel. All I could do is be obedient to God. I just went through a lot of situations that I couldn't do anything about. I said to myself every day, "I had never been through anything like this before." I was mad at God for allowing things to happen to me. The whole summer all I did was help my daddy with the family business, get high, and play basketball. I would often say to myself that my parents didn't know, but they knew what I was doing. I just prayed and hoped that I would snap out of it. My family was there for me all the time. I was just lost sometimes because of what I had been through. The trauma was so significant the doctor said that I had injured the right frontal lobe of my brain. I was devastated. I was having headaches, back, and leg pain constantly. I realized that I couldn't go through the whole summer talking about it.

I would go to basketball camps never saying a word about it to my coaches. It was just something that I knew that would disqualify me from making any AAU Teams. I wanted to impress my coaches and teammates. After going through all the traumatic experiences, I managed to play AAU ball for a team that traveled to St. Louis, Indianapolis, and New Jersey. All I was trying to do was get my life back together. I must say it was hard by the grace of God. When we look at other people's lives, we say, "I want what they have. " You don't know what they went through to get to where they are now. There were sharp pains in my feet, legs, and toes when I tried out for teams. I tried very hard to make something out of my life. I knew coming out of the accident, I wasn't going to be 100%. I knew that God was on my side. I was getting better daily. My thinking was not good, and I would isolate myself from time to time.

God was showing me different things when I started school that year. I was not myself when I started my freshman year of high school. I was a heavily recruited High School Basketball Star. I went to Memorial High for a short time because the school corporation said that I didn't live in the district to attend. The only reason why they questioned me was that it was about money. They wanted me to go back to public school so I could play for a school that I could generate funds for. I was so sad because after all I had been through in grade school, the controversy came in my freshman year.

All I wanted to do was play ball and get my grades. They had other plans for me because they had given me an ultimatum. I had to sit out a year and stay at the Catholic school or go back to my public school. In the meantime, I was still attending high school. I remember my classmates asking me if I was staying at Memorial High School. I told them that I was planning on leaving. They were like you should stay. Most of them wanted me to stay before we even set foot on the basketball court. It was an awkward situation, but I had to go because it was profitable for both parties.

My parents respected my decision, and I was satisfied with the outcome. I chose to go to the nearest high school. I wanted to be around people that I truly cared about, and people that cared about me. I was just an athlete to those schools. Some schools don't care if you get your grades or not. I kept on insisting that I wanted a better life. I was thinking about college. I was thinking about a career. I couldn't see myself without having something to fall back on. I was very ambitious, and I'm still that way to this day. I didn't want to disappoint my parents or my family. I was 15 years old during this time and very vulnerable. I never expected things to turn out like they have turned out to be. I asked God to help because sometimes, I felt helpless even when I knew what I was doing. Trust me, I acted like I knew what was going on, but I didn't.

Education is great, but God is greater. Basketball was great, but God and family are greater. I was trying to put the pieces together that made sense in my life and career at this young age. I knew that God is greater than life itself. This was in late September, and it was different in 1982. That year I was doing everything and anything under the sun. I was hiding something. I never told anyone about my problems. All I did was drink, smoke, and isolate myself from my family and friends. I was feeling different inside and outside of my body. I knew how to mask at home. I knew how to mask at church. But when I self-medicated, I took the mask off. I didn't like who I was, but I went through that situation, and it got me to where I'm at today. I was never a trusting person. I didn't like being around people until I had to mask being around them. Today, I don't have to mask because God has unveiled me to be his beacon of light and hope in this lost, dying world. I know the Lord has brought me a mighty long way. I know that when I was going through something and having a tough time, it was God who was with me while I suffered and pulled through. I did all these things repeatedly for the next three years until I graduated from high school in 1986.

Those years were hits, misses, ups, and downs. I was still going to church with my parents. I still wasn't ready to read the Bible and fully be engaged in the word. I would do what some ministers and preachers do to this day. They go to their favorite scripture and make it fit their interpretation of what they felt. I was going through and had the audacity to think that God was punishing me. I thought that I must have done something wrong for all of my hiccups. You see we can make God a saint and a villain. The truth is He is not what we think He is until we give ourselves to Him. I was a mess, and I knew it. Once you realize you are a mess people know you are as well. People are watching you when you think that they are not watching you. Through 1983-1985, I found myself going through the same routine. We went to church every Sunday with my parents. My brothers and I worked the family business during the week. We were always working with our father. We worked winters, summers, spring, and fall. My dad was no joke, and he wanted us to make an honest living. He wanted us to love God and be successful.

We made a good living back then. It was interesting because my dad was never into the money like we thought. He was teaching self-preservation and self-employment. He talked about being respected and helping others. My father fed the block with everything people needed. I was so happy to have a dad like him because he provided in so many ways. He supported us with love and respect. I loved and thanked him for the experience he gave me. He gave me jewels like diamonds, pearls, rubies, sapphires, and many other life-changing memories. They don't make men like him anymore. I watched how he conducted himself with other people. In 1986 I was ready to be just like him. I wanted to be more like my father. I know that somewhere between that time I thought about giving up basketball because I wasn't the same person anymore. I had to give up some things before I headed off to college.

In 1986, I graduated from High school. I was ready to move out and anticipating getting my life back in order. I was anxious and ready to get it together. I felt funny and different in all my high school years. I was not the same person from the automobile accident when I was 11 years old. The doctors said that I would never be the same and they diagnosed me with PTSD. I was like okay, whatever. I knew that I was a miracle because God had done for me what I couldn't do for myself. I didn't understand me, but God understood me. I cried, "Lord Help Me!! Please Help Me!" The Bible says, "They that call upon the Lord shall be saved." Up until this point I had been through hell and back. My family went through hell because of my ordeal. I want to thank them for being there for me through the good times and bad times.

Most of all, I thank God for my awesome mom and dad. I wouldn't trade my family for anything in this world. They gave me strength when I didn't have it. I just wanted to get the year over with so I could decide what college I wanted to attend and start preparing for my SAT exams. I was ready to do all I could to prepare myself for a better future. I thought that 1987 would be the best year of my life. I was preparing myself to say goodbye to my family and friends. I told my Biddy Basketball and AAU coaches goodbye. All I wanted to do was move out of the house on a College Basketball Scholarship. God allowed me to put everything into perspective. At this point, basketball had taken me to many states.

Many times, I was the only black man on the team roster. I loved the game of basketball until I met Jesus Christ. I remember bringing home every trophy before I entered high school. I had 40 trophies from entering tournaments in several different states. I remember bringing home MVP or Most Outstanding Player Awards. I had dreams and goals. I was even invited to the famous McDonald's All-American Camp. Even when I won the awards, I felt empty because my parents couldn't be there, and I had my medical problems. My parents were into church and family. I knew that God was there because He was the reason why I won the trophies in the first place. I understood my parents' situation because they were taking care of their brother's and sister's kids when they passed away. There was no one to care for them due to mental illness or natural illness. My parents taught me to visit other churches, praying for others and helping them. We had a house full throughout my high school years.

My dad did some things you don't see any more too often. When his sister passed away, he took full custody of her son. He made his nephew part of our family. One of my family members had a case of mental illness, and he came to our house and blended right in with us. It was never a dull moment in our household. I reflected on old memories because I was getting ready to move on. I knew that I wasn't prepared to leave, but it was time for me to go and do what God wanted me to do. I even asked myself, "Are you ready?" I had to experience what God had for me to go through at this time. God has been good to me, and I was so ready to make a move. I had to know that God was with me because I wasn't so sure. I thank God for His Mercy and Grace.

I was determined to do the right thing. I just wanted a better life for myself, and in between, I tried out for basketball throughout the summer. I was helping my father with his businesses. He had a fish and a food business. We would wake up at 6:00 a.m. and prepare for the business to run just like he showed us. We would put food on the grill. My father taught us how to marinate, tenderize, cut the meats, and everything else. It was a lot of work.

My dad met a man who owned several farms in Kentucky. The man was a friend of my great uncle, who was a tall man. He was about 6'5.' He had gray hair, a deep voice, and a big laugh. He asked my father if he would be interested in buying a farm. My father said yes. One day my uncle called my dad and asked him if he was ready to see the farms. We went to Kentucky to look at the farms. For the first time, I saw sheep, cows, ponies, dogs, cats, chickens, and pigs. The farm had a lake. I fell in love with the animals and the farm. I was like King David the chosen one after tending the sheep. I just wanted to get out to feed the animals as much as I could. We fed chickens corn. We fed ponies hay. We fed pigs slop bread with milk in it. I was so open-minded to animals and wanted to know what they wanted to eat and what they didn't like. What I loved about my father was that he wanted his own farm so he could pick and choose what animals he wanted to slaughter for his businesses. He was thinking of ownership. He no longer wanted to buy fish or meats from people. He wanted to own what they were selling to him. He purchased the farm in Kentucky that had about 5 acres of land. There was a white farmhouse on the property.

One morning we let the animals out, and the whole farm had animals everywhere. When it was feeding time, we had a ball. We would go to the farm at least every weekend for three months in the summer. What was so exciting was that we lived in Evansville, Indiana and the farm was in Kentucky across the bridge. It only took 15 to 30 minutes tops to drive over to the farm. It seemed like we were over there a lot more than I expected. We would buy the feed for the animals at different prices. Some of the feed we brought for the animals was very expensive such as 500 dollars for each different animal we owned. The upkeep of the farmhouse was expensive as well. I remember the first night we stayed in the house on the farm. We had to make the house livable because the man said the house hadn't been lived in for over a year. When we first opened the door, I saw cobwebs on the walls. We went in and painted the walls, called a plumber to fix some pipes, and an electrician to get everything running again. Once everything was finished, we moved some furniture into the house, and it looked nice.

The house looked big on the outside, but when you opened the door, there were only three little rooms. The whole house was refurbished from the inside and out. I was so young at the time, and the farm life was one of the best times of my life growing up. I didn't realize the values that my father was setting for us. My father always put God first in everything we did. It was God, his family, and friends. Once we left the farm, we would return to Evansville to go to our other home. I was lying in bed one night and was having dreams about what we had done on the farm. I told my friends how cows chew grass. They crunch grass as they chew the cud. I can hear the sounds to this day. I miss that farm and learned a lot from my parents and my siblings.

I remember going back to school still in pain, healing, and recovering from depression. I wanted to escape from reality, even though I was trying to drown everything out by playing sports or helping my father with his business ventures. I was banking on the Word of God. I had no choice. I knew through prayer and reading the Bible that I would find comfort in God. I had no peace at the time because I was still drinking a little here and there. My life was never the same. I never really read the Bible in its entirety. I just went through the motions. I encourage you all to read your Bible daily at least an hour a day. God loves us more than we can imagine.

CHAPTER 3

Adulthood

In 1987, I was ready for college after a disappointing senior year of High School Basketball. The whole year, 1986, was crazy. I thought I was going to be prepared for a nice summer and move on from my parent's house into a better situation. I underestimated my time that year. I spent most of that year preparing for my S.A.T. test for College. I didn't realize that my father taught me so many life skills and discipline until I became an adult. Those skills became useful to me. God is so good. I was trying to do everything in my power to work for my dad for the whole summer and work at home.

I worked wherever and whenever I could because I needed the money even though the date was getting closer and closer. We worked the farm for the entire summer. We woke up at 6:00 a.m. and fed the animals. My brothers and I worked side by side.

Sometimes my dad would call on me to do more instead of my older brothers. I was always by his side and called upon him. He must have known something that I didn't know. We were close, and I understood his language very well. He didn't have to say too much to me to get his point across. He was stern but not mean. I just did what I was told most of the time. The only time he ruled with an iron fist was when I rebelled against God and him. I rebelled by sleeping around, drinking, doing drugs, and staying up late.

I realized that I couldn't mix the two. You can't serve two masters. The Bible says, "You either love the one or hate the other." I was swinging on both sides of the fence. I felt the pain and anguish of that whole summer because I was still rehabbing. I was in pain long after the accident. I was still living at home at that point. I knew that it was a matter of time before I left for college, so I prepared. I told my family and friends that I was picking a college that was best for me to attend. I got a call from a coach who asked me to visit Olney Central College to see if I liked it. I will never forget it. My parents drove me there on June 10th which was on the weekend. I just wanted to go down there and explore the community and city. It was a three-hour drive, and we were tired once we got there. I looked at the campus, and it was a tiny school.

The community was small as well. I was surprised. We drove up in the parking lot of the school to meet my coach. He was there waiting for us. We all got out of our vehicles and introduced ourselves. We proceeded into the school. We met some of the faculty and professors. I felt good about the visit, but I didn't like the school because it was in a small country town and it was about 99.9 % white. I wasn't prepared for this school. I thought they had dorms and there were none. I had to get outside housing. So, when I was told that I would get a roommate, I thought it was going to be an athlete like me. I thanked everyone at the college for a visit. Afterward, we rode through the town in less than 20 minutes. As we were headed back home to Evansville, I planned to notify them of my decision. Honestly, I was skeptical. I wanted to visit another college to see if I was the right fit in their school, but no one else offered me a scholarship. I did what I had to do. I went home and prayed to God. I felt a peace about what was happening to me.

For some reason, I knew that I was going back to that college. I didn't know why God would put me there. I ended up getting a two-year scholarship. I told them that I was committing to them. I called the coach, and he hooked me up with my classes. He said that he was looking forward to seeing me on August 17 for an entire school year. I only had about two months to go. I was ready because, in my mind, I was always living a fast life. I was prepared to move on down the road from my parents. At times I felt like I was a burden to them. I wanted to show them that I could make it on my own. I tried to do everything in my power to get my heart, mind, and body right for a serious lifestyle change. I had seen a lot of good things happen and they were awesome. I couldn't see all the bad stuff that was waiting around the corner in my life. I lacked experience, and I was going out in the world on my own. I learned the hard way. Honestly, that summer was a turning point in my life. Nothing was ever the same.

On August 17, 1986, I headed to Olney Central College on a Saturday morning. My parents and my brother packed my things then we left for Olney, Illinois. I felt like I needed to take a chance. I was afraid to go off, but I didn't let my family know. I didn't know what would happen once my family dropped me off at the school. I didn't see myself being happy there. I saw a basketball scholarship and getting what I could out of school. I met my roommate once we arrived. He wasn't a basketball player. He came from a suburb of Chicago, and we didn't get along. We were cool, but we were entirely two different people. He was very proper and different. My parents met him and helped me load some things in the two-bedroom family house that we were renting. The house was okay because I had a big bedroom and a nice size kitchen. My roommate had the smallest room in the house. I spoke to him about the rules and regulations of the house. We were at odds with almost everything. I tried to reason with him. He would be mad at me because he knew that my attention was going toward my girlfriend and not school. I had everything going for me at school on and off campus. We had a chapel there, but it wasn't church. My church at home was my dad's church.

I had temporary fun in college, but it never brought me the joy that God has given me. I had to struggle some more by going through more pain and anguish. My parents were headed back home with my brother, and I missed them from the time they pulled off. I felt sad as they were pulling off. My heart was crushed. I stayed the course by staying in school because it was never about me. I tried to mend situations. I decided to make things right and looked at all the things that I was going through. As a result, I only found that there is always somebody going through something worse. I was tired of it being me, but then I realized it just wasn't me. I had to find ways to pray for others and become a problem solver. Also, I had to understand what it's like to have sympathy for other people. I didn't realize that God was tugging on my mind.

The next couple of days on the campus were opportunities to meet all the students, faculty, professors, and the donors of the community. I didn't get to meet everybody on the first day, but I felt brand new in school. I was shocked that many white people liked me. I went to an orientation during the first week. I received my books and study hall assignment. I thanked God because I lived up to my end of the bargain.

I met my girlfriend about two weeks into the 1986 -1987 school year. She was from Gary, Indiana. She looked at me and asked me where I was from. I answered her and asked her the same question. She was cool, and we hit it off. We started to call one another and were gelled together. We did everything together. It's funny when things go well, but there is always something that has a thorn in our side.

I had the college, the parents, and everything that I wanted, but it wasn't God's plan for me. It was my life as I saw it. I truly believe that God used basketball as a platform for me to get closer to Him. I knew that I was never going to see those people again once I do things God's way. I was going through the motions as I enrolled in all my classes. I thought, "This is not my destiny."

I met my college basketball teammates. It was cool. They were an awesome bunch of guys. I will never forget their faces. They were tall, and their heights ranged from 6'6 to 6'9. I was only about 6'0. God blessed me with a talent that I just was unstoppable for my size. Since I had no church to attend, all I cared about was school, my girlfriend, and parties. Most classes were in the morning, and the latest one was at 2:00 p.m. My basketball practice was at 4:00 p.m. to 6:00 p.m. During the weekdays, I studied and spent time with my girlfriend. I adapted to my schedule and thought about going home to visit my family for Thanksgiving. I had another girlfriend back in my hometown. Both of my girlfriends didn't know about each other. I knew that I wasn't going to continue down this path of unrighteousness. I had to make some decisions on getting my priorities right. I had to choose God or my life.

About one month into college I got myself together. I was headed down the wrong road by partying. I had no coping skills. I tried to fix my problems with drugs and alcohol. I thought that I had to self-medicate when I felt pain which was dangerous. I had to get it together and keep it that way. I guarded my heart and did not let things get to me. I understood that you could be in a healthy relationship or have healthy friendships. People can't see everything you do or think about daily. But God sees it all and knows all. You can run, but you can't hide. I didn't want friends of mine to know who I was without God in my life. I was a sinner. I was drinking on weekends and smoking marijuana. Before I knew it, I was partying every weekend and seeing more women than I could handle. Although that wasn't my intentions,

I put myself in those situations. I wanted to be something that I wasn't. Everything was routine and very predictable. The next thing I knew, I was having sex with lots of women from college, going to cookouts, dances, and bars. I had the college thing down to a science. I had no business trying to do other things that were no good for me. Sometimes a friend would call and tell me that they were having a house party. I would go, get drunk and get whatever I wanted.

There is a price you pay for sin. The first semester was okay, but I could have done much better. I was aspiring to get a degree in communications. I didn't have my priorities in God's direction. I was in my feelings and doing my own thing. I asked myself what did I do wrong? From August all the way to October and our first Basketball game, I would party hard. I wouldn't do anything during basketball practice, home game nights, or away game nights. It was difficult hiding and isolating myself to do wrong because I didn't want anybody else to know what I was doing. What I didn't realize is what is done in the dark will come out in the light. God's light cannot mix with darkness. I was in for a rude awakening. I was only 18 years old in late December. I had friends from school, the basketball team, the baseball team, and all over. They weren't the right kind of friends. They were people that party every day all day except when we had to go to school. These kinds of people are not your friends. They are your enemies. It took me a long time to realize that because I thought as long as they were doing what I was doing, everything was okay. It turned out that when we engaged ourselves into sin, we became lost in life. We couldn't see our way back like the

Prodigal Son until Jesus Christ our Father lets us come back in His Kingdom after repenting.

We can become like lost sheep that have been led astray only to see that you spend all your money and squander your life away. Where are your friends once you run out of drugs and alcohol? Where are your friends once all the money's gone? You are lying with the pigs and have nothing. You are down and out. I noticed that once the party is over, people act differently. Some are sick as a dog. Some don't want to go home because that's all they know. I was the one who spent all or most of his money by riotous living. I was the one who did everything his way. However, God still had His hand on my life. What an amazing God we serve. I didn't tell my parents everything. I was too ashamed to call them and confess everything. They had enough problems of their own and I wasn't going to give them a reason to make a visit unless it was what they wanted to. I would call them once or twice a week to say that I was doing okay, and I wasn't. I just didn't want them to worry about me. I know that many parents worry about their children going off to college. Pray for them and call them periodically. See how they are doing and make visits sometimes unexpectedly. I had to come to my senses and realize that I went to get my education. I needed help, God, my family, and Godly friends. I didn't have that in college. Everybody was getting high except for a few people. I wish I was one of them because they were on the cutting edge of getting their education, degrees, top jobs, and a better quality of life. What kept me going was God. I had stayed for that year because of His love for me.

I remember my first ball game. I scored ten points and like three rebounds. It was fun running up and down the court. I was involved in many positive things on campus. It was off campus and at home where I was not too happy. All I did in college was party like a party animal every weekend. God was with me the whole time. I was ready to go home. I thought, "What's the point?" I felt like all I did was bring the mess from home to college with me. I was drinking, drugging, and smoking in between classes. I talked briefly with my coach, and he would only say that everything was going to be okay. I realized that when your coach or mentor say things like that, they don't care anything about you because it's not them who are going through something.

It was late November, and I was with my girlfriend. My girlfriend was the one person that I could talk to. She listened and gave me positive feedback. That is why I wanted her around me. Even though we didn't see eye to eye all the time, she kept it real with me when some of my teammates were phony and gossiped. She would tell me about people talking behind my back, and everything else. She called me to come over and asked me what I was doing for Thanksgiving. I told her that I would call my parents and asked them if she could go with us for the holidays because she didn't want to go back to Gary, Indiana. I got my parents approval, but I had to stay with her at my sister's apartment. One week later, we had to get our clothes together and travel to Evansville to see my family.

My sister came to pick us up that weekend. I introduced my girlfriend to my sister. We got into the car and drove the highway. It was cold outside. We talked about school, our classes, and about a lot of positive things. I asked my sister how everybody was doing. She said all was well with our family, but I knew that she wanted to say more. I didn't want to tell her the truth that I was experiencing in college. I think that for me to get out of the house and move to college was a big deal. I wasn't fully prepared for the big picture. My education should have been far more important than a girlfriend. I told my sister that I felt like my priorities weren't right. I knew that I had to figure out some things.

Meanwhile, we made it home after stopping and using the bathroom. I was glad to be back and happy to introduce my friend to my family. I introduced her to my parents, and I knew right off the bat that they didn't like her. They didn't say anything about her to me. They just gave me a look that said I could do better than that. I was like wow. Here it is a person I liked, but my parents didn't like her. You must side with your parents, but I thought what God says about this girlfriend of mine. I was so glad that I could always get approval from my parents.

They never told me anything wrong. Later that evening, we went around town telling my family and friends about my girlfriend. We were preparing to go to my sister's house so we all could go out and dance at Tinker's or Allen Lounge. We went out that night at about 11:00 p.m. These lounges were black nightclubs where there were pimps, players, prostitution, drugs, and alcohol. Even if I didn't have any money, people were buying me drinks. I could never say no. Although, I said no occasionally I said yes almost 95% of the time. We sat around and watched people laugh, dance, and make drug deals in the bathroom. As we were watching them act crazy, I asked myself, "Is this the way I want to live my life?" I realized that God doesn't answer prayer in sin. I realized that I had my girlfriend to use her like she was using me. It was getting late at around 1:00 a.m., and I wanted to go home from the club. My parents were right about my girlfriend because when I told her that I was ready to go back to my sister's house, she said that she wasn't ready to go. I said, "Okay. I'm going to get a ride back to my sister's apartment from her boyfriend."

Psalm 66:18 (NASB) says, "If I regard wickedness in my heart, The Lord will not hear."

The next morning, my sister pulled me over to the side and told me that my girlfriend was asking her about a dude in the club. My sister didn't say anything but observed her. I couldn't take her seriously after we returned to college. The rest of the week went well. I talked to some of my old high school buddies and family as the days were winding down. We had some of my parent's cooking and went to church. After being in Evansville for a whole week, I was ready to go back to Illinois. I liked my girlfriend, but I fell back and just let the relationship run its course. The next morning, we said our goodbyes and headed back to college before it got dark. It was a 4-hour drive. I didn't know if it was going to be my sister or my parents taking us back. It was okay with me whoever took us. I gladly thanked my sister for allowing us to stay with her that week. My sister drove us back, and we were tired of going places because every day we did something. We were off and running back to college.

All I thought about were getting back to my classes, playing basketball, and going to practice with my teammates. We left the house at noon and ended up on campus at 4:15 p.m. I got our belongings out of the car and kissed my sister bye-bye. I was so glad to be back. As my sister pulled off, I knew that I had to make a change because there were distractions in my life. I had been through many things, and I was willing to change my situation. I could only look to God and my parents. I had to continue to listen and learn. Most of our lives are turned around because of the decisions we allowed God to make for us. When I made a decision, it was based on how I felt. I could no longer make decisions that way. I was four months into my first year of college, and I went through the stress of getting my class work done. Also, I was dealing with a relationship that was not good. The only good relationships that I had was with God, my parents and some family members. I didn't have a good relationship with my coach, teammates, or friends. We all wanted something from each other and there was no unconditional love like you would get from God or my family.

I felt stuck at times which is somewhere I didn't want to be. I went back into the routine that Monday morning by attending school and basketball practice. I thought I was doing something when I returned from break. I would get letters from family and friends. About a month away from another break, I thought about taking one of my teammates back home with me Christmas. My birthday would happen during the break.

I talked to my professor that Monday morning about my communications class. I asked him how far I could go with a communications degree. He said, "You can get into radio, T.V., broadcasting, and journalism with this degree. You can get your Bachelor, Masters, P.H.D. in this field of study." I thought communications would be good for me, but I didn't see that in my vision. I was never interested in the unknown. I wanted something for me to be set in stone, concrete, or solid. I had other classes that I was into such as Physical Education, World History, and Geography. I loved my class work and participated in everything that I could. I never could get close to some of my other friends because when I told them about God, they were not trying to hear it. They just wanted to party, and I was living a double life at this point. My daily routine was to serve God, go to classes, eat lunch, and go to study hall for one hour. Some days, I would go to basketball practice, home, hang out with my girlfriend, and then bed. Sometimes she would stay all night, but I thought about eliminating something before the new year approached in a few weeks.

As I was about to turn 19 years old, I had a chip on my shoulder. I was smelling myself and calling myself the man. All I wanted to do was go to school and eliminate some things from my life, but I couldn't do what was right at times because the temptations were too great. I thought that I could take days off from partying. The next thing I knew was someone called me. Someone I knew asked me if I wanted to get stoned after school. I needed a break, and I couldn't wait to take my friend T-Bone back to my house for the Christmas break and my birthday. I knew we had to be back by January 3rd for the 1987 school year.

My birthday is on December 28. I told myself that I was not going to party on that day. I tried to be serious about how I felt ahead of time. I realized that it was something that I had made a choice not to do. Besides that, T-Bone and I would talk. He would say to me, "We are good athletes, but it makes no sense to party and wear your body down. The two don't mix."

We would drink beer off and on occasionally. It was different because it was very boring. Sometimes it would get stupid when I would come over to a party for a couple of hours where people were drinking. Guys would start off cursing one another and then end up fighting. I was so embarrassed to be around folks like that. I would get invited to something decent from time to time.

All in all, I was tired of being around people sometimes. I would isolate myself and hideout. After experiencing all the things that were going on, I sat down one Saturday morning to ask God for forgiveness. I needed to get some understanding as to why I was doing what I was doing. Many times, we blame others for our problems when we are our own worst enemy. Sometimes Satan doesn't have to do anything; we do things for him. He laughs at us as if we are too stupid to realize what's going on. People talk, and Satan knows who loves God and who doesn't love God. He knows our weaknesses and our strengths. One thing I did that upset me was I did things many times without thinking of the consequences. There are negative and positive consequences. The positive one is not engaging in anything at all.

By the end of the second semester, I was on the edge of towards transferring to another college or going home. I felt like I was in over my head. As the three weeks were approaching, I had finally made myself get prepared for this trip home. This trip was different from being with my girlfriend previously because we weren't talking as much anymore. I would see her on campus sometimes, but we were not messing around too much anymore. My other friend warned me about her before I messed with her. He told me that she had a boyfriend back home and that they weren't serious. I felt so sad for her because I knew that she didn't know God as I did. I didn't want to mess around with her or date her anymore. The sin that we were continuously committing was bothering me. I had to apologize to her. What was interesting is that she still wanted to be with me. I was shocked and we still dated but it all faded away eventually.

I anticipated going home so Tyrone could meet my family. A couple of days after taking our college test, we got ready. We began packing for almost two weeks of fun. I was hoping that it snowed after we got to my house for the Christmas break. I called my dad and asked him if someone could come to pick us up. He said that he would let me know because he might be too busy. My brothers, Tim, Greg, Gary, and Robert came to pick us up this time. I was so glad to see them. I introduced Tyrone to my brothers. We loaded up our belongings and off we went. I noticed that my friend had brought a lot of clothes with him. He brought dress clothes and sportswear. I knew that most of my clothes were at home.

I didn't party too much this time when I went home. I just went through the motions and allowed Tyrone to enjoy his time with my family and me. Once we got to my house, Tyrone said, "You guys have a big house." I said, "Yes we do. Thanks to God and my parents." My parents were glad that I had a friend that didn't party and loved God. They liked Tyrone because he cared about himself and his family. All we did was sleep and eat the whole time we were there. I took him to see some of my old friends. We had breakfast, lunch, dinner, and snacks. We would go downstairs to play ping pong to occupy us whenever we got bored because we had a table down there. We would play every day. We always had something to do besides go to church.

I knew that I had a calling on my life. I didn't know what to do as far as what was going on in my life. I always influenced the people around me. I didn't know to what degree of influence to cause them to live right and honor God. My thinking was right, but I was trying to figure it all out. I didn't know why I didn't want to party or play basketball anymore. I had been playing ever since I was five years old. It was taking a toll on my body after the car accident. Later in college, I thought it was time to move on or just quit school and basketball altogether. I leaned towards that decision when I was home for the Christmas break. I remember going to the gym with Tyrone and some friends. We played hard, and we had a ball that day. We showered, ate, napped, woke up, and be gone all day. We did something positive every time we got together which is what I liked about Tyrone. He was positive when he even spoke to me and others. I loved him like he was my brother. He was a good friend of mine. After the break, we returned to campus and told people how much of a good time we had.

It doesn't matter who you are. Whether you do good or not, some people are not happy for you. You must be happy and allow God to show you how to love and bless others. By no means was I perfect, good or bad. I was average and had a very laid-back personality. I was introverted at times and aloof. I didn't care if you liked me or not.

When we returned from college on January 2nd in 1987, Tyrone and I were happy. We returned drug-free and peaceful. I did what I always did which was to thank God and my parents. God made it possible for me to go to different places unharmed. I am blessed and highly favored. My parents were genuine and real. They were all I had looking back on it. My backbone was Jesus Christ, my mom, and dad.

The rest of the school year I did the best that I could in the classroom. Also, I completed a solid basketball season until I got a call in February that my dad had been admitted into the hospital. I wanted to come home but I once I talked to my mom, I realized that it wasn't that serious. My dad's diabetes was acting up. His sugar was too high. I prayed for him and hoped to talk to him as soon as possible. I didn't speak to him until a couple days later. Once I was able to speak to him, I asked him if he was okay, but I could tell that something was wrong. I told him that I loved and cared about him. He said he loved me too and we hung up the phone. I cried because my earthly king was sick, and I was looking at the bigger picture. Later in March, I talked to my dad almost two to three times a week. He was a great man of God. He joked and laughed with me. I was laughing with him on the phone. It was getting close for spring break, and I was thinking to stay at school, but I had to go home to see my dad. I had a friend of mine drive me there. I only went home for a couple of days in the middle of spring break in March. After I saw my dad, I was happy to see him feeling better and healthy.

After sneaking in town for a couple of days, finding out my dad had diabetes and high blood pressure was overwhelming. He told me all the medications that he was taking. I asked my mother how she felt when I was there. I could tell everyday life was taking a toll on my parents. I missed them both. I had to return to college even though I didn't tell anyone once I had arrived. I made the decision not to go to college anymore. It wasn't for me. I anticipated coming home and not returning for the 1987-1988 school year at OCC. I had until April and May or the last semester to move on which I did. I was preparing for my finals and trying to get the best grades possible. I planned to go home, regroup, and transfer to another college.

As I told a few people that I was leaving and moving on, the word got out that I was leaving because I didn't like the school which was true. Some people know how to get rumors started and tell lies to keep things going. I felt like a big weight lifted off my shoulders. I wanted to be free and be true to myself. I wasn't getting that at the college. I didn't feel wanted or needed. I was an outsider who didn't feel welcomed. I knew the other 15 to 20 African Americans who were there that felt the same way.

Among several hundred students enrolled that year, I made a bad decision going there. I needed a change. I said my goodbyes. As time winded down, I was ready to put that year behind me. I said goodbye to my ex-girlfriend, Mark, Tyrone, and my other teammates. My roommate Hollis was probably happy that I was gone because he hated me. On my last day there, I remember we had all gotten something to eat and talked for hours. I had my brother pick me up and was ready to go home. I was happy to be coming home for good. I needed a change in life. I told my brother my decision as we were going back to Indiana. He knew I wasn't going to be there long because he knew that wasn't for me. He saw how I was acting in front of him and my family. He said I wasn't myself. I just wished I could have done two years instead of one year. I returned to my parents' home, and I immediately started working for my dad. He was still sick, overweight and exhausted. He was irritable at unexpected times. I loved him anyways and no matter what.

My life wasn't the same when I came back home. One month after I was home, my cousin called and said he was moving to Denver, Colorado to pursue coaching. I told him, "Sounds too good to be true. Hit me up once you find out what's going on out there." He called me about two months later in July and said that he was coming to pick me up in a couple of weeks to transfer me to a college. I went to Colorado for the summer and came back to Evansville in August. Nothing was going right in my favor. I was set on finding a regular job and going back to my dad's church. I did get a job, but something was still missing. I was bitter about what I went through. I had doubts and self-pity at times. I found odd jobs while still working for my dad.

My mom would tell me, "You know that once a crab climbs up to the top of the bucket trying to get out, there is always another crab trying to pull it down so he couldn't go where." I laughed at first, but it's true. What she was saying to me was to climb the mountain and even go around the mountain. Don't let anyone get in your way of reaching your goals. It was a sad situation in 1988 because that was when the crack cocaine epidemic was very rapid. I was using drugs off and on after I came home. It was mainly weed and coke. When I was 20 years old, I had a job but still lived with my parents. I was very vulnerable and very non-caring. I did what I wanted to do. I was just tired of a lifestyle that required structure because I had it at 11 years old and it was taken from me. So, I rebelled by holding grudges and hating myself for being a part of something that I couldn't understand. The enemy would always attack me in the things I liked or loved. I had quit playing basketball in an organized setting. I tried to give everything up and start all over again. That didn't happen. I rationalized repeatedly. I made a mistake coming back home because I was never the same. It seemed like trouble was all around me. If I wasn't in trouble, someone in my family like my nephews and cousins were. My dad was sick again. He would be sick off and on from 1986 until his passing in February 1989. By the end of 1988, I was binged drinking and feeling sorry for myself. During this time, I slept around again and did what I always did which was trying to figure things out. I still would go to church off and on. I would confide in my old friends, and they reassured me that I would be okay.

I thought, "Here we go again." I decided to get some help from The Rescue Mission which is a program for people with drug and alcohol addictions. The word of God is preached before you eat. If you stay there like I did it will help you stay off the streets. I wanted to get clean, and I was scared. I knew that Satan was trying to kill, steal, and destroy me. I checked in on a Saturday afternoon, and no one knew I was there. I was somewhat embarrassed and at a low point in my life. I know that the Great God Almighty was with me because when I checked in, there were guys that I saw that looked like they were dead men walking.

I saw murderers, gangsters, crooks, and you name it there. Some even got out of prison or suffered from mental illness. As they got information from me so I could get a bed, I asked myself, "What have I gotten myself into?" The first night was hard. I walked around feeling the building from the inside out. There were guidelines to follow and rules or regulations to abide by. I tried my best to comply with their strict rules. We woke up at 6:00 a.m. to do devotions. We ate breakfast at 7:00 a.m. Afterward, we made our beds and cleaned our rooms. Next, we met with assigned counselors so we could have an exit plan.

We could stay there for a year if we wanted, but I was determined not to stay that long. Anyway, this program would let you leave and go to work. If you didn't have an outside job, you had to work for them. There were around seventy men in this program. At times I saw guys arguing and acting crazy. I would stay away from those knuckleheads. I remained in God's word to find peace and comfort while I was there. Most of the guys in the program were crazy white guys and a few black men. I talked to all of them as we were telling our stories. I thought it is none of their business and they don't care anyway until we had a round table discussion one night. Many of us were trying to get stuff off our chest. I ended up staying there for over one month, and some days I felt like it wasn't for me. I found out that the program was for me because going there gave me structure again.

We knew that we were the black sheep, but God was turning us back into His lost sheep that had been found. We were drinking milk. We weren't ready for meat to chew and spit out the bones. We were all living our way until we gave God a chance to work in us. These were some of the best times of my life. I got treatment, stayed clean, gained weight, read the word of God, and practiced what the word said. I was taught about God's agape love which is unconditional love. I was taught about forgiveness and restoration. I was taught so much that I was given a job out of the deal.

I got a job at the Department of Correction Youth Care Center. I thought I was on cloud nine at this point, but I still was living at the Mission's Center. I remember how the job came to me. One of the men came to me. He said that some of the Ministry Directors had been watching me. I was around 21 years old at the time. They called me in the office one day, and it was a good feeling. I felt so good about myself signing paperwork and being hired to work with Youth. I helped them find Jesus Christ as I did so they could receive healing from their past. I got my uniforms, and a couple of days later I took a drug test. It was clean. I knew I could do it because it was healthy for me to be working. I finally got time after a couple of months of being there to leave and tell my family where I was living.

I tried to leave the program and was able to for a couple of weeks. However, I still ended up going back and forth from time to time. I remember feeding young men. I was so happy with the job. I was obsessed with tower controls, and they operated because the facility was a low to medium security building. We had to give them recreation for an hour, then lock them back in. We would do a devotion with them, and then a group of ministers would come to them. They had to sign in, and we had to prepare seating for them. I would watch them and see how they interacted with the ministers. I had fun working with everybody. This experience not only opened my eyes, but it changed my life. Everybody began to tell more about themselves and backgrounds from a trust standpoint. The reason why I was going to the mission property is that I started to start feeling myself and I started seeing this woman. It was only two months of me being clean, and I started thinking about getting in a relationship.

I went to AA meetings at night, and I had to get permission to go there if I stayed at the mission. Sometimes I would have one or two days off work from the youth center. I would go home or stay there. I had choices, but the decision I made with the girl I met at the AA meeting was terrible. We were both early in sobriety, and I spoke to her after one meeting. I saw her again one evening around the fourth AA meeting. Afterward, she said, "You want to go out for something to eat?" I said, "Yes. Okay." We went to Burger King. When we finished eating, we drove around in her car for a while. I noticed she started acting all frisky as I looked at her. She pulled over and started kissing me. We ended up doing all kinds of sinful things. I told myself that I wasn't going to do it anymore, but we ended up doing it many other times until I stopped going to AA meetings altogether. When you read the Bible, it cuts like a two-edged sword.

I was a full-blown sinner on the surface, very prideful and self-serving. I wanted to give up the player title. I just wanted to run as far away as I could after this experience, so I ended up moving back to my parent's home not realizing that those series of events had set me back. These events had a profound impact on my life because I never imagined getting myself clean. Not playing sports and trading one addiction for another was just another coping mechanism to help me draw near to God. I felt like the oddball and misfit because I had given up the drugs and alcohol. I held on to fornication and lust. I thought it was normal and I didn't understand about the fact that I shouldn't participate in it. I thought, "I'm a man and going to do my thing." So, one day when I had free time to talk to my father, he explained to me how fornication is wicked and wrong. He said when you are not married it's a sin. He told me that he had done the same thing when he was younger in the military. I was like wait a minute, and a feeling came over me that I was addicted to sex. I didn't want to tell him that I had been seeing different women on different occasions. I didn't plan on telling anyone that. I just wanted to start over and go cold turkey.

I did start over and still maintained a level of confidence to not give up on God. God doesn't give up on us. We give up on God sometimes and want to continue in sin therein. We even feel like we can't measure up to His standards. I stayed close to my family primarily, my parents, because I knew that my dad was sick. He didn't want any of us to know how bad he was. He was very ill because I saw him one day taking five different types of medications. I would read the labels and see what they were used for and why. He took a water pill for high blood pressure. I would give him 100 units of insulin. He also took something else for inflammation. He just accepted his life on life's terms, and he didn't complain. I watched my dad work extremely hard while he was very sick. He still trusted God to overcome his demons and failing health. I couldn't do anything but help him, and it was too late. I remember him telling me from time to time to take care of my mother if something happened to him. He was very serious about what he said. He would tell me to go to the park with him to walk around and exercises. I admired him for trying. He inspired me just off his sheer courage. He helped everybody, and I can honestly say he is the reason why I'm writing My Life Becoming A Minister.

CHAPTER 4

My King Passed Away

On February 6, 1989, I was at work when I got a call from my brother Greg. He said that he went to the hospital that morning with my dad because my father wasn't feeling well. My brother drove him to Deaconess Hospital and sat in the emergency room all day until they admitted my dad for an overnight stay. Early the next morning when I went to work, my dad, the Late Rev. Judge Lent Meriweather, passed away around 5:00 a.m. I was devastated, and it hurt so bad that I wanted to die. It was like my whole world just changed. I didn't know what I was going to do. My only thoughts were pain and suffering. I was lost again and had no hope. He was my everything and my role model. He was the man and a very powerful man of God. He was well respected and loved in the community and abroad. He was only 58 years old. He died so young, but I understood that my father served his purpose on earth. He did all he could to help us get our lives in order.

Later that day when I got off from work, I went home and looked at my family. I saw the devastation, hurt, and pain in their eyes. My brothers and sisters were very devastated as well. I never saw my mom cry so much. The next couple of days, we received calls from members of our church, family, and friends. I never saw an outpouring of people coming by the house to send food, flowers, cards and everything else before this. Our family was very appreciative for the funeral arrangements that were done by Gaines Funeral Home.

My family waited at least a week to bury my dad because he had brothers in California and Tennessee and a sister in Indiana. As they were preparing to fly and drive into Evansville, I had a bad feeling that this was going to be a hard pill to swallow. I went by the funeral home and stood around because I knew that's where my dad's body was located. I thought about all the good times we had when I was a little boy and the love that he gave. I remember when my dad led a delegation to Haiti one summer. He brought back Haitian boys and girls from his missionary trip. Also, he brought back gifts and sculptures.

My mind reflected on all the great things he did for the Lord. I felt bitter and angry. He had been sick for quite a long time. I thought he had a cold, but I knew it was serious this time. I just wanted to tell him how much I loved and cared for him.

As relatives were coming to town, we prepared for a wake. The wake was early in the week, but the funeral was on Saturday. The wake was from 7:00 p.m. to 9:00 p.m. on Friday, and it was packed. I remember taking deep breaths at first because I wanted to see how my dad looked in the casket. I was quite impressed. He looked like he was sleeping. All my family, friends, uncles, aunts, and cousins attended the wake and there was standing room only. I heard people saying he was a great man of God. I heard everything, but I heard from God that day as well. I knew I had to carry the torch. I just didn't know to what degree.

I couldn't sleep that night when we got home from the wake. I thought about paying my respects to my father and the legacy that he left me. I thought about wearing the proper suit and what I was going to do after he was laid to rest. I thought about all kinds of crazy things. I realized that the enemy could attack you when you are going through a bad situation. I was being attacked especially after losing my dad at a time when I needed him most. I lost my dad in my 20s. Saturday morning came, I was in a frenzy. I felt very sad and all emotional. I just started crying. I just wanted to tell him that I love him for the last time even though he was gone. I was very hopeful that he would wake up. I took a shower, got my suit together, and brushed my teeth. I anticipated all that was going to happen.

Once we were ready, the funeral home cars came by to pick us up. I looked outside, and I saw about four limousines waiting outside. You would have thought it was some big megastar inside the house. The star that day was my dad's home going service. We loaded up on the cars and proceeded to go into the direction of the church which was about seven blocks away. It seemed like forever. Once we all got there, we were led inside to the front of the church. I was so nervous to see all the people there. Our church was packed, and there was standing room only. People came from all over the world.

The community was saddened about my father's untimely death. He had given us all he had, and now it was time for us to pay tribute to him. I know that God was well pleased with my dad because of the relationship they had. "A job well done, my good and faithful servant." I thought that the whole time of the funeral. As I sat in the pew next to my brothers, I looked up at the pulpit. I saw some of my father's close friends. They used to come over to the house to visit. Some came over for counsel, advice, and ministry. I reflected when I was a little boy when my dad used to cook for me. He did everything possible to help his family. I mean he truly put his whole life on the line for his family.

The funeral lasted for about two hours. The songs, preaching, and remarks from everyone was incredible. I said to myself, "I hope someone will feel that way about me when the death angel calls me home." We got ready to leave the church to lay my dad to rest at Oak Hill Cemetery. I was a pallbearer at my dad's funeral. I recommend to anybody that when their parents pass to do the honors. It was an awesome experience for me. I felt terrible carrying his body, but I gained strength from the Lord Jesus Christ. It was the last time I was able to say goodbye to Dad.

As we were taking his body back to the funeral car, I thought about the times he would ask me to go somewhere with him. He would always have a positive conversation and considered others. We would stop by his mother's house and drop off food like fish and chicken. Also, he would drop off food and goods to church members, families and friends. I realized that my dad was a giver. He gave from his heart because Jesus Christ taught him that. I realized this when I was 15 years old. I witnessed my first encounter of both my parents praying at their bedsides on both knees. My mouth dropped wide open, and I started to ask questions. I'm glad that I had parents that believed in God. I feel their presence even today.

We drove out to the cemetery. The ministers, family members, and motorcade was there. Some friends came out to the burial site. It was a sight to see. It must have been at least 20 to 25 cars in the motorcade that day. Once we arrived, my father received a 21-gun salute because he was a Private First-Class in the military. He fought for his country in the Korean War. I was so proud of him and remain so today. Afterward, we had our final remarks and said our goodbyes to dad. I went back to the car feeling broken and scared.

Suddenly everything hit me of the kind of father I had. Often, he would say, "You watch when I'm gone what's going to happen." He was right. There was no peace, love, and going to church. There was no more anything because no one carried the torch, so I walked around in the wilderness for several years after my father's death. We went back to Mt. Olive Galilee Baptist Church to eat some food after the burial. We were all looking at one another. It was like being in a room full of people, and everybody's wounded except you. The only reason why I was able to press through was because of God. I had no choice but to do God's will. I was hurt, but not wounded. I had to carry the torch somehow and some way. As I ate at the church, I heard my brother Gary say that our dad passed away on his birthday. Then I listened to my sister Kathy say that our dad passed away one week before her birthday. I immediately thought that our father's passing had taken a toll on them as well. I found out that when someone you love dearly passes away, there is no amount of money, food, and whatever else you give can replace them.

These things help, but at my lowest point, and I couldn't eat or sleep. I felt like we were all being punished. At times I felt guilty which was a trick of the enemy. He wants to keep us bound, out of control, and useless. He tries to use every trick in the book to divide us. I realized at the repast that there were a few negative things said as well among family members, but the devil is a liar. I just wanted our family back together strong like it was when my dad was alive. A few days after my father was laid to rest, I started drinking again. My life was spinning out of control.

After everything my family and I had been through, the entire Black History month was a tribute to my dad. I didn't see it any other way. I realized that the rest of the year was going to be tough as well. All I thought about as the days and months went by is losing my father and the impact it had on my family and me. Life turned 360 degrees with my family, and we were never the same. This devastation took a toll on my family, and everybody went their separate ways. The foundation of my family was blown away like a brick house in a hurricane. Nobody communicated, stuck together nor bonded as we used too when my father was alive. Everyone grieves in their way. All I could do was pray and ask God for strength. What they forget is there is strength when a family prays together: they stay together. It seemed like every day there were distractions and mischief.

I remember times when we tried to handle our mother's affairs. She wanted to move out of the house, and I was skeptical about that. I saw that she needed to move to a smaller place. She finally sold the home and moved out. I was happy for her to continue her journey with the Lord. She returned to her old church home that she was raised in - the Apostolic Faith. She seemed a lot happier when I saw her after we all had to move out of the house. I knew it was coming. There are things God will allow you to feel and see before it happens.

I met this girl and moved in with her. We knew each other from high school. When I lived at my mother's house, I stayed with my girlfriend from time to time, so my only recourse was to move out and move in with her or go to the mission. On March 14, 1989, I moved into her apartment. We ended up having a son together, and our place became too small because she already had two kids. I knew I was in a bad relationship with her because the relationship was not of God. I was in a relationship of convenience, and I just got with her. It wasn't real love, and I felt the pain of that. When things got bad, they were terrible. I remember her telling me to help her kids. I thought to myself, "I'm not ready for this." We were acting like we were happy in front of everyone. It was so sad to put on a happy face when you know you are not together for the right reasons.

I remember moving out of town because I hoped that it could change our lives. My girlfriend did the most unthinkable thing that you could do when you are in a relationship: cheating. On top of that, she blamed me for her cheating. We were together for about six years, and I was glad it was over. The only things I was worried about were the kids. After I moved on, I tried to visit the children. She lied to them until they found out the truth. I would buy them Christmas gifts, and I prayed for them as well as hoping that they will be okay. The whole year of 1989 and 1991 were years of hell for me. All I did was go to work as much as I could. I got drunk and high and was a full-blown functional addict. I went from one program into another. I realized for the first time in my life that I hadn't surrendered to Jesus Christ.

I would tell every man not to do what I did because it only adds to the confusion. I wasn't happy with what I was doing. I was using drugs and alcohol. Kids know when you're high on drugs. They watch what their parents do. When I moved back to Evansville, I lived with a friend of mine and moved into the Mission. I didn't want to, but I had nowhere else to go. I stayed there for a long time until I got on my feet again. It seemed like every time I got on my feet, I would get high and mess up. I had no hope. All I thought was it's just a matter of time that my life was going to turn for the worst.

I would call my sister asking her for money and other things. She helped me out, but I didn't want to tell her that I was homeless. She knew it, and I knew that other family members knew it as well. I didn't care at this point in my life. I just wanted to get the help that I needed from the triggers and other things I dealt with. I experienced warm and fuzzy feelings. Imagine that you want to change your life after everything you have been through. You are at the mercy of drugs and serving God. That is how deep it was for me. I had to make a choice. I tried to serve both, and it was frustrating. I couldn't do it. It left me lost and very out of control. I was fighting for my life. I felt like I lost everything that I had. I was miserable, and I had to continue to fight.

I was in for a change. I attended AA meetings again, and that still didn't work. I remembered what I went through with another woman at one time. I tried to go to different churches on and off again. I remember going back to my dad's church several years after he had passed away. I wasn't ready for that anymore. It was over for me because a new pastor had come in and it just wasn't the same. I knew that was the end of an era. God had taken me into higher dimensions. I had gone through many heartaches, pains, trials, tribulations, and storms. I couldn't do anything but trust Him. By 1992, I was getting better.

I had joined my mother's church and sang in the choir. I was friends with the elders and pastors at the church. The same Jesus Christ raised my parents but in two different denominations. My dad was a Baptist, and my mother was Apostolic. We just went with the flow of going to church and worshiping God. I wasn't on the drug scene anymore. I concluded that it was no longer for me. I would be a member of my mother's church, and it was different for me. I had been there before, but I had no intentions of joining. I did join eventually. I thought about my mother's old church. It was a small building on Jefferson Street. It had been unoccupied for years and not used at all. It was the path that led me to where I'm at today.

All the old members of my mom's church on Jefferson were dead. My mother had been going to this church for a while because I remember it when I was five years old. My mother had moved on to a new church where the members excepted her. However, the new church she attended didn't believe in women ministers or pastors. The men were pastors, and the women were ushers doing praise and worship. People mask and do all sorts of things in life, but God knows everything we do. All I remember was when my father was alive if my mother wanted to go to her church, she went. Out of obedience to God, she chose to go to my dad's Church. I'm proud of her because they don't make them like her anymore. She prayed and tarried all through the night. The church today isn't like the church years ago. We prayed more and gave all we had back then. Everyone helped each other one by one. People were sharing, caring, and lovable. Today, there are clicks and organizations. I wondered if any of this was from Jesus Christ or someone else. I started isolating myself at times because I didn't want to be with anyone. I was like a loner. I found out that it was beneficial up to a point. I was hiding from my family. I was already thinking about leaving again, but I couldn't because every time I left, I would come back home. I was never homesick.

I thought about leaving Evansville for good, but I didn't know when. I ask God to reveal Himself to me. I wanted out of Evansville after the death of my brother-in-law and losing my dad. I lost all hope, and my only hope was turning to God. I might as well had packed all my belongings and moved into a cave. I was lost and lived whenever and wherever I could. I took a downward spiral and recognized the danger and state of mind I was in. I knew I wasn't delivered from drugs and alcohol. You may not drink or get high anymore, but the behavior that it causes us to believe that we can do anything at any time is a false sense of reality. I sat down and took a rain check on what was transpiring in my heart, mind, body, and soul. Suddenly, I didn't know what was going to happen. I called on the name Jesus Christ.

Out of all the things that happened that year, I couldn't rebound from this one. I chilled out until I bought a car. I would talk to my brothers: Timothy, Gary, Greg, and Robert. We got together sometimes and enjoyed one another. Sometimes, we cooked out and made hot dogs and burgers. I had to do things that would change my whole life, and I knew it wasn't going to be easy. I couldn't trust anyone nor myself. I needed some advice and guidance from my family. I wanted God to take me to a new place to start all over. I knew I wasn't ready to go, but at least I was telling the truth. I was in a do or die situation. I thought that if I could fake it until I make it, I would be okay. Major things were missing in my life.

All I could do was hope and pray that God would give me a new life somewhere that I could start over. Perhaps I could've moved away from Evansville, but I wasn't ready yet. I wanted to move out of Indiana. I had lived in Evansville for a long time. I had lived in Indianapolis for a couple of years and had been to Gary, Indiana several times. I just felt that I needed to go in a different direction. By this time, it was in the fall of 1993, and I was going through some rough patches again. Trying to stay in touch with my family was a huge task. Several years after my father passed, we all lived in the same city but were growing apart from each other. I hardly ever saw my sisters when all these things were going on because we were all doing our own things. I was over Evansville and didn't care anymore about anybody. I know now that is a weakness. I thought that if something were to happen to my mother matters would only worsen. I hoped that someone would step up to the plate by guiding or leading us back on track. For example, it was like Moses' brother Aaron leading the children of Israel out of Egypt to the Promised Land instead of Moses. We had no one to take us to the Promise Land because the Lord had to prune and change me.

I could no longer do my own things. I had to trust in the Lord and let go of some carnal ways. I was in rebellion and didn't want anything from anyone. I refused to visit people's houses asking for food, drinks, money, or anything else I needed. Many times, our character is no good once we are wasted on illegal substances or alcohol. I had been wasted and not happy with my life. I was around men doing the same things who were throwing their lives away. Many of us had God gifted abilities and talents. We just were not ready to take a leap of faith. My biggest fear was not knowing what was on the other side with God. It was the fear of having someone take control of my life. I can't see Him.

Is He Real? Oh, it's easy to say, "Yes Lord, I want to live entirely for You and only You," until an assignment to walk in obedience or sacrifice is given. I was still about 70 % to 30% ratio of giving my whole life to God. I wanted to hang on to my sins and do some sinful deeds. It wasn't that I had run out of things to do; it was me trying to find new sinful things to do. The only other choice was to move to God. I fought and lost many battles. One thing a man can never do is curse God. Our hands are too short to box with God.

I witnessed how celebrities have nice things that look glamorous, but on the inside, they are as miserable as they want to be. I was the same way. I was all torn up inside, and on the outside, I looked like I was happy. However, I was all busted and disgusted. I never wanted to feel that way again. I can tell you that the journey was well worth it in the end. Look at the part you played before you walk away from something. I realized that I should never have been a part of many things that I was involved in throughout my life. It was my fault that problems arose from the situation. I wanted no parts of sin, but somehow, I was surrounded by it daily. People were doing things that I didn't approve of when I went to the Mission or around my family. Sometimes I wouldn't say anything. I would turn my cheek.

I visited my coach's house one time to talk about old times. We both knew that I was going to ask for money. It was always that weed or alcohol beverage that I craved for $20. He would always give me money. I told myself that I was wrong for that. I felt guilty because he was there for me through all my successes and failures. I never told him how much I cared for him.

Rev. Barry Paddock was my AAU Basketball Coach even when I played for the mini Evansville Aces. God blessed me with some pretty decent male figures even years after my daddy had been deceased. I just missed my dad.

God put me in a position where I could do nothing but turn to Him. The winter of 1993 was the first time I decided to read the entire Bible in chronological order. I didn't realize everything that I was reading was ancient. I questioned some of the things I read. For instance, Jesus turning water into wine. As I was read the story, the first thing that jumped out at me was why did he perform such miracles and for what purpose? God also took some of the worst people and turned their lives around such as King David. It amazed me how God can take a person like Moses and use him to advance His people to the promised land. It gave me hope. I too can get free from bondage through prayer, supplication, and application. I wanted to explore my thinking at this time in my life. I was around 22 years old. I was no longer lost. I came out from the worst of many bad relationships. I tried to get employed and keep the jobs once I got employed. I didn't want to get terminated for drug and alcohol use or plain ignorance. I kept saying, "Lord this time make it plain to me what you want." I finally surrendered. It cost me friendships, and it also kept me out of trouble. I was a follower of Jesus Christ again. I attended my mother's church visiting many other churches. It wasn't easy reinventing myself.

I learned Matthew, Mark, Luke, and John. The Gospels are great examples of Jesus Christ's wisdom, knowledge, and understanding. I was into the Holy Spirit and Christianity. I learned everything that I could for the whole winter and spring of 1994. I was cold turkey and drug-free. I was working again and got my confidence back. I started seeing my family, and we were conversing again. We would still talk about the past for healing purposes. I just wanted to get prepared for the platform or the take off that would take me to a new level. It was so weird to be clean, and I was different. I envisioned myself having my own church. I dreamt, "Pastor Jerome Meriweather of the Potter's Wheel Church." The slogan would be "Jesus Christ is the Potter." I'm the clay that needs to be refined and refilled with God's purpose. I thought about being a role model for my son and family members. I understood the power of God and the permission Satan had to get from God to get at me through a storm, test, or trial. I wanted God to show me how to expose him through his wicked schemes. I no longer wanted to fight anyone physically or mentally. I wanted to do it spiritually. I was learning that I could do all things through Christ which strengthens me.

I was making progress. I had to lose some worldly people in the process. Also, I had to disconnect from some church people because some of them were holier than God which was too much for me. It seemed like they could do nothing wrong and they blamed others for their problems. They believed they were okay because they had more money or talent than me. They never acknowledged God as the One who gave them the gifts, anointing, and blessings. I would visit this all-white church sometimes and saw people go there for the word. Many people fellowshipped there for the food. They would serve breakfast before the service and the dinner after the service was over. They fed the poor and would send people home with a doggy bag to feast on later. I liked the sermons sometimes. The praise and worship were okay. Occasionally the pastor would preach about the major and minor prophets. He mentioned how some of them were poor, rich, and powerful. I realized in a situation like that you can have power. If it's God's power, you will be blessed and highly favored. You can have power without God like the Pharisees and Sadducees. You can have money and be at odds with one like they did when Jesus was on the scene. They formed alliances to keep God from advancing His calling. I wonder why people who have agendas don't have a purpose. If it's not a Godly purpose, it fails. I can't understand why you would build a church on quicksand and hope it stands.

Why would you bless someone with old clothes when you can bless them with nice clothes? Don't give someone something you don't want. Give them your best. Help them with God's love, joy, peace, and give them the fruit of the Spirit. I learned to stop pleasing myself and others. I taught myself to love God unconditionally. I was headed in the right direction and loved it. I felt God's presence everywhere I went daily. I felt Him in my house, church, grocery store, bible study, and many other places. I even convinced a few people to get saved because I told them that God is the way, the truth, the light, and that anyone that calls upon the name of the Lord God shall be saved.

I was never the same after being clean. I knew that God was giving me multiple chances to see things His way. I saw life on His terms only. I realized for the first time in my life that I could no longer live the way I used to live. It was difficult for me to hang out with people. When someone asked me to go out with them, I started thinking about it. I eventually said no. The reason why I refused to go out and party is because I needed to start over. I have been repeating the same stuff and going to different addiction programs for a while. I never made any good progress. I was no longer relying on anybody but Jesus Christ. It was different and a chance I had to take. It wasn't easy. It was the only I felt I could stay sober by not using anything at all. I did nothing except ate food. I drank juice and water. Sometimes I took natural substances.

At all cost, I avoided everything I could to stay clean. I wanted to change for God and wanted a better life for myself. I would have drug and alcohol dreams. The dreams were good to my flesh. I realized that I couldn't have anything in my hand. I was doing fine and didn't think about it. Some of the hardest times I had in recovery was watching someone use alcohol and drugs confess that they were not addicts. I was like that. I even had hard times going over to someone's house where they were drinking a beer. I knew that I couldn't do all sorts of things if I wanted God to use me, so I just remained clean for several months. My old friends walked away from me because I had been clean and sober for a while. I realized that once you start walking with the Lord, everybody is not going where you are going. God has a plan for all of us. His plans for us are not the same. He blesses us with different ministries and many gifts. Everything is to be used for His Kingdom. I was still in Evansville and wanted to move away because God allowed me to see over the horizon. I saw a glimpse of my destiny, and I didn't know where I was going. By this time God was preparing and letting me know that no matter what I did good or bad, He was going to release me from bondage. He would move me away from my old habits and lifestyle. It took a while, but He was pruning me and getting me prepared for a bigger platform.

I waited for this change because after having major setbacks and going through hell, I wondered how much I was going to be able to deal with my madness. I would pray to God every second, minute, an hour to help me navigate through my thought process. I made myself change my life. In 1995, I was changed in my heart, mind, body, and soul. I wasn't delivered though. I was a babe still on milk and the bottle. I had just come off one of the biggest binges of my life. I was surprised that I was still around. At one point, I thought my life was over, and I kept on living a lie. I knew it would have been over. What amazed me is that people liked me better when I was drunk or high because they could control what I did around them. When they saw that they could no longer do that, they were mad and didn't want to be around me. They acted funny because I no longer wanted to do what they wanted to do and started hating on me. They said, "You think you are better than everybody." I said, "Yes. I'm better because God made it better."

My life consisted of my work schedule of working from 7:30 a.m. to 5 p.m. I would eat dinner at 6:45 p.m. or 7:00 p.m. I thought that there was more to life than what I was currently doing. I dreamed of going back to school, and eventually, I went to Indiana Business college for a semester. I didn't value going because the professor didn't seem to care about the students. It was an online business college, and the campus was small. I worked at Sam Wholesale club and Bob Evans. I worked every day like a slave. I went over to Buckner Tower to see my mother from time to time. Afterward, I went to the mission every week and attended church when I could. Other than that, I was idle for a reason because I realized that God was saving me for something greater than me. I was nothing special in my eyes, but God saw something in me that I couldn't see in myself. I even thought about going into the military, but I knew it wasn't what God wanted, so I stopped doing what I wanted to do. In the summer of 1995 and 1996, I was so blessed to have things going in the right direction.

I wanted to be happy with myself. I had a good job and a part-time job. I had nice clothes and my own place. I needed to go on a higher level with God, but I didn't know where to start because I was afraid. I attended different churches in the area. People knew me and my father. Sometimes you can accomplish things off your parents' name, but I wasn't relying on them. I was relying on Jesus Christ which is the name above every name and the Great I Am. I felt out of place or like something was missing, so one Sunday I went to my mom's church and talked to the Bishop. I was so happy to see him because I needed his counsel. He seemed to care about me. I asked him about how he became a pastor and what was his calling? He told me that it was his calling. God calls whom He wants to feed his sheep, so they won't run astray. He told me that God would give you signs about what He wants from you. God will deliver you from bondage. The Bishop said, "We all have problems, and we need to pray always to God. We need to pray even when things are going well. God knows our hearts." It seemed to me that the only thing I was trying to avoid was not to get overzealous with my thinking. In terms of making progress, the only thing that kept me going was God. I was hurting internally, but I was carnal. I didn't know how to express my feelings as I waited for God to give me my final exit plan to move out of Evansville. His presence dumbfounded me. I wasn't too keen on believing in something that I couldn't see either.

I was very skeptical when the Bishop preached about God allowing the Children of Israel to pass through a parted sea. I wasn't too thrilled about hearing a sermon from my father at times. My father preached about how King David lured Bathsheba into his place to commit sin. I thought it was all hogwash. One day everything became real to me because I realized I did the same things. Christians can't blame God for their sins because He is not a sinner like we are. The things that Adam and Eve did in the Garden is the reason why we are sinners. I explained things in the Bible to people.

I would take my time reading the Bible because some things you can't explain. For example, in Genesis in Chapter 1 the earth, day, and night were formed. Why did God create 12 hours for daylight and 12 hours of the night? Why only 24 hours? There could have just been daylight since God is light. I thought, "It would be difficult to sleep in the daytime during 24 hours of daylight." I realized that you couldn't figure God out. I was trying to educate myself like a Theologian. I thought about going to seminary, but by 1996 and 1997 I was a long way off. I explored all the possibilities and told people that I wanted to be like my dad. I knew at some point in time that I was going to follow in my father's footsteps. I had to get in a deeper relationship with God. My days of going through the motions of pretending to know God were over. I had to study to show myself approved to rightly divide the word of God.

I wanted to have a girlfriend again because I had quit fornicating. I wanted to have a healthy relationship with a woman. I never had that experience. I had it with my family, but they had changed after my father's death. I wanted to walk with Jesus Christ, and it wasn't easy because people had their opinions. "Well, he didn't make it in basketball. What is he going to do now?" I asked God what the purpose of Him making me wait for a long time before He found a ministry for me to study. I needed Him to make me an understudy before He released me into unfamiliar territory. I felt like God was honing my skill set for several different ministries. I was seasoned in the Missionary Ministries, Community Ministries, and Outreach Ministries. I had hands-on experience with those ministries with my dad. I had to get prepared to do other things like preparing myself to worship, doing the Lord's supper, and get the proper training to be ordained some day. I would watch other Christians and saw how they prepared for worship. I was asking God to help me in every area of my life. He will deliver anybody from sin. He said all you must do is ask and you shall receive. Knock, and the door will open. Seek, and you shall find. That is all we must do when we call upon the name of the Lord. Don't let anyone take the Holy Spirit from you. He is your protector, provider, and comforter.

When things aren't going well, you pray. God will accept you as you are. When things are going bad ask Him for help. Don't wait until things get out of hand. God will show you how to get yourself together and get your life back on track. I was distraught at times because I would ask God why it seems like good people get the short end of the stick. He never answered me on that. I asked Him to reveal certain things to me because I was like I'm not doing the things I used to do. I just figured that if I stayed clean long enough that I was going to be rewarded. I knew that God knew my heart better than I did. I was okay by it though because I was determined to stay clean and sober. The fact that I was able to do this for myself was a good thing. I was never in trouble with the law. I abided by all the rules and regulations of Indiana.

In the spring of 1998, I was so tired of being in Evansville. I had been clean for quite some time and decided to have one drink daily. I was so bored that I wasn't happy about being clean and sober. I went to a cookout with a friend and decided that I wanted to drink a Bud Light. I felt so good, but I felt a little sorry for ending my clean time. I was taught through AA to call your sponsor and do various steps. Suddenly, I felt no better than any of the meetings that I attended. It was a warm and fuzzy feeling when I started to drink a little more.

God knew I was going to fall again. He warned me early on in our relationship that I was going to be okay whether I made a mistake or not. He loved me no matter what. All I had to do is not be prideful and stop thinking that I was perfect. I was facing this guilt after I finished drinking. I had to tell someone I relapsed. I did and was embarrassed. It was hurtful. I knew one day that I was going to have to tell someone. Most people don't realize that when you are an addict, others are hurt that aren't addicts because everyone is affected by your disease. I had no intentions of hurting people or no one for that matter. I needed to get sober quickly and in a hurry.

I felt good about going to AA and NA because I was dibbling and dabbling in all sorts of stuff. This time I went with a different frame of mind. I no longer wanted a woman from AA or NA. I wanted a peace of mind so I could figure out why I did what I did. I finally left that scene because when I was in a meeting one time, a sponsor said something about a higher power. He said, "If your higher power could be your doorknob or any object of your imagination..." That turned me off. I felt like it was starting to be cult-like. I just wanted not to get bent out of shape for what I had done.

My family was okay with it. They never gave up on me. I sometimes wished that I wouldn't have done certain things, but you can't ever get those years back. I was running from myself again knowing that I was connected to God. He never made me feel bad. He comforted me. He moved me out and over. He made me believe in Him so that I could see the light. In a way, I knew it was going to happen to me. I realized that we are never prepared for what is coming our way: good or bad. I truly believe that God wants us to acknowledge Him when we do good or bad. After my dad passed away, my child was aborted. The accident I was in almost cost me my life. I had to rehab after that and had to deal with the psychological effects. Take nothing for granted.

Don't put God on the back end of your problems and use him when you want to.

Say no to the world but not to God. There is a difference. Pay attention to detail and the people you encounter. Everybody is not for you. Some people want to see you fall on your face. It's family members and friends who want you to go down. I realized that for me to get any real breakthrough I had to move away and start all over. I could only dream and wait on God to allow this to happen for me. I was still using off and on. Even though I was going to church and living dangerously on the edge, it wasn't worth it. Can you imagine going to work with a hangover Monday morning? Among other things, going to work broke because you spent all your money on drinking, smoking, and partying. Imagine being tired of yourself.

By the summer of 1998, I was so worried about myself and my Family. We needed each other badly. We had not cleared the air for some things that happened when my father passed. I was upset about me sinning and failing to uphold my end of the bargain of staying clean and sober. I witnessed different friends get sick with cancer or something tragic would happen to them. For example, a friend called me one Monday and asked if he could borrow my shoes. He wanted to wear them to work because he needed some work boots. On Saturday night he was partying at a club. While he was clubbing, he and another guy got into it. An argument broke out, and the guy swung and hit my friend in the face. Well, my friend got the best of him. The guy got into his car and drove away. When he came back, and he shot my friend several times in the chest. My friend died on the scene. I was sad for several days when I heard the news of his murder. It affected me for quite some time, and I didn't want to be a part of any tragedies that happened to people I knew. I knew it could have happened to me. None of us are excluded from things going wrong in our lives when we are not with God. We can only change what we can in our own lives without Him. The struggle was real. I looked forward to the days where God would make a move for me. I couldn't do it. Even though I didn't know everything about being obedient or sacrificing, I knew how to wait on God.

One Thursday on my day off from work, I went to the mission to get something to eat. They preached, and we blessed the food to be nourishing to our bodies. I went to see how my mother was doing because she lived down the street from the mission. I knocked on her door and asked her how she was doing. She said to me that she wasn't feeling well for quite some time. I asked my mom, "Why didn't you tell me or anybody for that matter? Are you seeing a doctor and getting better?" She told me that she didn't want to worry me or anybody else. I said, "Mom please, we love you." I was so hurt that I felt like we weren't there for my mom and she felt like she didn't need us anymore. She had high blood pressure, and she lost her husband years ago. I knew something was wrong once I saw her face. We hugged each other. She told me that she felt terrible because my dad was gone, and things were not like it used to be. She was lonely and felt like things were not getting any better as far as her health was concerned. Family members had changed as far as people coming over to see my dad when he was alive, but she knew who loved her. She knew her enemies as well. She was a very discerning woman of God.

By the end of 1998 and the beginning of 1999, my family and I were on good terms again. It wasn't because I was sober. I was still partying from time to time. I just toned it down a notch where it wouldn't be visible. I hated being around negative people. I could only wonder how it was for my family when all hell broke loose around them when I wasn't present. Not to say that I'm a tough guy, but nothing terrible had happened to me except for me creating my demise. I was delighted that God had taken good care of me and had kept me out trouble for a long time. I thought that if I got in trouble, I knew that no one was coming to bail me out. People care about themselves and the things they want. God gave me a different outlook on life, and I had only a few years for it to manifest. I went on an isolation mode again once I saw that people expected me to fall. There was talk about me falling on my face again, and people started making bets if I would stay sober or not. I thought it was low, but that's the nature of the world we live in. I just toned it down. I moved slowly into what God was trying to get me to do which was always be myself and allow Him to do a work in me that I couldn't do for myself. I had to go on creep mode sometimes for fear of trouble trying to suck me in. I was on pins and needles. I had graduated from this scene, and everything was getting old to me. I wasn't the same person anymore. I wanted to be out of the nest for good and away from my family helping me. I tried to get closer to God and my mother.

Reverend Judge Lent Meriweather

CHAPTER 5

My Queen Passed Away

In the early morning in the summer of June of 2000, I was at work working on a roof with a friend that was paying me by the day. We had been working on several houses, and I was so excited because it was a new job. I took off the old roofing and put firestone glue back on the new tiles. I got a call from my brother telling me that our mother was in the hospital. I was so shocked because it was unexpected news. I asked my brother was she okay and my brother said no. I was ready to walk away from that job to see my mother as quickly as I could. It was around 2:00 p.m. when I got the call. I asked Mr. Green to take me to see her, and it took us about 15 minutes to arrive. I went to St. Mary's Hospital to visit my mother. Once I got to the 5th floor, I saw my mother unconscious and hooked up to a respirator. I knew immediately my mother was very ill. I was angry at this point. It was around 3:00 p.m. and everybody was in the room. The doctor came in and said that my mother was brain dead because of the brain surgery that she had received a couple of years before this all happened.

The family was together in the waiting room and my mother's room. Everybody was in and out of the room. We were nervous. I overheard someone saying something about turning off the respirator, and we had to decide to keep her on it or not. I wanted to see a miracle from God like always. I figure I have come thus far myself into my journey. I felt good about her chances, but I also knew that if it was her time to go, no one could stop what God already planned for our lives. I looked at their eyes and faces. It was full of disbelief and uncertainty. All I could do was pray and talk to God. This time it wasn't about why God? It was let Your will be done. No matter how good or bad a situation is, Christians must believe that God is in control. We could only wait on God and make the situation as calm as we could until about 8:00 p.m. that night. I watched with agony knowing that a decision was going to made soon about my mother's fate. I remember going to the cafeteria occasionally and then going back and forth to her room talking to family members.

The whole night felt strange until we went home around 10:30 pm. I kissed my mother goodnight, and the next morning I got a call from my sister that stayed up there all night that she passed. I cried because now I had to deal with my queen passing away. I felt lost and hurt at the same time. Her death was worse than losing my father because it was so painful to see her like that. She gave birth to me. She was my mother and couldn't be replaced. I just wanted to see her one last time, and I went up there that morning. The doctor told me it was high blood pressure and life long illness. I said my goodbyes to my mom which was the hardest thing that I ever had to do. I had a dreadful feeling as I thought about her passing. My sisters Christine, Geraldine, Doris, and Kathy made our mother's funeral and burial arrangements.

I would never have dreamed that my mother and father would have passed twelve years apart. They were both young when they passed away. My dad was 58, and my mom was 56 when she passed. I truly miss them both. I found out that when you lose your parents, a part of yourself goes as well. I felt empty or a hollow feeling as though something in my body was missing. I was at the church where my mother was going to have her funeral, and something came over me a couple of days later after she had passed. I had a feeling of despair and worry for my family. It was real and was a series of growing pains for my family after our parents went home to be with the Lord. I was glad that they weren't in pain anymore, but I was very distant from everybody after my king and queen passed away. My mother's wake was at the Apostolic Church where I joined with her after my dad died. I was never big at looking at obituaries or people laying in the casket. I knew that it wasn't for me, but there was a lesson to be learned. It taught me that life is not promised to anyone. I don't care how good you got it. Man is appointed once to die. It does matter to God how we live our lives.

God and family are all we have as Christians. We have the word of God always, and we need to be reminded that when things go wrong in our lives, we need to be there for one another. At my mother's wake, I watched people cry and voice their opinions about how things should be. I felt like we all could do better in many areas of our lives such as lose some weight, get a gym membership, start working out, stop eating fatty foods, start eating healthy, start fasting, and stop procrastinating. Stop living a lie when someone asks you a question. Don't beat around the bush or take my kindness for weakness. I saw my mother go through many things like this.

The day of her funeral wasn't a good day. I wanted to stay home because I felt pain and anger. Nothing else matters when you're grieving. My mind was full of uncertainty and not doing too well. Many people attended both of my parents' funerals. God was there and made the whole experience peaceful for me. I know now that God can do what He wants to because I thought that my mother's funeral was going to be bad, but it wasn't. I think it's only bad for someone if their relationship was bad or something of that nature.

When we go through things in life, we ought to thank God for His mercy and grace. He allows us to go through happiness and sadness at the same time. I learned that pain, hope, love, and forgiveness is a part of life. Bearing our cross is a part of our lives if we are His children. Jesus bore his cross, and we must bear ours. Our actions must line up with God's word. We are to exploit and exemplify our Father in heaven. You see I knew one day that God was going to release me from bondage. I didn't know when God was going to release my ministry. I knew I would go through many more things before He would show me my new land of milk and honey if I wasn't obedient. I also realized there are things you can't change and people you can't change. Everybody is not going to love you. There are people in your family that don't like you. There are people in your church that don't like you. But God loves you and if we are God's children, how can that be? He loves us unconditionally, but with us, it's always conditional.

I learned a lot from my parents in the church that we grew up in. I will always love my mother for playing the piano and organ. She wanted a piano in the house, and my dad made that possible for her. I love the days when I woke up and spent time with them. I long for the days when she cooked great meals because she could cook just about everything. She was a woman to be reckoned with and a great minister of music. She sang songs, and I watched her in choir practice every week. I saw her in action. I hold great memories of my mother. I will always love, pray, and fight the good fight for the Lord. I was very happy to be her son. She loved me no matter what. When I was doing right, she hardly said anything to me, but, "I love you," "You All right?" and things like that. My heart and mind will always be with her because she left a lasting impression on my life. I will give her my all no matter what because she allowed God to use her and my father to build God's kingdom. Therefore, I'm the recipient of their labor. I never dreamed of being in a position such as this to serve God. I went through hellfire and brimstone to get to where I'm at today. It's all possible with God.

I decided not to go to any other churches except for my mom's church so I could get the full teachings and settle down. Eventually, I knew there would be a time when I would relocate elsewhere. A few days after we buried my mother, I went back to work. It was very different getting up on those roofs, and it was still hot in Evansville that summer. It was very humid and musky. I just tried my best to not think about her, but it hit me that mother wasn't coming back. I tried to mask my feelings, and it just wasn't working. I needed to talk to someone about feeling sad when losing both parents. I found out unless you have been through these things yourself, there is no use of talking to someone who hasn't been through what you experienced.

In the Fall of 2000, I wasn't healed from my mother's death. I was doing all I could to keep my sanity. I wanted to give up and throw in the towel. My heart didn't allow it. I would always get one job and quit another job. One day I said, "I'm going to try this and do something else." I started making excuses for my lifestyle. I thought that I lost my parents. Who was next? Me or someone else in my family? I felt sorry for myself and started drinking again. I would go off the deep end again. I concluded that I couldn't take it anymore. "Having a drink of Bourbon ain't gonna hurt." It did hurt and hurt badly. I ended up being a functional addict and depressed for the next five or six years before God released me to move out of Evansville into a huge ministry in Ohio. I was a dead man walking around. I had given up. I almost lost my life as a result of giving up. Satan had me bound, and I thought since my parents were gone that I didn't have any reason to live. He lied to me all the time and told me that I wasn't going to be anything or worth anything. I didn't care to say, "Devil you are a liar, and the truth isn't in you." I believed that for a while until I saw how God had changed many other people's lives who had similar problems that I had. You will see how you can be easily persuaded once you get down and out. We need to come to realize that God will snap you out of your misery if you let Him.

There were good days and some bad or weary days. Some days I didn't speak to anyone in my family. It's sad when you have family in the same city, and no one seems to care. All I did was visit my brothers. We got high and drunk every time we got together. I knew what that was going to be like because it wasn't our first rodeo. One afternoon, I was at my older brother's house. I stopped by to see what he was doing because I hadn't seen him in a long time. The next thing I knew people were knocking on his door. It was a bunch of chaos everywhere I went.

I was like Lord, please help me. I wondered what it was going to be like because he knew that I had more sin that needed to get out of my system. I was going place to place again. I was homeless and agitated that I let my home go. I didn't want to be in Evansville anymore. So, I would live with my brothers Gary and Greg off and on. I felt safe at times although we were getting high every day or at least three times a week. Reflecting, that was bad enough. I don't see how I made it through those dark days of drug use and sleeping around with different women. Every time I think about it, I get goosebumps because I probably slept with about 100 women at this point.

I wasn't done yet. I was slowing down, but I was a very sick, prideful individual. I wouldn't listen to anyone. If someone said we were going to go do this or that on a particular day and they weren't there, I wouldn't show up. In other words, I wouldn't believe them and anything they said. I would continue to do my own thing. I was glad to be their friend but not get close to them. I kept my distance to keep myself from getting hurt. There were certain things that I didn't let anyone know about me. I changed when my mother died. In 2000, I got so drunk around my birthday which is December 28th. I didn't feel anything. I smoked weed and felt no pain. I just had a thing about being that way around my sisters. That was one thing that I couldn't bear was allowing my parents and my sisters to see me in a drunken state.

I self-medicated secretly for several years. I made it my business to respectively stop going to church after the year of 2000 and 2001. These were the years that I got into trouble. I had just purchased a car, and this was before the world trade centers blew down. I remember filing my income taxes in February and purchasing a silver Mercury Cougar. I wrecked it because I fell asleep at the wheel one night. I don't remember how I got to the hospital. The police officer said that I was pushing my car down the street trying to go to the gas station because I ran out of gas. I was charged with a DUI in February 2001. A couple of months later in April, I did it again. I went crazy because I realized what I had done to myself. I worried about going to court, jail, and figuring out my situation.

That summer I didn't realize that George Bush the President of the United States came to Evansville. The secret service pulled me over on a routine traffic stop to ask where I was going and what I was doing. I told them that I was with my brother and we were hanging out. They asked me for I.D. and told me to wait. While my brother and I waited I looked in the rear-view mirror. I saw a SWAT team of cops with big guns and gear on. They were ready for combat orders. We waited for five minutes, and the police officer gave me my license back. He cleared us to go and told us to be safe and have a nice day. I felt good that he let us go because the day before we partied hard. It was around 4:00 pm, and we were on the verge of just getting started again. I was so happy that day, and we were glad to get some more drinks in our system. Later that night, we went to everyone's house that we could. It seemed like we were having fun that weekend.

I went to my friend James' house. If I gave him two or three beers, he would let me lounge on his porch, eat his food, curse, and do everything else if he was getting something out of the deal. I could tell when he had too many beers because he would fall asleep and go into his room. After everybody came over, we would buy more booze for about 10 to 15 people. It also came along with all the extra bull crap because many times the girls would come over. They would get the drinks, food, and crash over his house. I was tired of it because they had money to pitch in on stuff. After a while, it got old. I was done. I truly wanted to go in a different direction. I dropped my brother off and called myself relaxing over a girlfriend's house. We were just friends and she introduced me to her friend that she had worked with at a nursing home. She told me all about her and that I would like her. I went out on a blind date with her. I was like no this is not right, but I went anyway. It was one of the biggest mistakes of my life.

I met her in October 2001. She drank and partied with me. I went home with her. She told me the truth about who she was and her past. She said that she had recently come out of a bad relationship where her ex-boyfriend cheated. She was angry at him, and they had a daughter. We saw each other at least three times a week. It was not serious at first. Then we started seeing each other four or five times a week. That time increased to every day which lasted to the beginning of January 2002. I lived wherever I could. Sometimes, I stayed with both of my brothers. One day she offered me to move in with her. We only dated for four months when she told me that she loved me and wanted to get serious by settling down. I was skeptical because I saw that something wasn't right. I knew God was speaking to me about her. I knew that she wasn't the one for me, but I wanted to see if our relationship would work out. I moved in, and it was okay. The expectations were not met. She wanted things her way, and I wanted things my way. I should have known to never move in with her. I was not good at playing daddy especially if the kid wasn't mine. I did that for a while and got another job because she wanted to move. She had lived there for five years. She said that she was going to apply for a new place to live. I waited for a couple of weeks after she applied for the place.

Several weeks later, I was at work when she got the good news that she was approved for a new place after applying. I was happy for her. While we were preparing to move our stuff out, she talked about getting married. I was like no way because I was okay the way we were. I saw that she wasn't over her previous relationship. On a Saturday morning, we moved into her new house together, and two of my brothers helped us. We started moving around 9:00 a.m. and finished at 2:00 p.m. There was a lot of furniture and clothes. We threw away junk and kept some things. It took me days to recover after this move. I should have just helped her move and cut the relationship off.

I blamed myself for getting in a bad relationship that I knew that wasn't going to work out. It was doomed from the beginning. It was my fault because I could have said no. We lived together on and off throughout the year. We went out and partied all night sometimes on weekends during the summer and fall of 2002. It was a rocky and unstable relationship. It was that way because we had nothing in common. We were together for the wrong reasons. I didn't love her. We argued over stupid immature things like taking the trash out of the house. I was living with the enemy and realized it was too late because we had a sexual relationship. After I got home from work all we did was sin. I felt like I was in the weirdest relationship ever. I found out that she was using me to get back at her ex-boyfriend for what he did to her. I didn't want to be a part of any of that. I tried to help her see that she was setting herself up for failure. She wouldn't listen to me. We were both stubborn and thought that we knew it all. By the end of 2002, I was trying to get away from her by being with my family and friends. I believed that we spent too much time together. She would go over her parents' house, and I wouldn't go with her. I didn't feel wanted or needed by her family. I knew that they didn't care for me like I didn't care for them.

I woke at her house one Sunday morning and started to go to this church not too far away. I looked at this church one day as I was coming home from work. I thought, "Maybe if I ask her to go to church with me one Sunday, I can rekindle our friendship." For some reason, I couldn't bring myself to ask her because when I would talk about God, she would look all crazy. I hoped that God would help split us up. We were not on the same page.

I remember we ate dinner at the same table, and I felt distant from her — this time I had all I could take. Enough was enough. In March 2003, I told her that I needed to talk to her. After an on and off again relationship, I wanted to end it. Our relationship was up and down. It was unstable and full of fornication. For two to three years, we wasted time and money. She was acting funny as I told her that we needed to talk. I was so tired and weary because our relationship wasn't going anywhere. One Friday evening we sat down and talked. I was in for one rude awakening. I thought about breaking off our relationship as she told me that she was pregnant. I hoped that she wasn't and didn't believe her. She went and got an EPT test, and it was accurate. Then she went to the doctor for a checkup, and sure enough, she was pregnant.

We were not on good terms after that. It seemed like we would argue all the time. I would see my family and tell her that I would be back later. She would get an attitude. I was concerned about her well being. One morning when she woke up, she told me that she didn't want our relationship anymore. I agreed with her. The best thing that came out our relationship is our daughter whom I love dearly. I looked at the part I played in this volatile relationship. I thought, "She is having my baby without me." I felt I didn't deserve that since I never beat her up or anything like that. I thank God that I had enough sense to move on. If I would've stayed, then I would never be in the position where I am today. I apologized to her. I asked God for forgiveness. Even though we never got along, I forgive her for all the things she did to me. I hope that she forgives me for the sinful things that I did to her. It was not her fault but mines. I thank God that I can admit when I am wrong. We must stand up and be honest with people. We must tell them about what God wants versus what they want from themselves and others. I respect her, and I adore my daughter.

My daughter was born in October 2003. Even though we are not on good terms, I trust and believe that God will reunite us together someday soon. It's not easy not being able to talk to your daughter because of what someone says or thinks about you. When my mother died, I was going through things like this. I felt like it would never end.

I thought, "I didn't play the field and was real with her." I did have some mixed emotions after moving out. I had to go because it wasn't where God wanted me. I did this to myself. I moved back into the mission and was very ashamed. I was around 32 years old and unstable. I bounced back and forth all over the place. I wanted God so bad I thought about running away all the time. I was always doing something that I had no business doing. Either I was in a bad relationship with a woman or around bad people. It has been said that people are attracted to bad people and things. By the end of 2003, there was no communication between us after she had our daughter. Eventually, I got to see my daughter for the first time when she brought her up to the mission. It was a blessing. She looked like me around three or four months old. I never dreamed that I would be going through this. I wanted to play the field when I first start dating and messing around with women. I thought that it was easier not being in a serious relationship. I realized that I couldn't get hurt that way. I felt good about this kind of relationship because I didn't have to put up with someone's baggage.

God began to deal with me when I started settling down. My thinking started to change because I realized the truth. I thought that if no one got hurt, we will be okay. This way of thinking is far from the truth. I was hurt even when I was single. Years ago, I truly loved someone and that was the person that got away. She was younger, and I was more in love with her than she was with me. I realized that I had to move on from her because I was more mature as far as having a job and taking care of myself. I didn't want her but wanted to have fun with her. We need to check our motives and our thinking about how we manipulate people, places, and things. When I was weak, and out of control, I was reckless. I felt abandoned. By the of 2004, I was a veteran at the mission. I had been through the mission quite a few times. I went to church there and been through discipleship training several times. I attended Bible study there and fed the homeless. I didn't care because I knew that God would get all the Glory. I just felt like my time was up at the mission.

For five years, on and off, I lived at the mission and took their ministry training classes. I told my brother where I was staying. He asked, "What are you doing back in there?" I told him, "Man this time I had nowhere else to go." He said come on, and the rest was history. I told the clerk at the front desk that I was leaving and going to live with my brother. I had a decent car. I always had a decent job and car. I moved in with him, and all we did was party almost daily. We got high on everything that we could get our hands on. If we weren't drinking, we were bored. I was getting ready to move away from Evansville until I met this other lady. I started dating her, and it was a two-year bad hit and miss friendship. She lived in Newburgh, Indiana. I was living with my brother and doing okay. I still felt out of place over at his house.

I believe because I knew the hood, I wanted to upgrade and be somewhere people didn't know me. I realized that I was trying to get away from my past. By the end of 2004, I started messing with this lady. She was tall, well-built, young and had lots of secret baggage. After we dated and messed around for a while, she told me that she had some personal tragedy. She said that her daughter died of crib death. I felt sorry for her and prayed for her. We went to her church together a couple of times but still fornicated often. I knew that I was a preacher's kid and I couldn't stop sinning. I stayed at her place sometimes and eventually moved in. I wished I never did because it seemed like I made one bad decision after another.

We were carrying on like we were an item. One weekend as we went riding in my car, she said, "I want you to meet my mother."

I thought to myself, "No way." I had enough meaningless bad relationships. I had no reason to be her friend. I felt sorry for her and wanted to tell her it was over. I just went along with what she wanted to do. As I got to know her more, she told me her life story. Her father divorced her mother, and she resented him for that. Her dad cheated on her mother before he divorced her. We need to pay attention to the warning signs when someone tells us about their past. I found out that she was upset with her dad for twenty or more years.

It's sad when we get involved in relationships with someone who blames themselves for their parents' divorce. It's not their fault. Their parents were two people who probably never should have been together. If their mother had mental illness and their dad was sarcastic and aloof, that is a dangerous combination for a toxic marriage. We all need to own up to what is going on in our relationships with other people. Many of us are in relationships today for the wrong reasons. Some people stay in relationships based on what the other person does for them. It could be money, sex, clothing, or vacations that drive the relationship.

It's hardly ever Jesus Christ that is responsible for your unsuccessful relationship or marriage. If the relationship goes south, it's his fault or her fault. I realized that every unsuccessful relationship I was involved in was my fault because I knew what I was getting into. I wanted what I wanted and did what I wanted to do without seeking counsel. I was blind going into a bad situation. I truly believe that God gives us His free will to do great things for Him. I also believe that once we make mistakes,

He still blesses us along the way. We may think that our way is better but it's the world's way of doing things.

I stayed with her at the beginning of 2005. It was okay but not good because she smoked cigarettes constantly. I was annoyed by that. It seemed like something was wrong every time I came home from work. I applied for a new job at a government food processing plant. They called me early in the new year for a position. I went to the interview and they hired me soon after. I went to take the drug test and passed. I wasn't surprised about passing the drug test. I was still doing drugs and alcohol off and on. I just stayed clean long enough so I could pass the exam. My next step was to go to orientation for the rules and regulations of the job. I knew my relationship with my new girlfriend would be over soon. We only lasted around two years. Our relationship was based on what we could do for each other.

I had been through countless relationships where there were no strings attached. I wasn't trying to move in, marry, or get engaged to someone. One weekend in the early part of May 2005, she told me that her father wanted to meet me. I agreed just for her and asked what day we were meeting him. She told me next week, and I agreed. I anticipated meeting her dad. I honestly didn't want to do it, but here I was again making someone else happy. We went over to his house, and I stood face to face with Satan. The man was introduced to me and me to him. The handshake was soft, and he gave me a fake smile. The look on his face said, "Where did she meet him?" He had no idea of who I was or where I came from. Later I found out the real reason why he wanted to meet me. He was concerned for his daughter because she had a major health issue that she had not revealed to me yet. She had hidden it from me for almost two years before I moved back in with my brother. Her parents knew. I asked myself, "As much as I was going over her mother's house with her, why wouldn't she tell me?" Then one day her father needed to talk to me on the phone. That's when the secret was revealed. I found out some bad news. She had been diagnosed with M.S. back in 2001 before I had started dating, courting, and moving in with her. I was tired, and I thought about permanently moving back in with my brother Greg.

I had trust issues all my life. After being involved in many terrible relationships with women, I could no longer blame them. I had to look at myself and focus on why I did certain things. I wanted to see a clinical doctor at some point. I knew it was very costly and I couldn't afford a doctor of that magnitude. I realized that I was a womanizer and I wanted God to deliver me. I was addicted to everything. Drinking and drugs were the underlying factors. The accident caused the trust issues and the internal damage which made me feel inadequate and different. I had to start over, physically and mentally. God was there to heal me and hold my hand, but it was time to let my hands go.

In the summer of 2005, I moved back in with my brother. We were always close, and we talked about old times and our hopes and dreams. I told him that I was tired of Evansville and was praying that God would get me out of here. I told him that God showed me in a dream that if I don't get it together now, I was going to wind up dead or in prison for the rest of my life. In the dream, I was partying with some friends, and there were some guys that I didn't know watching me. However, they knew me. I was dancing with this girl, and this guy came out of nowhere on the dance floor. He said, "Hey! What are you doing dancing with my woman?" I said, "I don't know." Then he pushed me, and we got into a fistfight. The rest was history. I ended up hurting him really bad because my name is MERIWEATHER. I was like wow. I had so many close calls like this in the past when I was younger and single. I wanted to stay put, go to work, stay away from women and drugs for a while. I wanted to go cold turkey for several months before God move me on down the road.

I was a basket case, and I knew it. I cried out for help but didn't have any power to do anything except be around family and go through the motions. I felt sorry for myself, especially when it was time to go to bed. It was the first time in my life where birthdays and holidays like Thanksgiving and Christmas didn't mean anything to me. God was still in my life. I had to learn that if I wasn't obedient, I would continue to go through some things, and He could not release me into the ministry that he had chosen for me. I thank God for His Mercy and Grace. His love for me was and is unshakable.

By the end of 2005, I was lost and was hanging on by a thread. I would go for a routine cocktail until I saw the light of God. I would get up to go to work at my brother's house on Jefferson street. I took a shower, ate breakfast and got in my car. I drove about two or three miles every day to head to the government MRI food processing plant. I was there for quite some time and wasn't happy. I was sick without the drugs. I stopped going to church because I felt betrayed and had trust issues towards God.

It came from my accident because I didn't understand what I was going through. I was furious because I had been cold turkey for a couple of months. Then comes the devil one day when I got off work. This girl tried to get me to pay to have sex with her. I wasn't the kind of guy to would mess with prostitutes. I thought that I wasn't going to do anything, but I was wrong.

I made a big mistake because she asked me to buy her some alcohol. Initially, I told her that I wasn't going to buy her any drugs for sex or anything. Well, I didn't stay true to my word. I was a weak person and bought her some beer and liquor. We went over to my brother's house. We started drinking and dancing to devilish music. I stood on my word and didn't have sex with her. She asked me again to buy some drugs with her. I resisted, but I was drunk. She kept asking, "Can you buy me some weed and whatever else I want?" For some reason, I thought it was Friday evening, that I didn't have to work, and it was okay. I gave her $150.00 to get all she wanted. God knew that I intended to have sex with her. Well, guess what? She ran off with the money. I was upset, and I went looking for her after my brother had come home from work. I told him what happened. That was unexpected, and I felt like a sucker.

I was looking for her and didn't run into her until about two weeks later. I asked, "Why did you run off with my money?" She told me that she had a drug addiction. I said, "Okay. When are you going to pay me back?" She said that she wasn't going to have the money no time soon. I looked at her and said, "You know what? I'm not going to sweat you. Get some help. If I were a drug dealer, the outcome for you would probably be much worse." I took it as a loss. I left her and went riding around with my brother that day. I felt terrible as the day went on because I thought about my family, my son, and daughter. I hadn't seen my children in a while. I didn't see them during Christmas and at the end of the year. I prayed for everyone. I was so bored that I told my brother that if someone came by or called to tell them I wasn't there or available. I didn't want to be involved with anything. I was in and out of church. I felt like my back was up against the wall. I tried the New Year's resolution thing on my birthday towards the end of the year. I prayed to move away on good terms.

At the beginning of 2006, it was freezing outside. One morning, there was snow on the ground. I woke up and took a shower. My brother asked me what I was going to do that day. It was about 8:00 a.m., and I told him that I was thinking about going to The Potter's Wheel Church down the street to get something to eat. They had a soup kitchen every Saturday that opened at 9:00 a.m. I would eat there often. Sometimes the volunteers would let you eat lots of food and take to go plates home. Sometimes I would come back with bags of food, clothing, shoes, undergarments, deodorant, etc. We had access to a lot of good things. I gave a lot of stuff away, and it came back to me. I wasn't going to church that much because I thought that I didn't have that much to do. I would walk to the Potter's Wheel church to attend their services and volunteer sometimes. The leaders were Pastor Mike Ballard and Co-Pastor Mike Kough. They are some great Men of God. They welcomed me because they knew that my dad was a minister. One day they asked me what I did for a living. They acted like they cared.

I had fallen back into my addictions on a small scale. I drank mildly, but nothing like I was doing early in my addiction. I realized that I was going on a downward spiral. I had been there before, and I wasn't ready for death. I needed to get into a program or ministry. I was thinking about it while I was talking to them. On March 16, 2006, I started to go to their church services. I went to bible study at 9:00 a.m. and then to the regular service at 11:00 a.m. I noticed that if they didn't serve anything to eat, people wouldn't show up for church. I started going either way because it didn't matter to me. I couldn't stop drinking and would mask going in their drunk. It was time for me to break the cycle. My weight was up and down because I would eat when I wanted too. The only time I would eat was when I smoked weed or early in the morning when I got up. Sometimes I would go over to a relative's house and eat whatever they had available.

God will protect and guide you. I know He will. I was ready to walk all the way with God. I was volunteering for God. I started talking to people more and more at the new church. I felt safe around them. Also, I felt a sense of peace and comfort around them. I respected God and them because I knew that they loved God. They had all the power in the ministries there. I avoided them one day because I was high. I hadn't been home yet and was drinking. I stood in the soup kitchen line. They looked at me and were embarrassed because they knew I was high. They started asking me questions and I would avoid them to keep them from asking me anything. All I wanted to do is get some rest so I could sober up. I was close to my healing and transformation to Jesus Christ.

My love for Jesus Christ, myself, and my family was getting stronger. I went through some tough times in my life. I lost my brother-in-law at the age of 11. I lost my kid through abortion, and I lost my parents. I contemplated suicide, but I was too chicken to do it. I realized that wasn't God's plan for my life. I was still going to the Potter's Wheel Church. I was at work, and I was ready for the restoration that I needed. I talked to anybody that I could at church. I saw it all because people were coming over there that I have known for years. There were alcoholics, drug addicts, prostitutes, gays, lesbians, and whoremongers. I was one of them. I saw people with physical defects and mental problems. I saw people who worked every day and still struggled to put food on their table. I saw it all. I saw God, Jesus Christ, and the Holy Spirit there.

On July 25, 2006, my life changed forever. That day was the day that God said, "It's now time to get your restoration, healing, and transformation." I will never forget it. I did my usual routine on a Saturday morning. I woke up, showered, and headed down to the church to eat breakfast. My brother was asleep, so I decided to go by myself and left the house at about 8:30 a.m. I had no idea what was about to happen. It couldn't have come at a better time.

The doors opened at 9:00 a.m., and I greeted Pastor Mike Kough with a good morning and a solid handshake. He said, "How are you?" I said that I was okay. He said that he needed to talk to me about something. I asked, "Did I do something wrong? He said, "No. After you get done today, come to my office before you leave." I didn't know what he wanted to talk about. The Potter's Wheel Church served breakfast, and lunch from 9:00 a.m. to 1:00 pm. I was on pins and needles just thinking as I was volunteering and eating. I was in a good mood that day for some reason. Many times, when I was there, I wasn't doing well at all. I walked around the facility cleaning up and served food.

Finally, towards the end of the day before they closed, Pastor came to the kitchen. He stood right beside me and said, "Come on to my office." I went with him, and he said, "Sit down."

"How have you been doing Jerome?" he asked.

I said, "I've been doing all right."

He said, "I hear you came from a good family of ministry."

I said, "Yes. My parents were ministers."

He said, "I saw you walking down the street one day close to where you live. I saw you going over to a known drug dealer's house."

I was in denial at first. He asked me was I getting high on things other than weed. First, I was going to lie but I couldn't, so I told him the truth. "Yes. I'm doing coke and whatever I can get in my hands. The day you saw me I was making a run for me and someone else. You see when you are getting it for someone else, you get more for yourself as well," I replied.

He told me that I needed help and this program in Cleveland, Ohio would be the place where he would recommend me to go. He said if I went and stuck it out, I would never be the same again. He told me that I probably wouldn't come back after graduating from this program call Jesus Christ Ministries. I was to report to them by bus or airplane once I arrived in Cleveland. He asked, "If I called them and they had a bed or a placement for you, would you go A.S.A.P.?" I told him yes. He called the ministry staff and told them about me. The rest is history. After he hung up the phone, he asked me what mode of transportation I would like to go there. I said that I wanted to take the scenic route, which was the bus. I wanted to take it all in as I was headed there. I knew that after committing to Jesus Christ Ministries I would have to go back to my brother's house and tell him what had happened to me that day. Pastor Mike Kough arranged for me to leave on a Greyhound bus early Sunday morning or the next day. I was so happy and thrilled. I was smiling from ear to ear because I knew that God used Pastor Mike Kough and Pastor Mike Ballard to get me away from my familiar surroundings. Meanwhile, we talked about the routine of how things were going to go down there. He prepared me for what the deal was there. He bought me a bus ticket and gave me $100. I was on my way to the best thing that ever happened to me.

The late Anna Louise Slaughter-Meriweather;

CHAPTER 6

Jesus Christ Ministries/Ohio

I packed my clothes at my brother's house that night because the next morning I was preparing for a long ride to Cleveland, Ohio. I was anticipating how it was going to be there. I told my brother that I was going to stay in touch with him and I was coming back home to visit. I knew that God was going to move me away because the signs were there for the renewal of my life. I knew that I wasn't going to be able to say goodbye to everybody because I didn't have enough time to make rounds around town. I trusted the Lord, and I took a chance because I saw a dead end in my life in Evansville. I felt shut out from family and friends. I also knew that I had accomplished a few things in Evansville, and I was known for playing basketball. When God told me that it was time to go, I obeyed. It wasn't a hard decision to make. Greg and I had talked about it many times. Finally, God answered my prayers.

We had a great dinner together that evening after I came back from the Potter's Wheel Church. I laid down that night and couldn't stop thanking and praising God. I needed to rest and told my brother that I was going to bed by 10:00 p.m. Also, I told him that everything was going to be alright. I fell asleep around 10:30 p.m. I had a dream about God taking me to foreign lands and transforming my life. He blessed me from the crown of my head to the soles of my feet. I knew that I was on my way to something greater than me. I woke up the next morning at 7:00 a.m. I yawned, took a shower, brushed my teeth, and got dressed. I went into the refrigerator and ate some fried eggs, bacon, and orange juice. While I was eating, my brother came out of his room into the kitchen. I said, "Good morning." He said, "Hey. You are going to be okay?" I said, "Yes. Thank you, Bro." It felt right, and my bus wasn't leaving until 9:15 a.m. I asked him to drop me off downtown to the bus station early so that I could get checked in. I got my suitcase and luggage as he was getting ready. I was a little nervous because everything was going to be new to me.

We got into my brother's car, and he said, "Man, I'm going to miss you!" I said, "I'm gonna miss you too brother." We only lived ten minutes away from the bus terminal and were there in no time. He dropped me off, and I promised to call him once I arrived and got situated in Cleveland. I still had about 20 minutes to board the bus and show my tickets to board. I sat down and was gazing outside the window reflecting on my journey.

It was about five minutes left when they called for boarding to Cleveland. I said that's me. I gave the clerk my tickets, he clipped them, and I boarded. He put my suitcases down below the bus, and I said, "Free at last! Thank God Almighty. I'm free from bondage and worry." For some reason, I sat in the middle of the bus and was so comfortable. I knew that I wasn't going to be back in Evansville for quite some time. I saw that the bus wasn't going to be full headed to Cleveland, so I got a little closer to the front. We left the bus terminal at 9:30 a.m. Once the bus started backing up, I froze in time and braced myself for this big move.

It was like a big load was lifted off my chest. The bus driver took his time because he drove very slowly. I imagined the finish line of making it there as I looked out over the seats. We stopped at some small towns in Indiana and Louisville, Kentucky. We crossed into other small towns in Cincinnati, Ohio. There was another 7-hour drive before we made it to Cleveland. I stayed awake for the entire bus ride. I realized I was hungry. The bus terminal in Louisville was huge. The driver said that we could get something to eat and we needed to get ready to board the bus by 1:30 p.m. He talked to us about being on time for the bus schedule. I was like you don't have to tell me twice. I started walking swiftly to find a McDonald's so I could get the meal deal which was popular at the time.

It only took about 15 minutes to get something to eat. I had a Big Mac with cheese, large fries, coke, and two apple pies for dessert. I was ready to eat, so I got back on the bus. Some people went to different places and came back a little late. The bus driver waited a few minutes over, and I ate my food. I started to get a little sleepy after I ate all my food. At 2:00 p.m. and we were just outside of Louisville, Kentucky. The bus driver said that we might arrive in Cleveland a little earlier than expected. He said instead of 7:00 p.m. we would arrive in Cleveland by 6:30 p.m. I said to myself, "I hope so." I took a nap and woke up. An hour later we pulled up to a huge bus terminal in Cincinnati around 3:15 p.m. It would be another three to four hours when I would have to get off the bus in downtown Cleveland. I was bracing myself for this big step in the ministry. I couldn't sleep anymore because I was not going to miss anything along the way from here. I realized how far it was from Cincinnati to Cleveland was on the bus. I thought, "I hope the people are nice where I'm going. What if I don't like it? What if I don't like them? They might not like me." I knew thinking like this was a distraction from the enemy. I just was ready for the challenge. I was determined to make it work. I reflected and saw where I had come from to where I was going. God had His mighty hand on my life. I was on a journey.

We eventually stopped in a town called Steubenville, Ohio which was the hometown of Dean Martin. I noticed that some movie stars that were popular in the sixties were born here. It was about 5:00 p.m., and we were 140 miles outside of Cleveland. I looked at the signs that we passed by on the highway. I was getting hungry again, so I thought about using the bathroom on the bus before we stopped. That way if we stopped again, I could focus on getting a snack before we took off. I noticed that in small towns where we picked up two or three people, we didn't stay long. We would stop about ten minutes then take off again. The driver wasn't playing. It seemed like we made 20 stops before we made it to Cleveland. I thought that we shouldn't be stopping so much since we were so close to the city. I guessed wrong because the driver had his schedule in check. It was late in the evening as it approached 6:00 p.m. I was anxious and couldn't wait to get there. I looked at the mile marker, and we had only 50 miles left. I took a deep breath and said to myself, "God help me and make this work."

We arrived in Cleveland at 6:45 p.m. The bus driver pulled up to the bus station and parked. I had to stand up and get my legs underneath me. I also had to wait for my luggage underneath the bus. I stood there looking around to see if someone had a sign or something. I finally got my bags, and I saw a white van pull up. Some other cars were pulling up at the same time picking people up. I saw a man get out of the van with the Jesus Christ Ministries logo on his shirt. I approached him and asked, "Are you here for me?" He said, "What is your name?" "Jerome Meriweather," I replied as I showed him my identification. "Yes. It's you," he said. I was so happy that I forgot to ask his name. I jumped in the van, and he told me his name was Andrew Carson.

Before we drove off the premises, he said, "Look they are making a movie just down the street from the Cleveland bus terminal." "They are making the Super Man 3." I saw remote controlled cars and movie scenes. I saw how they cover the Ohio plates and put New York plates over them which gives an illusion that they were filming in New York City.

I put my stuff in the van, and we drove for an hour. Jesus Christ Ministries is located near the banks of Lake Erie. We drove from downtown Cleveland to Chester Ave. We passed the freeway to Lost Nation Highway in Cleveland. I saw a huge mural of Lebron James on the side of the Cleveland Cavaliers stadium. I was in awe because I loved basketball at the time but not more than Jesus Christ. I realized that Andrew was giving me a little tour of the city. We met some church sponsors before he finally showed me my new home and the school that I would be attending. I was so glad to be in a better situation that had meaning and substance. He asked me if I wanted to get anything from the store before we went home. I said yes, and we stopped by a convenience store to get a snack. I felt appreciated again at that moment because the whole situation was right for me. We were approaching the place where I was going to live for six months to a year upon finishing and graduating. I looked up, and there were big substantial brown adjacent houses up on a hill. A school was at the bottom of the property when you first drive in off the road. Next to the houses was a church on the hill with a pulpit and sanctuary. It was about 8:30 p.m. and I was amazed because the property was about 40 acres of land. I got out of the van and was so excited. I was smiling as he had the keys to my room and board. He let me in my room, and it was nice. I laughed and was pinching myself all night. There were other men in the building, and we introduced ourselves. I looked around the house. I was amazed to see how clean it was and how they lived. I couldn't unpack all my things right away. I took a shower and called my brother to tell him that I made it to Cleveland. I told him that I liked it already even though I hadn't been on the premises that long. It was getting late, and I was getting sleepy. It was hot in the summer of 2005 in late July. August was just right around the corner.

I couldn't wait to meet the rest of the crew in the morning because they knew I was coming. I got into the shower and said a prayer. I asked God to order my steps. I got on my knees on the side of my bed and said, "Thank you Lord for giving me a new life and freedom." I was in bed by 10:45 p.m. because we had to get up for roll call at 6:00 a.m. Breakfast was at 7:00 a.m. and morning devotions were at 8:00 a.m. Everyone had to be on time. I liked the ministry because they were strict. I met Brother Murray and Sean. They were some awesome Men of God. I walked in and met them the first day, and they were good to the other students and me. They were around 20 members of the ministerial staff. They had people in charge of fundraising and donations. They had people in charge of the educational curriculum. They had jobs for us to do. We cleaned churches, made crosses, called on the phone for donations, did mission outreach, prayed for people, cut the churches' grass, picked up food, dropped food off, and went to the nursing homes. We were so busy the first day. I wondered what I'd gotten myself into. I heard constant preaching about how God could use whomever He wants to use to accomplish His mission. I was looking at how a well-oiled machine this ministry was, and the hand of God was upon it. I decided to finish and stay if God was in it. I was 100% sold on this ministry, especially when it was explained to me who the founder was and how it was founded. I couldn't believe God chose me. I didn't think that I was from a royal priesthood. As far as I was concerned, I was just a piece of crap that got lucky and rolled into town. God didn't see it that way. He saw me as a man of God who needed His help and for me not to see things my way anymore to see it His way. I went two to three days thinking that it was all routine until we went to church. It was a requirement. We had a Bible study during the weekdays and weekends. I had some of the best times of my life teaching bible study and preaching in the classes. I was getting ready for something great. Before I arrived at the ministry, they implemented a new way of teaching, and it was required before we graduated.

After lunch, on a Thursday afternoon, the staff told us that we all had to recite three hundred scriptures of the New Testament and keep a record of it which was part of our graduation requirements. We practiced Saturday mornings because we had to learn what we needed to graduate. The ministry would keep you until you passed the scripture requirements. It was a little overwhelming, but I started to recite and told the staff that I was going to pass. I thought, "Please Lord get me out of here in six months." I was prepared to push myself to become a better man of God.

On the weekends, we had some downtime until we had to do chores or run errands. I just wanted to study the word of God. Brother Sean oversaw the curriculum. He had us studying the New Testament and Acts of the Holy Spirit. We studied the Major and Minor Prophets. I had to go through these scriptures several times a day because we had to understand the interpretation, the meaning of these scriptures, chapters, and verses. On Monday we would study in the morning from 8:00 a.m. to 12:00 p.m. Lunch was at 12:00 p.m. Afterward we had work detail that consisted of everyone getting their tools, and a man would pick us up. We would do a job on a work order that the man wanted to be done in his house or a place of business. We had a five-man crew of cutting grass, and two sets of them cut at least four lawns. We would have two guys per job for a house or business.

We would also have people doing things back at the school for disciplinary reasons. Those men stayed back and couldn't go anywhere. The reasons why they stayed back could have been because they smoked a cigarette or disrespected a staff member by letting their tempers flare. I was a laid back kind of guy. Reading a book wasn't my thing, but the Bible was. I stayed busy and got into my routine. For the most part, I stayed out of trouble. When I wasn't reading the Bible, I would clean up. I washed my clothes every weekend and my dishes daily. We watched movies at dinner time. We had a good thing going on for a while.

In the middle of September, it was starting to get cold. After two months, I was comfortable. I knew who I was supposed to be, when to do it, how to do it, where to be, and who to do it with. Jesus Christ had me in check, and He took care of me. Nobody ever disrespected me. Every day wasn't a bed of roses but had meaning. God was ordering my steps. I had faith, hope, and love for Him. I was talking to one of my friends whom I'd known for a month. He asked me what brought me there. I told Him the truth. I was on my last leg and fighting for my life. I wanted to give up and throw in the towel, but God said no. I had been thinking about negative stuff. I said, "I'm tired and very weary. Lord, fix me. Help me!" There is nothing worse than a man who has potential but feels he has nothing else left in the tank. Suddenly he gives up. I told myself that will not be me because I wanted to change my life and reinvent myself. That's why I came here. He told me his reason why he came. He had been messing around with methamphetamine, and that drug had him all over the place. He said that it made some of his teeth rotten. He said he just started snorting it with his girlfriend one day. The drug burned his nose, so he started smoking it in foil. He said that it is a wicked drug. I told him all drugs are wicked. We all gave our testimony to what happened in our lives. We had some awesome days there that I will never forget.

By November 10th, I was well broken in. I even had the nerve to help other guys who might not have their work in order. Some of them lacked in areas of the ministries. I would try to help them accomplish their goals. I would help anybody. I didn't care what they were going through or if they were black or white. I just needed to help someone. People were helping me all the time. I had to get my life back on track, and it was going great. One thing that crushed my heart was when I saw a guy check in and three days later, he checked out. I heard people saying, "You know the guy that came here a couple of days ago? Well, he left early this morning walking down the road with his bags at around 6 a.m." He had cold feet, and I prayed for him because some guys never came back. I had hoped that once he came to his senses, he could be strong enough to return or go somewhere else. Four months into this powerful life-changing ministry, I started calling home more frequently. I would call my sisters and brothers. I was always thinking about my kids. I thought about making the journey back home and maybe staying home after graduation. I knew that God was taking me on a mission. One day I was talking to Brother Murray. He said that God had some great things in store for me and I would be surprised at how He will lead and guide me. I respected Brother Murray because he knew the word of God without the Bible being in his hand. I would watch him recite scriptures. He was a beast when it came to memorizing God's word.

Kevin was another staff assistant that was helping all of us not only memorize God's word, but he would go the extra mile for all the students. He had a gift of helping in many areas. He told me to break down my first two lines of scripture memory if the scripture was several paragraphs long. I listened to him, and it worked out well for me. Lisa was another staff member that was there for medical issues. If a student got sick, she would take their temp and help them get some antibiotics. She did everything by the book and was a nice Christian lady. Brother Murray and Brother Sean were married men.

Most of the staff members were young and weren't married. I had so much respect for them because they not only cared for me but cared for others. A couple of weeks before Thanksgiving, we were preparing ourselves for a big feast. Some of the guys asked if they could go home. Some of them stayed back as I did. The ones that went home had to fill out paperwork. I watched how happy they were. That was when I realized that I could be happy for others because they missed their families. Some of the men had children, wives, and girlfriends. They introduced them to me. I had a ball talking to them. Most of them, as I remember, were ordinary country people. They were the type of folks that would give you the shirt off their backs. I concluded that we were all family. On Thanksgiving Day, we had three nicely sized turkeys, cranberry sauce, deviled eggs, pies, cakes, coffee, corn, green beans, spinach, potato salad, and all kinds of other foods.

When God has put His hand in the fire and in anything that he blesses, you can forget it. I'm going to be where the blessings are. God makes no mistakes with what He said He would do. I ate everything that I could, and I was so full.

We started to clean up after the feast around 6 p.m. We were exhausted taking the trash out because we took out ten huge bags of trash. We washed the dishes, cleaned off the tables, swept, and mopped the floors. We watched movies, and Thanksgiving shows like Charlie Brown and The Grinch That Stole Christmas. Those movies were funny. I went to bed that night late. I slept in the next morning because we had some downtime because of the Holiday. I wasn't hungry, but I was in awe of what I have accomplished since joining the ministry. After all the festivities were over a couple of days later, everything went back to normal.

CHAPTER 7

Jesus Christ Ministries/Missouri

Over the next couple of days, we ate leftovers from the Thanksgiving Feast. One of the staff members, Kevin, announced that some of us would be leaving before Christmas or after the New Years. I had a movie spinning in my head hoping that it was going to be me. I worked hard and well after Thanksgiving. I recited more scriptures than usual, and I was doing more than required. I went the extra mile, and it was funny because I was willing to go on to my next assignment. I was preparing myself for something greater. I got on my knees and asked God to show me the way to advance in this ministry. He showed me, and I realized that the most important thing to God is being in a relationship with Him. I prepared to read the bible more. I found out that's the main way God talks. I prayed more and said, "Father in the name Jesus, I love you, and I need you. Lord, God, guide me. Show me the way to your Kingdom. Thank you, Lord, for your mercy, grace, and kindness. Oh, God, give me the strength." That prayer put me in the driver's seat. I waited on the list for the names of the people who will be going to the next level of Jesus Christ MINISTRIES in Cape Girardeau, Missouri. I anticipated the wait time. I thought they were bluffing.

Finally, on December 14, the list came out. Out of thirty men, there were only four names listed. I was so happy as I stood in line to see if my name was up there. As I walked closer, I saw my name. I laughed and celebrated so hard with the other guys whose names were posted on the list. I was so glad to be headed to a bigger and better ministry. I called back home to let Pastor Mike Kough and Pastor Mike Ballard know that I was graduating December 23, 2005 and headed to Missouri the next morning. They were so happy for me. They told me that the whole time I was in Ohio, the ministry never called them to report that I was doing anything wrong. They said they knew after a month of me being there with no calls that I was going to make it. I felt sorry for the guys who didn't make the cut. I realized that some of them were there before I arrived and didn't make it for whatever reason. I prayed for them anyway. I realized that we had to get things together quickly. We had to fill out the application for Cape Girardeau. I started cleaning up my place. I accumulated some things. I threw stuff away and gave stuff away. I said my goodbyes to everyone including staff. I also thanked them. I made sure to say goodbye to Brother Murray and Brother Sean because they were responsible for helping me get my life back on track. God chose them to help me. I'm forever grateful.

We tried out our cap and gown for the next couple of days. They looked like they were used, but we didn't care. I tried my clothes on, and they didn't fit. So, I tried on the biggest cap and gown they had, and it fit. It had already been cleaned. I put it up in my closet and went to get something to eat with the other graduates. We were encouraging the other students to get themselves together so they could experience the graduation and their accomplishments. We realized that God not only gave us our lives back, but He gave us all ministries. Some of our family members were there. We had food and lots of fun. We took photos together before the ceremony. When the ceremony started, we were on the stage smiling and in tears.

Brother Murray started the ceremony at 11:00 a.m. and gave us the benediction at 12:00 p.m. I was so happy because the ceremony didn't last long. All the graduates spoke. We had a big feast on that Friday afternoon. When the feast was over around 5: 00 p.m., we looked up and saw two vans pull up from Jesus Christ Missouri Ministries. We made sure that we were all packed and ready for the morning drive. We walked around the compound and talked to people for the rest of the evening. We spoke to the drivers of the staff in Missouri. They told us it was going to take six to eight hours to drive to Cape Girardeau from Cleveland, Ohio.

I remember the Jesus Christ Missouri drivers' names were Larry and Mark. We stayed up talking until about 10:00 p.m.

because they had said that they wanted to get an early start in the morning. I remembered that one of the vans was for luggage, clothing, and shoes. The other van was for the passengers. We went to bed that night and awoke at 6:00 a.m. Saturday morning. I had a good night's sleep. We took our showers that morning, brushed our teeth, and put on our clothes for the day. We loaded our luggage in the van and got into the other van by 6:30 a.m. We said our goodbyes to everyone that we would see later down the road after they graduated from Cleveland Jesus Christ Ministries. I was glad to have been chosen to move up in the ranks to further my calling and assignments. We got into the vehicles and prayed together for traveling mercies. It's a prayer we pray when traveling to long distances, short distances, and everywhere else we go. We got into the vans after the prayer and started driving down this country road. I looked back at one time and then never again. The memories are fond. Brother Murray was funny and had a good sense of humor. All the jobs and work he had us doing was very beneficial to our ministries. We cut grass and played sports. He baptized us in Lake Erie. The lake was only a half a block from us which was on this high hill and street. You couldn't see the Lake until you drove up this steep hill. I thought about everything that morning because we knew it was going to be the last time to come back to where we got our blessing from God. About 30 minutes into our road trip, we approached Lost Nation Highway.

The drivers were conversing back and forth about where we were going to eat breakfast because we hadn't eaten anything that morning. They decided to take us to a store in Cleveland before we drove any further. They stopped, and we all got out.

We got a couple of store-bought sausage and egg biscuits, orange juice, and snacks too. We got back on the road for a long road trip. All I could say was, "I'm hungry, and I want to try to stay up as long as I can." The drivers were playing all kinds of music for us. Some of it was corny country music. I thought, "Let me get some sleep now." It seemed like they were driving slowly, but the odometer read 65 and 70 miles per hour when I looked up. The only time we stopped was to use the restroom or get food.

By noon we were crossing the Illinois state line, and we were hungry again. We stopped for lunch at McDonald's in a small town called Mt. Carmel, Illinois. We used the bathroom before we ordered from the menu. Some of us got back into different vans. Some got into the van with the clothing, and some went into the empty van with no luggage. We drove through the small town to get back on I-70. We were only three to four hours away from our destination. I remember it was a cold day as we drove through St. Louis, Missouri. It was snowing a little bit with snow flurries. The heat was up high in the van. I was so tired of riding in the vans that I wished we would have flown. We were getting closer to Cape Girardeau.

After some time passed, I looked up and saw that we were 60 miles outside of CGM. The drivers told us what to expect at the ministry. They said we were going to like it because it was much bigger and better than the previous ministry. I thought, "Okay, let us see for ourselves." I knew that once we got there, it would be 4:45 in the evening. Once we got to the city and started driving around a whole bunch of hills and corn fields. In a town of 20,000 residences, there was nothing there. I looked at the other guys and thought, "Man, we just left the fields and we are going back into them." They looked at me and probably thought the same thing. I prayed silently, "Lord, help us because we don't know what we were getting ourselves into." We got up this long windy hill, and we saw this big colossal building that read welcome to Jesus Christ Cape Girardeau Ministries. I was in awe at first, and our jaws dropped. We got out the van and slowly went into the building. We saw many men. I found out they came to Cape Girardeau from ministries all over the United States.

There were about 320 men in this ministry program: 70% White, 20% Spanish and 10% Black. We greeted everyone when we walked in. We talked to some staff members and some other people. The men asked us where we were from. I told them, "Indiana." I asked them how long they have been a part of the ministry and where they were from. Some said they were from Ohio, Texas, California, Utah, Georgia, Arizona, Florida, Oklahoma, and many other states. They checked us in, and we got all our belongings out of the van. Some of the older students helped us get our luggage into our dorms. I was assigned to Dorm Room B. We had some pretty big dudes in our dorm. The dorms were huge, and I had never seen anything like it before. The first night was not too good because I had to feel these guys out. I didn't know them and introduced myself. Some of the guys were very friendly, and some of them weren't. Some of their parents ordered them to come. Some of their wives told them, "If you get some help, I will give you another chance because you drink too much alcohol." Some of them were court ordered. I heard so many different stories.

We would ask the new guys we met, "So what got you in here?" They would tell us what happened. It was either a life-controlling problem or an addiction. The ministry had men who were 18-60 years old. It was sad, and I was apart of it. The most important thing that I needed to do was to pray the first night. Before I went to bed that night, God spoke to me about everyone. He said, "The race isn't won by the swift, but the race is won by those who endure forever." I stayed in my lane and did what I was supposed to be doing that whole year. Some days were tough because there were lots of testosterone flying around. We ate that evening at 7:00 p.m. in a huge cafeteria. They served spaghetti and meatballs, juice, salad, and cake. It was good. Sometimes I felt like I was in jail although I wasn't confined. It seemed like all we did was go to church, work all day, go to the classroom and study hall.

The faculty members were some characters. They were husband and wife teams in the ministries. Some people were missionaries. Some of the teachers loved the Lord. Some students and faculty were there as spectators. I could tell that they weren't there for the right reasons. They didn't want God in their lives. They just faked it until they made their parents happy. They should have been going to get their lives in order. My reason for attending the ministry was because I had a purpose and meaning. It got tougher on me. What I went through would be very tough for anybody. On Sunday morning, we were assigned to go to three different churches. We had to decide on Friday. I was so tired of going to all white churches. None of the churches we went to so far were black churches. I realized that if I wanted to get out of the ghetto than I had to go to different places, but that wasn't the case. I didn't understand their process except for they wanted you to change for the better and it helped me.

Some of the rules and regulations were crazy. Ten o'clock at night was bedtime during the week. We went to school during the week from 9:00 a.m. until noon, and we ate lunch. One o'clock in the afternoon was the time we worked every day except for the weekends. For 16 months we had the same routine. We went on the praise and worship ministries. Also, we were on the radio and T.V. ministry broadcast. We did a lot.

My birthday was approaching at the end of 2005, and I was bored. I wanted to be back home in Evansville. I knew that I would have relapsed into my addiction. I thought, "Well I'm glad I didn't make that move." All in all, it was okay that I had a boring birthday. To me, it had no meaning, but it did in God's eyes. I was clean again and sober.

The New Year was coming in 2006, and it was cold. I was contemplating going home. A week into the ministry program, I thought, "This isn't for me. I'm better than this, and I'm better than them." I wasn't ready for someone planting a seed in me to stay. I met a guy named Ralph who helped me get myself together. He had already been there for at least six months. Ralph was from Gulfport, MS. We met in the chow hall. I was coming through the line, and he looked at me. He was sitting down eating, and I thought, "Wow, I'm going to be in this line for a long time." There were at least 80 men in the chow hall line. They would call us by different dorms with letters and numbers. They had their system down packed. People would be scheming through the line where guys would trade food from one to another. It was crazy and sometimes very out of order. With God's help, I made it. God allowed me to be pruned and get some work ethics in my DNA.

I remember one Sunday morning we were getting ready for church. We went to church a couple of miles away for morning services. On the way back the bus slid off the road, and we had an accident. It was scary as were slid down. Some students and I were screaming. I was glad to get off that bus as they summoned us another bus. As we were transferred, we were all checked for injuries. There weren't any major injuries, so we went back to our dorms thanking God. After getting ourselves together, the authorities took all our names down. I said to myself, "What is going on?" I found out it was for confidentiality purposes.

We took a shower and got ready to eat dinner. Ralph and I had planned to sit together. We were prepared to have a heart to heart or man to man talk. We did that day at lunchtime. We talked about doing ministry God's way. We knew that some ministries were not of God and some were because the evidence of God being there was real. We talked about the curriculum there or the finishing time which is the time in which the second phase of the ministry begins. He told me that the land that the ministries owned was about 500 to 600 acres of land. I saw all that I needed to see because he showed me. It took me at least a month to learn everything about this new place. We had two church services on Sunday. One in the morning and one at night. They had breakfast for all the students. We had food, clothing, and housing. We had access to tractors to move things. We had access to vehicles to drive us places we needed to go. God was blessing us. I settled down around March 7, 2006. After having various conversations with Ralph, I opened up a little more as time passed. I had gotten friendly with a lot of people. I had probably had around 20 friends by this time. They would come by to see me at my dorm. We would interact on various levels from the classroom to the fields planting strawberries or other projects we were doing.

On Monday morning, I thought that I was going to do my normal routine. They put me on a cutting grass crew of ten men. They had guys who were doing it all: raking leaves, cutting hedges, bagging leaves, putting up equipment and cleaning it up. I was glad to be a part of this team. We had a bond. We helped each other out all the time. It wasn't about racism or color barriers. We had friendships that lasted for a long time. All I thought about the whole day was being filled with the joy of the Lord. I started liking the faculty staff of 200 members. The first place I graduated from had 10 to 15 staff members. This second phase of the ministries was hands-on, teaching, preaching, and covenant blessings. I was very close to Ralph and he had a lot of friends. He knew the bible very well and would quiz me on certain topics.

I met another friend Adam who was a younger student from Arkansas. He was a big guy. He wanted to live for God and do God's will. However, alcohol was overtaking his mind and his body. He wanted to leave on several occasions. I just kept on telling him that he is going to be okay. I told him to settle down. I was going to have Ralph talk to him, but it wasn't needed. I told him, "All that we have been through means God is going to take us on another level once He gets done with us." He said, "Okay. I hope so." I said, "Don't trust me. Trust God's word, my friend." By this time, I was used to seeing the same faces every day.

I was very bored on some days. I got used to being around everybody to the extent to where if I saw someone leaving the premises, I knew where they were going. The rules were very strict. I encouraged myself to stay and thought, "You are getting all that you need." I wanted to leave, but I also wanted to complete what I had started. The whole week people were watching each other. People wondered what everyone was doing on the weekends. You had to be in the program for three to six months before you could get a pass to go home for a week on every holiday. I wasn't too big on that idea. I knew that going back home too much wasn't an option. I knew God had other plans for me. I proceeded to kick back and move forward with God's plan for my life. I watched some men come and go. The men that stuck it out were blessed. I knew that God was going to use me. I couldn't resist where he was taking me.

I learned a lot from being in the program. I learned teamwork on a massive scale. For example, if something wasn't done right when working with a bunch of men, we corrected each other according to Matthew 18. I was corrected on how the ministry did some things. I didn't have an attitude because I saw how Jesus Christ corrected people in the Bible. They were humbled. I found out that there is humility in correction. There is humility in training, rebuking, and righteousness. I would do my own thing often. I just wanted to be a servant leader. I care for people but not for their nonsense. You must put up with a lot of things. People were waking up in the morning mean mugging each other and saying slick words behind their backs. No one gets away with anything. They disciplined me on a lighter scale for talking back. I told them how I felt without cursing. The faculty knew by the tone of your voice if you were frustrated about being there.

I met another friend named Mike while I was there. He was a white guy who had a good heart. He just liked me for who I am. We met in the book store, and he told me he was from a small town in Louisiana. He had a drug and a woman problem. His girlfriend left him because he was buying weed every day or every time, he would get some money. He was so addicted that he wanted to leave to smoke some marijuana. He said that it calms him down and makes him feel better when he smoked it. I told him that I had graduated from it.

I wanted to see what God had for me instead of drugs. I had been doing this and that all through high school and college. I told him that I had been thinking about going into the next phase after I finished up here. I knew that my mind was made up on going on as far as God wanted me to go. We do have a choice in the ministry. God will take us further and further. That is what I did. I stood my ground on Genesis to Revelation. I had no disputes, problems, or reservations. I had one affiliation, and that was Jesus Christ. God had me to trust only in Him and no one else. It was worthless for me to hear about anything else. I was sold out on my relationship with Jesus Christ. By May 3rd, 2006, I had been empowered and completely settled down. I stayed in His word daily from that point forward. I begin to measure my life by the word of God. God made me realized that it wasn't anyone helping me or blessing me but Him. There was no one making me feel better about myself other than the word of God.

By this time, I had two children that I hadn't communicated with for a while. I didn't know where they lived. I hoped to see them once I graduated from Phase 2. I had a long way to go at this point. My mind was on my family and my kids. I wanted to be right for myself and them. I needed to be delivered from everything. God knew what I needed. I hoped and prayed every day for a change in my life. I knew that it would be a process and it would take some time to heal. I thank God for bringing me out of my madness because I knew I was on my way to hell. I was blind, and the wool had been pulled over my eyes. I never imagined that when God changes your life people are amazed, but they don't want what you got because it's going to cost them something.

I truly understand what it means to give up something in your life. First, it is not easy to give up or quit doing something that you have been doing practically all your life. I had decided that I needed to change my life because I was in the program. I couldn't see myself thinking about doing wrong and not wanting to stop. I'm glad that the pain was over, and I had put the damage behind me because it was nothing I could do at this point. All God told me was to look at their faces and see Him in them. I saw faces that were changing: faces that were bright or full of light and a few faces of darkness. Some of the faces of darkness tried to blend in. But darkness can't mix with light. The men with the dark faces had limited days in the ministry. It was sad to see because they were demons only there to start trouble.

What was so amazing is God allowed me to see some of the mess before it happened. I was astounded and shocked sometimes to see that out of 300 men that were there, maybe about 240 were men of God. The other 60 to 70 men were gone in large numbers. Some left one by one, two by two, and three by three all in one day or the weekend. I saw the wrath of God on these men's lives. The next thing I know I heard some of the students talking. "You know I heard Tommy left today." "Oh yeah, what happened?" another asked. "He woke up this morning and said that his girlfriend said she was going to leave him if he decides that he was going to stay in the program for a year." I said to myself, "Misery loves company."

The war stories about how they got on drugs and what they did were the normal stuff you heard from the men full of darkness. In other words, they weren't done with getting high. They were on the fence with everything. I didn't feel sorry for them because many were court ordered. I was God ordered and pulled out of the miry clay. I would go to the chapel every morning and at night before I would go to my dorm to shower or snack. I prayed to God faithfully every night. My prayers were long, and sometimes I said nothing but just closed my eyes. I couldn't see the old me anymore. I knew that Jesus Christ was working on me inside out. Satan works on us outside-in. He made things appear to look good. I saw that I could decide based on what he presented to me. I asked God to help me see all things from His eyes and not mine anymore while I was there.

I saw that some staff members or teachers were dark and had nasty characters. One of the teachers there always wanted attention from the students. He would do things to make you laugh. He had a spirit on him that was not good. When I first met him, he made me laugh because of his antics and his ignorance. I remember he taught a class called Church History. When he asked a student a question, and the student was right, he would test the student on other biblical questions. If the student was wrong, he would show the student up instead of correcting them. Sometimes I felt like I was in a cult instead of a ministry. Other teachers there were okay.

I had a culinary ministry teacher that had a group of men for breakfast, lunch, and dinner. There were ten men for each culinary ministry at meal times. I was impressed. We all had to sign up and do our chores. We cleaned, took out the trash, made the bed, and made sure the linens were clean daily. We had to brush our teeth and shower two or three times a day. We were getting it together for real-life situations. I wanted to do everything so that I could prosper in life. I couldn't see myself going through a year program and not get all that God had for me. I excelled in all the different ministries.

We had another teacher that had a Farming Ministry. He was a strict older white male. He didn't play and told us one way to plant strawberries. If you planted them any different than the way he wanted it done, he would be upset. Then he made you do everything over his way. He paid attention to detail, and he was on our tails all the time. He got on me for not putting enough water on the plants after planting before going to the next ones. He watered the plants every other day. We were on our knees so much it was crazy. We planted strawberries in the fields for at least four hours a day. It was hard work because we had to get on our knees and dig in the soil. We had about five acres of strawberries. There were about twenty men in the fields.

Some days were better than others. Our teacher wanted the strawberries to come out right. He would talk to us in groups and split us up. He told us what to do when things go right or wrong. He was always teaching us teamwork skills. I like him for that. I thought he was a bigot, but he wasn't. He was old school. He talked to us like we were his sons. He even told us a story about his real son getting involved with a girl in the ministries. The girl wasn't allowed to be around us because it was an all men's ministry. The girl lived on the premises because her parents were teachers as well. I felt that was something we didn't need to know about, but he just kept it real with us about some of the mistakes me make as men.

I remember most of the teachers there. The Praise and Worship Ministry teacher was an old guy about 69 years old. He was very sarcastic and asked me to come and try out for the mass choir. I did, and to my surprise, he put me in the front row to sing at tryouts. I learned about alto, soprano, tenor, and baritone. I learned a lot from him. He had me laughing because he would sing all kinds of songs to us. We would go on church ministries trips to sing at various churches in Missouri and Illinois.

Most of the churches were Assembly of God or Methodist, and they were far away from us. On Sundays every month, we would drive five hours on the road to sing songs. We visited about fifty different churches that whole year. They gave us some nice donations when we finished too. I remember the first time I went after trying out for the Praise and Worship team. We went to this Church in Illinois, and I thought that I wasn't ready. This was the first time that I had sung in an all-white church. I was nervous, but they looked at us and sang along. We were well received because God was blessing us. It was a fifteen-member choir. When we went out to sing, it was our testimonies about how God changed our lives that made them bless us with donations. A portion of the donations was used to take us out for a meal after we finished singing. Some of the money was used for gas, the upkeep of the church van, and used to help other ministries. The teacher's salaries were paid through many ministries. I obeyed what I was told, watched their operations, and never asked questions.

There was an older husband and wife team there that was a great addition to the ministries. They helped the men get their G.E.D and other life skills. I called them Mr. and Mrs. Firestorm. They looked like they were so excited helping me get to the next level. Even though I never needed them for those services, they would ask me about going back to college to get my degree. I admired them for that.

All I thought about at the time was that I had about five or six months left because I had been there for about six months. I knew the ropes, I was deep into the ministries, and I knew everybody. I could do just about anything because I had mastered the program to a tee. My old friend Ralph and I were still talking. He was nearing graduation on June 9, 2006. There were two graduations a year: one in the summer and one before Christmas. I was graduating at Christmas. I had a long way to go because my schoolwork wasn't complete. God wasn't done with me yet.

I was bored sometimes, so I talked to a teacher who didn't have many students in his drama or radio class. I ended up joining in the second week of July of 2006 because I was running out of things that interested me. I was doing the things I liked to do. I knew nothing about radio broadcasting or drama classes. I ended up dropping the drama class but stayed and worked in the radio station booth. What I didn't understand was that the radio broadcasting station was an A.M. station in Illinois. We would travel there a couple of times a month to use their free services. I only went three or four times because something happened to the point to where we just stopped going. I believe that it was too far away to continue to go. It was only one other boy going to this ministry training radio station and me. I remember I was doing a live show and said, "Caller, you are on the air." The caller asked me a question about God. I was shocked that I was even doing this and had I not pursued it, I wondered what I would be doing now. The caller asked me why God gave us second chances. I told the caller it was because He loves us so much like He loves His son. I also said that God gave us wisdom, knowledge, and understanding. I reminded the caller that we needed to always look to Him for answers and not just when things are going well, and that we needed to call upon Him when things are going good as well.

I had been involved with maybe ten to twenty different ministries at the time. We even had a teacher that got a mission's team of at least ten people to go to Mexico, England, Europe, Africa and to various ministries to minister to people in those countries. I thought it was cool because I wanted to go. I had dreams that I would be going with them someday. I never did go with them though. When people signed up for the mission's trip, I didn't put my name on the list because I thought the odds were against me since there were hundreds of men in the program. I never found the will power to sign up. The teacher asked me why I didn't sign up? I probably would have gone with them because I did tell him that my dad was a missionary early on when I first got there. I was in a good place. I needed to stay where I was for another five months. After already being used to the program, I was doing all I had to do which was going to school and working very hard every day.

On September 24th, I got my first letter from my sister Kathy. She had sent me a card with a letter and some funds. As I read the letter, I broke down. I was glad to hear from her. I found out by asking some of the students how far St. Louis is from Evansville that I was less than 200 miles from home. It would be a three-hour drive if I got a pass home for the weekend. I hoped my sister, or my family wanted to come to pick me up because I wanted to see them. My friend Ralph had graduated, and I didn't have anyone to talk to after he left. I remember saying goodbye to him and he said like they all say: "Man, I'm going to stay in touch with you." Well, I only got one letter from him after he left and two phone calls. After that, I never heard from him again. I knew that when I was preparing to go, I couldn't tell people that I would stay in touch with them. I would say I will see you on alumni days.

I didn't run out of things to do. I was looking at all phases of the ministries at this point. I had been there now for several months and was looking forward to December so I could graduate on time. I had to make some decisions in my life. I was debating if I wanted to stay in Missouri and go to this internship. I didn't know if I wanted to become a staff member in this St, Louis, MO Ministry. I had enough time to think about it because it all came fast before my graduation. I knew I wasn't going back home to live anymore. That was not an option for me anymore. I started making positive decisions in my life and they worked out well because I felt weird going back to visit sometimes. I felt unwanted and the vibes were real. I felt God speaking to me about being one slip up away from messing my whole life up completely. I was in no shape to go backward currently in my life. I did all I could before I left the ministries. I hated to go. I was so happy with what I accomplished there.

It wasn't like God was saying don't do that or don't do this. I was ready to leave to do more and learn. I felt I had done all I could do in Cape Girardeau. Some of my friends went home and had problems with everything. They couldn't find a job. Their parents kicked them out. I wondered how they were going to make it after they graduated. I listened, learned from their experiences, and stayed in my own lane.

I was in my last phase on October 16, 2006. I never will forget studying for the test and tying up loose ends such as saving my money. I knew that I wasn't going back home. The ministry taught me to trust in God and no one else. I wanted to achieve success in ministry. I did, and I knew I had more to do because I knew that it was more to God than I was exposed too. On Wednesday afternoon, I was called in the office by my counselor who was assigned to make sure that I was on the right track. My counselor made sure that I was succeeding in my classes, ministries, and everything that was in my case file. Things were going in a very positive direction towards graduation.

I started to say goodbye to everyone again because I was preparing as best as I could for the graduation and move. It was in November, and I was thrilled as I told my family and friends that I was almost done. I told them that I would be teaching ministry classes in St. Louis. It didn't hit me until I had filed an application acceptance letter. I filled it out when my counselor called them to upload the app for me to fill the paperwork out. Two weeks later I got an acceptance letter saying I was accepted as a teacher/staff member. I was so happy until I got there.

Every morning, I thanked God when I woke up because He gave me a chance to move into the Re-entry program where I could teach ministry classes to the students. I thought, "If I can do this, then I can go on to do greater things for the Lord Jesus Christ." By the end of November, I finished all my classwork and prepared for finals. I had to study church history, Old Testament, New Testament, Major Prophets, Minor Prophets, Epistles, and Acts of the Holy Spirit. It was very extensive, and we had to pass the classes to move to the next Level. I studied every day and night for months before it was time for testing. After we did our daily morning devotions, we would go to breakfast. Afterward, school lasted for three to four hours. Next, we worked another five to six hours that afternoon. Sometimes we didn't finish until dinner time, relaxation time, or study hall before bedtime at 10 p.m. I had mastered this system so well I was prepared, and I loved it. I knew that God was moving in my life. No matter how much someone would try to make me do something that wasn't godly, I just moved out of the way of what they were trying to do to destroy me. I kept myself sharp in God's word, and I would live it. I told people about God who truly didn't understand what or who God is. Many students didn't know who God was. I found out that some of the staff didn't know who God was either. Some of the staff would be homeless if they weren't getting free room and board from the ministries. I prayed for myself and everybody that lived on the compound. The compound had about ten nice size homes on the property.

I remember before I left, I had gotten a special assignment to move some furniture and clean this wealthy person's yard while I was there. One of the stipulations was they would feed us while we were working for them. Five men were picked that day. I will never forget it. It was on a chilly Saturday morning around 7:00

a.m. We got up, got ready, ate breakfast, and did our morning prayers and devotions. We checked out our lawnmowers, sheers, and everything. We were preparing to leave for this work assignment at this house. We didn't know who lived there because we had just gotten the paperwork for the address to this house. The house was like five miles away from the ministry. As we were approaching this long driveway filled with gravel rocks, it seemed like the closer we got the bigger it became. We looked up, and sure enough, it was this big brown mansion on this property. It was very nice on the outside and inside. We found out that the house was owned by a very rich family of a newspaper publishing company. We never met them and didn't know who they were.

The mansion looked like something straight out of a magazine. We got out of the truck and was greeted by the caretaker of the family. He said that it was a seven-bedroom house with four bathrooms. The house had a three-car garage and it was on 30 acres of land. We cut grass and hedges. We moved the furniture around. It was about six hours worth of work. We were delighted to see this huge home, and we were surprised to see a house hidden in a small town like this. The property had a lake on it. The rooms were huge, had high ceilings, and were spacious. It reminded me of a palace. That stuck with me because I thought that I would like to have something like that someday. The day was getting away from us because it was going on 4:00 p.m. We had done all we could there. The caretaker gave my friend a check for $600.00. The work and labor that we had done was okay. I knew that everyone would pay us more for the work we did for them. They knew it was for the ministry. After loading up everything, we left at 4:30 p.m. We said goodbye to the guy who let us come on the property. We took off down the road. When we got back, we told the other guys, and a couple of them said that they had been there before. I asked, "What did the house look like?" They described it to a science.

That weekend we were getting ready to graduate. We all were rehearsing for graduation. We had a couple of weeks left to go. I could tell some of the men were crying but I wasn't. I knew that I would never see them again. I kept a visual in my memories. I went to the classrooms and studied until I got an 85 or above on all my class work. I had taken every class that I could to get myself together. I had packed up all my belongings except for my toothbrush, toiletries, and miscellaneous things that I had and put it all to the side. I had gotten close to a couple of teachers, staff, and their families. I kept it professional. I broke down the week before I graduated because I was looking back at how far I had come. I reflected on other men and their lives. Some of them were going home, and some were homeless. Many of the men had children and a spouse. I felt sorry for them. I wanted them to get it together. I had children with whom I had no contact with in a long time. I didn't have custody of them. I didn't have that luxury. I had to find my kids if I wanted to see them. I went through because I had flashbacks thinking about my children and how I messed up. I felt that I was never going to see them ever again. That is how Satan talks to you when your back is up against the wall. I wanted to do all I could to help any and everybody.

One thing about me is I didn't care if you were white, Black, Hispanic, or from any other country. I knew God is a forgiving God and a God of righteousness. I had to do the right thing from this point on. I graduated and got a certificate in Biblical Studies afterward. The ceremony started at noon. The food was served at 2:00 p.m. I thought, "Wow. I'm not going home." It wasn't because I couldn't go home; it was because I knew God had a better plan for my destiny and life. I said goodbye after eating dinner and talked to some students that were left behind. I told them that they were special, and God had plans for them too. I told them to look to God for answers and pray without ceasing.

CHAPTER 8

Jesus Christ Ministries/St. Louis

The afternoon was getting late, and I went back to my dorm to get my things. I put them in a front area where I loaded them once my ride came to take me to the St. Louis re-entry program. I was restless because I saw other guys graduate, eat, and leave with their families. I had no family at my disposal. I was all by myself. It was just God, Jesus Christ, the Holy Spirit, and me. They put me on submissive lockdown. At 4:00 p.m. a van pulled up that had St. Louis written all on the side of it. A tall guy gets out of the van and walks in. He says, "I'm looking for Jerome." "Jerome who?" someone asked. He said, "Jerome Meriweather." I said, "Here I am." He called two other people's names. We all repeated goodbyes to all that was left behind. At 4:25 p.m. we loaded up everything and headed towards St. Louis, MO which was about 80 to 90 miles away. The guy that came to get us was Steve. For three years he was a staff member in St. Louis and oversaw the crew there. He told us everything about the re-entry program. We were on Interstate 40 driving at night. I said to myself, "I hope we get there soon." Steve told us the things that were going on in St. Louis was much better than where we had just left. I asked how. He said that I had to wait until we got there then I would see. We were waiting too. I noticed that we switched over to another highway when we were about 15 miles outside of the St. Louis city limits. We started going in an entirely different direction than we had been driving that evening. I asked him, "Is it much better than place or compound?" He said, "It's way better. The food is better." I asked him, "Are the people better?" He said, "Sort of because it's a smaller ministry. It is cleaner and easier to manage than a huge ministry like the one that you came from." We were getting closer to our destination, and we were all tired from the festivities earlier in the day. As we were approaching St. Louis, MO, I thought, "We are about five minutes away from our destination." It was about 6:40 p.m. when we arrived at the Re-entry Program.

We pulled up to the house and facilities where the ministry was. I was shocked because it was a lovely building with other buildings next to it. Everything was in a nice clean country town outside of the St. Louis city limit. Steve stopped the van. He told us to get out and get our belongings. We went into our living quarters. We met about 20 students who were going through the program trying to reach Cape Girardeau. I was there to teach them about God so they could experience what I had experienced while there. I went there to teach and spread the Good News. I saw their faces that night, and they looked like me when I was in Cleveland. I was the only black man there; not just the only black man teaching, but the only one there period. He showed me my room and where I was going to stay. I was in a room by myself which was a big change because throughout the entire ministry, I was in the same room with a dorm full of men. I knew that I had earned my privacy not only on a ministry-level but on a personal level. Steve knocks on my door as I was putting up my things. He tells me what my morning details were, what to do with the students, and that I was going to meet two people tomorrow morning. Their names were R.C., the Director, and Big Tony, the Program Director. I was a little hungry, but the students had already eaten. Steve took the other guys and me for a bite to eat at Burger King. I got a full meal and brought it back home.

We were all so happy and talked about our trials, tribulations, our demons, and our shortcomings. We knew to put them in God's hands before we would act out. There were no more excuses for me. I did what I would always do: pray and ask God for His direction. Then I would proceed. Other than that, He would let me know what the deal is. I wanted God to move in my life without me looking towards a man to move me in his own way. It was getting late, and I felt a little out of place because I had been on my own for a while. Honestly, I stayed away from Evansville because I knew it would be over for me had I gone back there to live. God knew that I had to be rebuilt and made whole again.

Before I laid down that night, I was set to do whatever God wanted. I was so glad to be able to advance in Phase 1 and 2. I was a teacher teaching New Testament classes. I also worked at the front desk as many times as they wanted. That night all I thought about was getting involved and helping the students get their lives together because I knew that I wasn't going to be there for long. I was looking forward to meeting The Executive Director and The Program Director in the morning. I went to bed that night at about 10:30 p.m. and was knocked out cold. I remember praying and falling to sleep. I awoke at about 3:00 a.m. to use the bathroom and went back to sleep. I knew that I was in the right place. I woke again at approximately 7:00 a.m. and Steve knocked on the door!! "Hey, Jerome. Breakfast is at 7:30 a.m." I said, "Okay." I was still very sleepy, but something told me a few minutes later to get up and shower before I missed breakfast.

I got some clean underwear, brushed my teeth, got my clothes, did everything I could do to get ready and made my bed. The first impression is everything when it comes to meeting new people for the first time and being around the students all day while learning their names and letting them know I care. I got in the breakfast cafeteria at about 7:45 a.m., and it looked like a hotel lobby breakfast bar. It had bacon, eggs, sausages, oatmeal, toast, orange juice, cereal, milk, juice, and water. I met the Director and the Program Director. They were already in the cafeteria as I was in line getting my breakfast. I introduced myself and shook both their hands. It was cool as we all received one another very well. Some of the students were looking and talking to me. They asked me where I was from and I told them. They said that they have never heard of Evansville before. I told them that it was less than 200 miles from St. Louis, and it would probably take about three or four hours to get there. I told them that it was a town of about 100,000 people on the banks of the Ohio River.

As we were eating, I noticed that Steve was staring at me. He said that he wanted to show me some things to help them with their job assignments that morning. After breakfast, he showed me around the other housing areas and facilities. I was somewhat impressed. I was happy that they had their ministries together because I heard that some of the ministries had been going down and led astray. He gave me a program for how they do things there. I even received a program on how they wanted me to answer the phone. I walked all over the place that morning. He gave me the curriculum to teach them and how to introduce myself as the New Teacher/Staff member. I tried to build relationships and get my feet wet in the ministry. I wasn't trying to be like anyone else. I just wanted the freedom to do God's will. I stayed focused that first day, and it went smooth. It was quite an easy fit for me.

The routine got easier for me as time went on. It was cold towards the end of the year. My birthday came, and I treated it like it was another day. I didn't do anything on that day because I was too into God. I wanted not only to change my life for the future, but I also wanted a Christian life full of wisdom, knowledge, and understanding. I just followed their curriculum, and I did what they wanted me to do. I was obedient and blessed. I had to set the classes up, and I did. There were some days where I could have slept all day. I would have some bad days. The students treated me badly to the point where I had to discipline them. They plotted against me. They acted out because they didn't want to hear about God. They even had problems with many other staff members as well. We also had one student leave because he said the programs suck. He called his parents and said he wanted to go somewhere else. They came and got him a couple of days later. We tried to talk them out of it. The students would keep secrets among themselves about the staff they liked and the staff that they didn't like. I was tried very often early on in my teaching debut. I was called names. I was talked about in the face of other students. I realized had I given in and did what they wanted me to do, I wouldn't be doing what I'm doing now. Christians must stand firm on the word of God. We can't be lukewarm and scared to teach or preach God's word. Love always cast out fear. They feared me for some reason. I just kept on helping the students who wanted help. One thing about me is that I never showed any favoritism with the students. I worked with them as they allowed me too.

The curriculum stayed the same the New Year of 2007. The director told me that if I wanted to get a regular job, I could at the beginning of the New Year. I was only getting a stipend for teaching the classes plus room and board. That was the deal we made before I had got there by signing the agreement. It was only $25.00 a week. I was thrilled to see that I could do what God had called me to do. It's not easy going into foreign territory doing God's work. Many are called, but few are chosen. When I joined any ministry, I stayed with God's plan for my life. I wasn't doing my own thing as so many people in ministry do. One month after being in St. Louis, I decided to call my niece Tracy to tell her that I was in the program. I knew she probably wouldn't understand why I was there. I didn't want to explain it to her. I called her and told her that I was in the St. Louis Teaching Ministry. She said that she was happy for me and that her daughter Vivian lived in Cape Girardeau. I said, "If I had known that, I would have been to see her already." Deep down I knew that I wasn't going to see anybody. I was always busy and under time constraints. I never looked forward to seeing anyone until after I completed the re-entry phase of my life.

Monday, January 11th, I asked permission from the Program Director to find a full or part-time job. I went to the nearest grocery and appliance stores, but the response was that nobody is hiring right now. It was after the holidays and people were bringing stuff back for returns. I stood there and said, "I'm out of here." In an all-white community, God was teaching me something. I couldn't find any extra work to save my life until about three weeks later. I got a call from a company that made street light poles. It was a foundry that had great benefits and had a production line. It was sweltering in the building. They called me for an interview. I asked them what time and date. They said that I could come in the next day at 10:00 a.m. I continued to do my ministry class that day and went through my daily routine. I told Steve and some students about the foundry job interview that I had tomorrow. They were happy for me until Steve said that Foundry doesn't keep anybody long. I asked why and he said, "It's too hot in there, and it's hard work." One of the students named Eric said, "Don't listen to him. He doesn't know what he is talking about. Go for it. Try it out. Just do the best you can.". Another student Terry came to me before the end of the day and told me good luck! I noticed that it took the students a good while to open to me. I believe that you must meet the student's where they are daily.

I went to eat dinner that evening, after the day had wound down. I went to look for a shirt for the interview. I had some slacks already, but my dress shirts weren't okay. It was time to get something new and different. I went and bought a white dress shirt for $10.00 on sale. I came home quickly because I had learned the bus route. I prayed to God for the job because after a while, it had become boring. I asked God to enlarge my territory. Be careful what you ask for because you might get it. I read the Bible that night, prayed, and shouted, "Thank You, Jesus! Thank You, Jesus!" I read Psalm 24:1, "The Earth is the Lord's and everything in it, the world and all who live in it."

I went to bed around 10:00 p.m. and I was ready to make the change in my life. I got up the next morning in prayer and prayed several times before I left home for the interview. I took a quick shower that morning and put on my clean interview clothes. I wore a nice clean white shirt, black slacks, black tie, and black dress shoes. I didn't want them to think that I was going to a funeral. I just wanted to look presentable to get the job. I prepared as best as I could. I was dressed and ate breakfast by 8:30 a.m. I was ready to go but still had some time. I didn't want to be there too early and not too late. The foundry was only like a mile away. I had a feeling that I was going to get the job. I really couldn't believe that I was going into a bi-vocational situation where I was doing ministry teaching classes and working a job.

I decided to leave at 9:20 a.m. and arrived on the bus at 9:45 a.m. I got off the bus and walked up to the foundry. I felt a very bad feeling approaching the building. I think that God was warning me to be careful. I went into the foundry office, and there were some rednecks inside. I told them my name and that I was there for a job interview. They told me to wait, and I waited for 10 minutes before a big dude came out. He told me that the man that is supposed to interview me is coming. He was on the plant floor. I guess he was doing inspections throughout the plant. I waited another 10 minutes, and he came with my application in his hand. He shook my hand and sat down. He asked me what I was looking to do there. I told him that I wanted to do foundry work. He asked if I had any experience in it. I told him I didn't. He said, "Okay. I will give you a shot. Be here by next Monday to start training. You will get the drug test, sign your W-2's, and paperwork today. It's hard work but rewarding. Some guys have been here for 5 -20 years and some have retired." I was so glad to get all that done in one day.

The job has benefits after 90 days such as dental and health insurance. They had a 401K, and the starting pay was 16.50 per hour. I finished all my paperwork and everything else by 1:00 p.m. because I had to go to a clinic to take a drug test. My employer wanted to see if I had any drugs in my system. I was clean, and I just waited for my start date. I was told to start next Monday at 9 a.m. to 5 p.m. After I made it back to the ministry, I had a long day. I was so happy to have been hired. I changed my clothes and got back into my ministry life. I thought, "I can do this. To whom much is given, much is required." When I first got there, I got my feet wet into teaching ministry in the daytime. Now I was working another job in the daytime while I taught and helped on the weekends. I was all for it. I couldn't wait to get an apartment or stay there. When I told them I got the job, they told me that I had to pay 100 dollars a week to stay there. I thought it was wrong because that wasn't the agreement. I remained obedient and paid what they asked. I started working and that first week of training was hell. It was hot in that plant 24/7. I was drinking water left and right. The first thing we did in the morning was turned the heat up in the kiln. It was a casting machine. It was huge, and they had hundreds of them. They made many semiconductors and die casting light poles. I mastered that for three months. I worked very hard every day and taught ministry classes at night.

On March 17, 2007, I got up for work. I took a shower, got my clothes on, and prayed. I ate breakfast, and I was still sleepy. Something told me to get some coffee. I made myself a cup and got ready. When I arrived at work, one of the mean supervisors calls me into the office. He says, "You got to produce more if you want to stay here." I told him that I wasn't aware that I had to meet a quota. He said, "Now everybody has to meet a quota. If you don't meet it soon, I'm going to have to let you go." I noticed that I was the only black man in this plant. I had my safety glasses and gear on. I felt like he was a racist because he gave me a look like I was nobody to him.

Despite all the hell my supervisor Perry put me through, I never told anybody at the ministry. I just talked to the people in HR. They told me that he has always been like that. I noticed that when I came in, he would have other employees watch me.

They knew that I was a Christian because I told them. They would follow me through the plant and would watch who I would talk to. One day it was a bunch of new hires there: a bunch of women and just a few men. One of the new hires spoke to me at lunchtime. They were all looking at me like I had committed a crime. She talked to me for a while before I could get two words out of my mouth. I worked hard every day to keep my job at the foundry until my 90th probation day. He fired me for no reason except to say that I didn't meet my quota. They had me running the machines and kiln by myself. They would always have two people helping each other. I turned in my badge and said to myself, "Thank you Lord for the experience." Truth be told I didn't want to be there anyway. I wanted to see just what a kiln was and how it operated. It was very hot in there and it wasn't for me. I really felt for the people who worked for him and for that place because it was the first time in my life that I really felt like a slave. They worked me so hard that when I got off, I showered, fell straight to sleep sometimes when I wasn't assigned to do ministry. God is with you when you think He isn't. I came home that day and told Steve and R.C. what had happened. They said that they heard of some things that were going on in the foundry of people doing drugs. All kinds of problems were going on in there. They told me that they were concerned for me. They said, "Find something else that you like Jerome." I felt a little bad, but I was relieved.

By the next week after winding down from all this, I talked to a friend who had told my other friend Michael that there was a tool and die company not far from JM Ministries on Biltmore Ave. I went there after getting a few days to recoup from teaching classes. I went that Friday to fill out an application. The secretary was a skinny country lady who told me to fill it out. I said, "Okay. Are you hiring?" She said, "Yes." I sat down and filled it out in about 15 minutes. She looked over the application and told me that she would get back with me as soon as possible. I wanted that because I had a bad taste in my mouth after I was fired from my last job. I just wanted to do ministry only, but I needed an income. I called back the following week to ask Shirley the secretary if I could get an interview. She said, "I will talk to the general manager and ask him if we can hire you." Lo and behold she called me back that same day. She asked me if I could come in that day for an interview. I asked her what time. I asked, "What time?" She said, "2 p.m." I said, "Yes."

I will never forget that. The interview was on a Wednesday at noon right before lunch. I had to get it together, eat lunch, nap, shower, get dressed and get there on time which wasn't too far from me. I was sitting in the lobby at 1:30 p.m. I saw Shirley in the office, and I saw the general manager. I was waiting to see if he was going to call me in the office. She came to get me before 2 p.m. I was ready to be productive again. I sat down in the interviewing chair before Jamie the general manager. We introduced ourselves. The first thing they asked me was, "Do you have any experience?" I told him that I worked with many tools before. He said, "We don't work with tools. We make them through the die casting machines." I told him that I could do the job with proper training. Jamie was so sincere that he gave me a shot and the job lasted until I could give them a two weeks notice. I started that job after we agreed. I took a drug test and completed more paperwork. I felt so powerful and good again because there was no justification for what happened the last time. I realized that some things we may or may not understand until the day we pass. I have come to realize that the God I serve is Almighty. What a Mighty God we serve. I was hired at $14.00 per hour as a tool and die inspector. I was inspecting nuts and bolts for all kinds of businesses.

I was delighted to be employed once again and very happy to be working in ministry while having a bunch of students that I was assigned to by God. On April 3, 2007, I knew that my time was getting near to move on. I saw that after I got my second job. The director wasn't interacting with me as much anymore. Steve, the staff manager, was not on the premises too much anymore. Everybody was acting differently as if they were doing their own thing. I didn't speculate anything. I was listening to and studying God's word. I was always thinking about my family. I couldn't forget about them. I wanted to leave. I felt so uncomfortable being there and I knew at some point I was going to be leaving. I went to the program director and started talking to him about what I should do about my future. I wanted to go to Bible College because that was on my mind since entering the first ministry in Cleveland. He told me that I had a choice to go to a Bible College in Oklahoma, Florida, or California. I told him that I would get back to him on my decision. He said whichever one that I chose, he was going to call them.

I needed to decide and was leaning on California or Florida. Oklahoma was out for me because I was tired of the country. I prayed every day until I made Florida my destination for Bible College. May 12th was my start date to enter the Ministry in

Jacksonville, Florida. I was so glad that the Program Director helped me get into Bible College there. I was only in St. Louis Re-entry for about five months. I was not getting what I needed there. Sometimes you must recognize when your time is up somewhere. God will let you know. He let me know fast.

I got an application from Jacksonville for Bible College and filled it out within an hour. As I was filling out the application, I knew that God would be moving me soon. I felt peace about the process. I just was ready to move on because going to Evansville wasn't an option. I was fighting to save my life. I needed to talk to my family. I just wanted to say hello to my brother. I was busy getting prepared to leave that following month. I washed my clothes and saved as much money as I could because I was accepted two weeks later into the Jacksonville Jesus Christ MINISTRIES. I told the students the next day that I was leaving. They acted like they were happy for me, but I said to myself, "I'm happy for myself even if they're not. I'm responsible and accountable for myself."

I was still working at my new job as a tool and die inspector. I didn't want to leave, but I knew that at some point and time I had to put in a two-week notice. I was friends with the general manager because we had a conversation about Jesus Christ. We were at work, and it was one of the best times that I had with a decent group of white men. These men were hard workers. Every time they saw me, they would talk about their families. They would ask how I was doing. Some of them were of different denominations and backgrounds. They were brilliant and very intelligent men. I wasn't there that long, but I realized they cared about me. Even today, Jamie and I still stay in touch. We developed a love of God and friendship through meeting on the job. Neither of us works there anymore. I knew that while I was going through situations, He is in total control. It is God who blesses us. It's not the Pastor, Bishop, Prophet, or business owner but it's God Himself. I knew all along that what I was seeking this time was a deeper relationship with God.

I moved out after putting in a two week's notice on the job. I talked to the students and staff about my destiny and faith in God. I repeated my goodbyes. There were some sad faces. I was not expecting some of the things that were said before I left. One of the students who didn't like me when I first got there said, "I hate to see you go, but I know God has a better plan for you."

CHAPTER 9

Jesus Christ Ministries/ Jacksonville

On May 1st, I headed back home to Evansville to spend time with my family before I headed to Bible College. I remember saying goodbye to everybody back in Cleveland, Cape Girardeau and St. Louis Ministries. The ministries were global in every State and many different countries. I was at the bus station in St. Louis at 7 a.m. Steve dropped me off, and I was so glad to go home briefly. I knew my assignment wasn't over. I was there for a moment.

Riding the Greyhound home was different. It was the most boring ride that I had ever been on because Evansville was my Egypt or Sodom and Gomorrah, although I was glad to be home for a short time. I made into Evansville at about 2 p.m. After staying with my brother Greg for a few days, I was ready to leave again. All I heard on my first day back was all the bad news about family members and many personal problems. My parents had already gone to their final rest. All the people that I looked up to were gone. After being home briefly, I realized that I was living off the legacy that God had blessed my parents and my grandmother with. I went to see my sisters, brothers, cousins, and nephews. I spoke to everybody about Jesus Christ. They said that I had changed, and I told them that I knew. Those days that I was there went by fast. People asked me to stop by and talk to them before I left. I told them that I would, but I was getting restless regarding ministries and doing God's work. I was not going back to my old way. I had developed a love of God so tight and bright. I became one with God, which means that I was not into the things of man. I needed to get more in-depth with God. I ministered to family, ate well, and visited my old church friends at the Potter's Wheel Church. Pastor Mike Ballard and Pastor Mike Kough were my mentors.

I got ready to leave Evansville on a Greyhound bus ride Saturday morning. I had already been in Evansville for about eight days. The next day I purchased my one-way ticket to Jacksonville, Florida. It cost me $100 and I was leaving one day before the class semester started.

We left early in the morning, and I didn't get to Jacksonville until about 9 p.m. It was a 12-hour bus ride from Evansville to Jacksonville. I got there on May 10th. The bus stopped in four states from Kentucky, Tennessee, Georgia, and Florida. I was so exhausted from this trip that I couldn't even make any phone calls once I checked into my room when I made it to Florida.

I saw all I could see that day as we arrived in Jacksonville. A man was holding a sign at the bus station with my last name and the name of the ministry. The man introduced himself to me as D.J. I liked him and he was cool. It took me about 20 minutes to get my luggage because I had to wait for the bus driver to open the bottom of the bus. As I put my personal belongings into his truck, he told me some things about this ministry that was to my benefit. He said that the Executive Directors were a husband-wife team and they were helping people at the Bible Institute. I was telling him about all the ministries that I have been involved in. I talked to him as we were leaving the bus terminal. I needed to see what I was getting myself into. As we were approaching Phillips Highway, I saw how far we were from the waterway to the bus station and airport. We were very close to our destination. He asked me if I wanted to go to the store to get something to eat before we got home. At the store, we got some snacks and drinks. We were in the store for about 15 minutes which was down the street from our place. He drove about six more blocks on South Phillips Highway, and my mouth dropped. I was looking at a remodeled motel that was turned into a ministry. I was completely turned off, but I kept it to myself.

We drove up and parked his car. Some of the students came out and said, "Welcome to the Jacksonville Ministries." I said, "Thank you." and pretended to be happy, but I wasn't. I couldn't fake it at this point. I got my things out and asked him where my room was. He said, "You are staying with another roommate and me." I thought, "What!!" because of the small rooms that I saw when he opened the door. I got a top bunk bed and one drawer. The rest of my belongings had to be in my suitcase until I had a place to put them. I never could understand why I was always sacrificing.

We moved things around that night to make room for me and the things that I had. I shook my head and felt that I had made the wrong move. I stuck it out and waited to start the school year on a good note. I met the directors, Mr. and Mrs. Santos. They were nice people and had some connections in churches in the community. They told me that a van comes on Wednesday night and Sunday mornings to see if anyone wants to go to church. I was all for it. The church was called the Potter's House Church under Bishop V.M. I waited for the opportunity because it was the end of the weekend going into the weekday. Going to church stuck in my mind because I knew that at some point, I would need sanity from being in a small motel.

By the time that I had made it to Jacksonville, I had been affiliated with over 500 churches since joining the ministries. I wanted more of the things of God. I had all I could take from the world. I have been a part of some great ministries such as fundraising ministries, donation ministries, cooking ministries, storefront ministries, selling crosses, making crosses, and going door to door ministries, outreach ministries, preaching ministries, teaching ministries, and animal ministries. If God is in it, the ministries will last. If man is in it without God, then it won't. Never bite the hand that feeds you. God is eternal life and the Great I AM.

I was there trying to unwind and trying to make the best of it. I knew something was wrong. God was showing me bits and pieces of what I was seeing. I never understood why this church ministry was using an old motel to run its operations. I walked inside the office the next day for orientation, and I was blown away with what I saw. The office was nice, and the classrooms were tiny. The kitchen was big, and the location of the ministry was okay. The only thing that kept me going was Jesus Christ, Tara, Bettye, Angela, D.J., and a few others that I was acquainted with. I was there briefly because of some circumstances that came up. I never truly settled down. I was relaxed at times. I experienced trial and error. I received lots of training in the ministries. I saw people form into clicks which turned me off.

On the first day of School, everybody introduced themselves. We all were excited. I kind of liked the atmosphere as well. I was so glad to be where God wanted me to be. I made friends quite easily in every ministry. I learned many things in ministry by being hands on. Our schedule during the week was a little bit different.

Monday through Friday we go to school in the mornings for about four hours after breakfast. We sold crosses in front of department stores for the rest of the day and on the weekends.

I sold crosses at Walmart, Costco, and 7-Eleven. The small crosses were $30.00, and the real big crosses were $50.00. Some weekends we would go to Jacksonville Beach to have fun. We would run up and down the beach then go out to eat at the local crab and lobster restaurants. Some of the students and I even went to the Jacksonville Jaguar Games which was pretty cool. We spent most of our time studying at the motel where we stayed. It wasn't a regular building. It was a building that was turned from a dope and whore house into the Jacksonville Bible Institute. I mastered the ministry there because it was just school, and they didn't care if you worked. They just wanted to keep their doors open as long as they could.

By the end of May 27, 2007, I enjoyed going to church at the Potter's House Church in Jacksonville. I saw many gospel singers visit and sing some beautiful songs. It seemed like every week they had ministry conferences. I went to a couple of prosperity conferences. I went to a lot of their Bible studies on Wednesday night. I talked with the leaders of the Church as well. I was engaged in everything that they were doing. The Church had a bowling alley. The Church owned clothing stores and restaurants. It was one of the best 21st-century churches that I have ever been a part of. I thought that this church had all the trappings and I wanted to be a member. I knew that I had to be obedient to God and stay right where I was. I witnessed how the church functioned. I was so involved with this church that I hated to leave when it was time.

People were trained during the week. I was happy to be in Jacksonville. I would always call my family and friends to tell them how I was doing. Since I was very active in ministry, I got an opportunity to meet several different people almost daily. I met several Baptist and Methodist pastors. I was the new kid on the block. Every day when I woke up, I hoped that God would make and mold me into what He wanted me to be. I couldn't run around with everyone. I stayed away from them because I didn't want any trouble. I wanted to change my life. I had some run-ins with some students when I didn't agree with what they were doing. I never mistreated them nor tried to sway them to serve God any other kind of way. If I disagreed with someone, I didn't go all spiritual. You have to meet people where they are at the time. You can lose them in a conversation by not listening to their language they want to talk in. I hung out with DJ mostly because he was a roommate of mine. We didn't always agree with one another.

We got along with each other because we left all our problems and sufferings with the Lord. It was hard for me to be there sometimes because I was bored. I had gotten very used to being there. I studied long and hard daily. I felt like I was in a camp sometimes because we had to sign out to leave and sign in to return. I was upset when one staff member asked me where I was going one day. I had not been there for a long time, only for a couple of months. I was being watched and followed from time to time. I was tired of being there because I knew that it was a drug and alcohol ministry. It was more like a deliverance ministry. The only thing that got me through the ministries was Jesus Christ. I never got homesick, but I thought about home at times. I just knew that wasn't where God wanted me to be. I tried to stay as busy as I could by playing basketball and throwing a football with my friends. Going to the beach was fun and going fishing was cool sometimes. I had some downtime. It was so good to be drug-free and stable. I just wanted a better life.

We had at least 30 to 40 students there. Some were leaving, and some were staying. I saw demons on many people. I had them on me when I was using drugs. I understood the evil that was involved in using drugs. You lose family, friends, and your mind while going backward. I almost lost mine. That's how I know. It used to get on my nerves when I saw people acting all proper in church and I saw them doing things that were contrary to God's word. I know I'm not perfect. I want to be righteous before God. I love the Lord from Agape love. I realized after being involved with hundreds of ministries, and to many states serving God, I knew that I had to stay in God's word. I also knew that I was called and chosen to serve God to the fullest and not get caught up in the 'I'm God' thing.

By the beginning of June, things started to get a little better around the school. We began to get our curriculum together at the Ministry Institute. I saw that students were getting a little bit apprehensive and very cold towards the staff members. They seemed like they were somewhat unorganized in their choice of classes and where they wanted to start. Many things were going on around me. I had to rely on God. I had no choices. The only thing I had was to pass or fail. Going back home wasn't an option. I had to think about all the good and bad choices I had made over the years or even reason with myself. I was deeply involved in serving God. I would read the word, pray, and fast. I knew that the Lord was changing my life.

I didn't want to be with anyone until I met a lady named Patricia. She worked at the Potter's House Church where I went to Bible Study on Wednesday nights. She was the bus driver and talked to me every time she would come by and pick me up. We had become good friends. She invited me to her house for dinner and a movie one night. I went over to her apartment at 7:30 p.m. She made lasagna, garlic bread, and tea. I ended up staying until 10:00 p.m. I was full, tired, and ready to go home. She asked me if I wanted to stay the night. I thought about it. It wasn't a good idea and it wasn't right. I was going to have sex with her if I stayed. At that moment, I made the right decision by telling her no. I remember after we ate and cleaned up, we sat down on her couch. We almost kissed. She was a very nice-looking lady and was maybe five or six years older than me. She was a well-established woman of God. I had to remember why I had come to Jacksonville in the first place. I had her meet me in the parking lot at least three to four times a week away from the Bible School because I didn't want anyone to know that I was dating her.

I knew that by not having sex with this woman of God, I was respecting her. I also knew the reason why I was doing what God chose me to do. I didn't deviate from doing what I came to do. I managed not to get intimate with her every time we were together. She let me know what the deal was. I never did anything with her except love her unconditionally. I struggled with God at first because I wanted it to be my way. I had to give up the sin to see things God's way. She asked me why I didn't do anything with her besides kissing her from time to time. I was more intimate with Jesus Christ. I realized that to fall in love with Jesus

Christ, you had to first believe that He is God and is our Savior. I would read the Bible front to back and sleep with it. I understood that Jesus loved poor people. I realized that the worst of all types and all kinds of people could enter heaven. The Bible had murderers like Moses, drunks like Noah, and Peter was a liar. John the Baptist ate locust and honey. I said, "Thank you, Lord. You mean a sinner like me can be saved?" I figured out why I didn't pursue her. It was because God had me choose Him and not her. It was that simple. I went home that night after leaving her house late that night. After that our friendship blossomed. I would go to the store with her on weekends. We went to the mall together and had a good relationship. I had to balance school and work. The relationship I had with God came first. I knew she would understand, and she did up until a point. I knew that our friendship wasn't going to last that long, so I stopped seeing her too much.

I started to hang around the students more and continued to establish some continuity between my roommates and friends. Angela and I, a staff member, were good friends. We would go to the church of her choice sometimes. Angela was COGIC, and I was feeling my way through Baptist and Non-Denominational churches. She was an ex-heroin addict from Detroit. She explained to me that she had been homeless and was on the streets for a long time before she had got saved. She eventually ended up getting involved in the ministries.

I had more female friends than male friends. I also learned that 60 to 75% of the churches all over the world are made up of women. They are running the church. I genuinely believe that men don't want to go to church unless they are benefiting from something. Men don't want you to see the softer side of them. They feel like they are weak. I grew up in a nurturing household. I had a huge family, and I put up an 'I'm hard mask', which is not who I am. I also learned that God can use a prostitute to hide some people to keep them from getting killed: God chose Rahab and the spies. There are many people and illustrations in the word of God where God used many different types of people to do His work. Honestly, none of us deserve His mercy. His grace is sufficient. He has made us all come back to life just by eliminating sin out of our lives.

I tried to look at Angela the same way I looked at Patricia, but I didn't see her the same way. I saw our relationship as strictly platonic. She acted like a tomboy, and I couldn't understand why she liked me. I guess she liked my conversation because I would build people up and not tear them down. I saw these things happen far too many times. She hated to see me, and my friend go somewhere off campus. My friend had a vehicle, and we would ride everywhere on weekdays and weekends. I made sure my homework was done before I went anywhere from May to July. It was a good summer because we got new students and some nice sizable donations. In the evenings and on the weekends, I went to the gym and worked out on the treadmill. I had my routine together and mastered it well. I had some enemies and some real true friends. I devoted my time to God no matter what. I did get invited to social functions while I was there. I did many good things and had some great times.

I didn't care who you were nor where you came from. I could care less because even when I got bored or when all hell would break loose, I still would read scriptures in the Bible to allow God to manifest Himself to me. There was so much going on because of reorganizing and rebuilding of the school. I had only been there three months and a few days when I overheard a faculty member and staff member talking about a Bible College will soon be closing. I thought, "I hope he isn't talking about us." I left it alone and found out later it was true. What they did was tell certain people at first. The students were the last ones to find out what was going on. I was so mad because I didn't know the truth about what was going on. I wanted the truth and nothing but the truth so help me God. I finally found out that we were preparing ourselves for a staff and students meeting on July 1, 2007. I would never forget a few days before the Fourth of July. We all were on pins and needles wondering about our future. I needed peace and love to be done with the college. Honestly, I felt like I was leaving again. Usually, when a move of God comes, it's by surprise and how it happens is suddenly. Thirty-five of us met at 10:00 a.m. on the day of the meeting. The room was so intense you could hear a pin drop.

The meeting started with a prayer and then some staff spoke about the school and what the budget was. I knew there was a school downsizing or a school closing with new faces coming. Bobby, a staff member, was chosen to tell us that the school was closing due to lack of funds and that they were making this motel into a Re-Entry school. I thought to myself, "Why are they doing this to us?" People wanted to leave right then and there. I took it as a wake-up call from God after being told that they were leaving, and we had to find a new school to attend. I had not finished even one semester at the Jacksonville Ministry Institute. They gave us a school closing date of August 23, 2007. I had Bobby and my friend Sean to call two schools for me to finish my ministries. One school was in Oklahoma, and the other one was in California. I noticed that when it was announced that they were closing, some people did pack up and leave. I wasn't shocked. They said they were going home. They didn't want Jesus Christ anymore. They wanted to party and play the games of life: hang out, stay up late, and do many other sinful things. I called my family and told them what was going on. I even told my friends.

I was glad that it was over. I wanted out myself, but I had to prepare myself for a new start before leaving Jacksonville. They called Oklahoma Ministry Institute, and it wasn't for me. I prayed about California and Oklahoma Ministry Institutes. I was leaning more on California, and it was that simple for me after talking to the Oklahoma people. I spoke to the California Ministry Institute. A week later, I choose the California Ministry Institute. My good friend Bettye and I decided to continue our ministries with the California Ministry Institute on campus in South Gate, California.

The Fourth of July was upon us, and we had lovely festivities on campus. We ate well and said goodbye to one another. I was so happy to see people go because some of them hardly did anything while they were there. They looked dead when I met them and while they were there. Some of us had accountability issues. Many of the students were so glad to leave. It made me understand that this was a move from God. It seemed like everything was planned behind the scenes. Suddenly as the students were bailing early, Bettye and I had become good friends. We used to sell crosses and go out on church outings together. She was fun to be around because she told me some things about her life. I was thrilled that I had somebody who I knew going out there to be with me as a friend. I got my clothes together, threw things out, and cleaned up my room.

A couple of weeks from when we had to go, they brought in a Regional Director from Chicago. His name was Mike. He had four kids and a wife. The new Regional Director told us that he had bought a house near Jacksonville Beach. He asked us to help him move into the new home he had purchased. We all volunteered to help him. At 7:00 a.m. Saturday morning, we got up and ate breakfast. We waited for Mike to come and get us to help him move into his home. About 7:30 a.m., he arrived with his family, two u-hauls full of furniture, clothing, and many other furnishings. I thought, "This man has a lot of things." We all said hello, got into vehicles, and headed about four miles outside of the city limits. I remember going over this tall slanted bridge. We rode all over the city and helped the new director out. Once we arrived at his new home, we noticed it was in a gated community. It was a mansion style home with pillars out front. Everyone and their vehicles had to get inspected before we went through the gate. His house was clean inside and outside. It was a newly built Mediterranean style home that had three bedrooms, four baths, a pool, and a three-car garage. I wanted to ask questions such as where did they get the money to buy it? Does God approve of Christians living lavishly? I never had the chance to ask him. It was a thought that came to me frequently. We worked all day long for at least seven hours. We were sweating and moving large appliances back and forth off the trucks. We took breaks frequently: water, bathroom, and lunch breaks. They took care of us all day long. His kids were nice, and all they would talk about doing was chilling at the beach and golfing. I thought, "What a life."

Sometimes we think that the life that somebody else has is better. It's not. It's how we perceive that person's life. For instance, I don't want to pay the price like some Hollywood star who had everything but died of a drug overdose. I want the blessings of God and everything from God. We worked hard that day and didn't get home until about 7:30 p.m. that night. We were so tired and sore, but we still went to church that Sunday morning. He gave us 100 dollars each. We earned it, and we gave some to offering and tithing.

We only had about 15 to 20 students left. I had just about two or three weeks left before I would be going back home to Evansville to spend quality time with my family. I was hoping that I could see my kids. It was hard for me at times because I wanted to give up but persevered through mental toughness. Weakness was never a part of my DNA. I was just tired of crawling and not walking. The old saying is that you must crawl before you walk. That was me throughout these ordeals. What is sad is some folk may think that they have arrived, but God is on the throne the last time I checked.

I only had a couple of weeks to say goodbye to my family and friends in Jacksonville. I truly missed the ministries there because it had served its purpose. I truly believe that I was there to serve for a short time. The thing that got me is how God put names of churches together. Potter's Wheel Church was the church that got me involved in the ministries, and the church ministries that closed in Jacksonville was the starting point of my ministries. God can put things together that makes sense to me. The name of the church that I was leaving was Potter's House Church of Jacksonville. Jesus Christ is the potter, and I'm the clay who needed to be put back together again. God had done to me all He said He was going to do.

I called my family. I told them I was coming for a week or two and that I had been accepted into the California Ministry Institute in Los Angeles, CA. I was so happy and talked to people about it. I was so glad to be leaving this ministry. I cleaned up my room and every day I had to get rid of some old things I had accumulated. I gave things away and threw things away. I had to think about all the blessings from God and all the things God had done for me. He put me in good company in the ministries that I was involved in.

I said goodbye to D.J., Angela, Bettye, and Mr. and Mrs. Santos. I knew that I was never going to revisit Phillips Highway unless I was going to be in town to visit the church. God changed my life, and He deserved the credit from day one. I didn't know how to fast and pray. All I knew how to do was speak God's word into existence. Sometimes I had to be reminded of what I came from and what I had become by telling God that I needed to continue serving Him. I told God that I needed to be exploited more so I can learn how to serve Him. I truly believe that when we serve God, we sometimes think we are serving man and become self-serving of ourselves. I knew my time was up. It was time for God to send me on a new journey and worship experience. I only had a few days left to go to Evansville and be with my family. I left Jacksonville a couple of weeks early to be with my family on August 21, 2007.

I was so happy to go home and get to see my family. I hadn't seen them in quite a long time. I was packed and ready to go. I left early in the morning and got a ride from Angela. The bus station wasn't far away. I awoke that morning and said goodbye to the five or six students that remained there. I was glad that I wasn't the last one to leave. I got to see how it looks when things go south in ministry. I witnessed many other things as well. I saw times when other students had to rely on others because they didn't have money, food, or clothing. I had my family and trustworthy friends from other places supporting me. When God takes good care of you, it's imperative that you help someone else.

The blessings were flowing to me. Other people got up and ate breakfast at 9:30 a.m. I was ready, so I loaded up the van and told her, "I'm ready." She started up the van and we took off. Angela took me to the bus station, which was only 20 minutes away, and we said that we would stay in touch. The bus was leaving Jacksonville for Evansville at 10:15 a.m. I thought, "Thank you, Lord. We had made it before 10:00 a.m." I was so glad she dropped me off.

I got my things on the bus and at 10:40 a.m., I was headed to Evansville, Indiana to be with family and friends for a couple of weeks. Before I had to either catch a flight to California or catch a bus. I had one suitcase and a backpack. I put the suitcase underneath the bus. It was on a long 12 to 14-hour journey that started in Jacksonville, Florida. The next states were Georgia, Tennessee, Kentucky, and Indiana. I went through many small towns. It seemed like we were on the road for 30 minutes at a time before we either stopped to pick up people or got something to eat.

I was annoyed. Especially, when there was a loudmouth on the bus from time to time. I slept most of the way and got plenty of water to drink. I thought about Bettye because she told me that she was leaving to go to California. She told me that she wasn't going home. She was flying there and that she was going to go out there ahead of time. She had come a long way from the lifestyle she used to live. I hoped that we would unite again out there. I anticipated coming there. I just was ready to go to Evansville to make a 7- to 10-day pit stop and say hello and bye to my family and friends. I arrived in Evansville at about 11:30 p.m. I rode the Greyhound all day and night. When we arrived in Evansville, my brother picked me up. I stayed with him for about three days and then I stayed with my sister for nearly a week. I was glad to see everybody that next day.

I had to put all my things in my brother's closet. He cleaned it out for me that night. I was so glad to be there, but I told him that I wanted to get some rest and we could go out to see everybody the following day. He said that he could tell that I had changed. I told my brother that we could do whatever he wanted as long as we are not using drugs or drinking. I was so glad to see him. The next couple of days, we were running around, and I was tired. I wanted to rest, so I told him that I needed to relax after I got to see everyone that I wanted to see. I wanted to see my kids, but I knew that probably wasn't going to happen because I had such a short time to visit. I ate healthy food like salads, apples, oranges, nuts, and grapes. For the first time in a while, I was happy despite not being able to see my kids and not knowing what the future was going to bring. I was a very different person because I was no longer using drugs or alcohol. I was very spiritual and wanted stability in my life along with clarity. I had no parents because they were deceased. There was no one there to tell me right from wrong anymore. I relied entirely on God's word and Him speaking to me. I wanted to know everything I could about God and wanted a new life that He had for me. I fought very hard to clean-up my life. I had to keep fighting to maintain the fight to stay in God's hands. I was up against all the odds.

I didn't let that stop me because some of my old friends and some family were saying, "Hey man, you can take a drink." I said, "I can, but it doesn't serve its purpose for me anymore." I was glad to see Mr. Paddock, my old basketball coach from Lakeview Optimist Basketball league when I was six years old. He wasn't my father, but he was when my father had passed away. I called him often asking for advice or prayer because he was a minister and a friend of mine for many years. We all need good solid friendships. God is all-knowing, and He knows our hearts, mind, body, and soul.

CHAPTER 10

Jesus Christ Ministries/California

I was leaving for Los Angeles, California on September 3, 2007, to start the fall semester at the California Ministry Institute. I was at my sister's home on the morning of August 29th in 2007. I received a sad phone call, and I lost it. Everything was going as planned that morning as I did my normal routine. I woke up at 8:00 a.m. or 8:30 a.m. I showered, brushed my teeth, put on clothes, ate breakfast, and talked to my brother and sister. I went upstairs to take a nap, and thought, "Okay. I can rest for the next four to five days before I leave because I have seen everybody: church friends to immediate family. I went out to dinner with them and ate at their house. I talked on the phone to many of them. I met them places, and I am restless as I prepare for a long journey to California."

As I was taking a nap, I awoke at 12:30 p.m. I got a call from the old director. Mrs. Santos called me, "Did you hear the news?" I paused as she said that my friend Bettye was in an accident. I asked, "Is she okay?" She said, "No. She was killed." She explained to me what happened. She said on Saturday morning Bettye had gone to cash her check at the bank. After cashing her check, she left the bank and was crossing the street. As Bettye reached in her purse, she dropped something. She bent down to pick it up. When she resumed crossing the street, a dump truck hit and ran her over. I was so hurt, and I was so supportive of her. I said to Mrs. Santos, "What a tragedy." All I could think was, "I wish I had been there with her because it probably wouldn't have happened." I thought if that could happen to her, it could have happened to me. How could this have happened to her?

I made phone calls to the California Ministry Institute. I asked the Director what happened, and he said the same thing. I thought about not going to California. I told my sister and my family what had happened after I had got off the phone. I breathe a sigh of relief. I prayed for Bettye's family immediately after I had found out. I felt terrible the remaining days that I left. It was one of the worst days of my life. My journey to California was a slow time and a long bus ride. I chose to take the bus instead of a plane to LAX. I called the California Ministry Institute to tell them that I was coming in on a Greyhound bus which took 2 1/2 days, would leave on September 1 and arrive between September 3rd or 4th, and would call once I arrived in Los Angeles for someone to pick me up.

I planned to take it slow because many questions arose about how Bettye died. People were calling me saying many different things about what happened. I prepared myself to leave my sister's house and said goodbye to my family. I didn't know when I was going to be back in Evansville because L.A. is almost 3,000 miles away. I thought that I had to find a way to get back to see my family on the holidays because to graduate ministry school you had to go all the way to the course terms and conditions. I was getting ready to get all deep again. I had to investigate her death. I had to do it my way. I hoped that it wasn't any foul play. I left Evansville, Indiana for Southern California on September 1, 2007, at about 7:20 a.m. For about three to four days straight, I was sick of thinking about what happened to Bettye. It bothered me, I was sad, and I had a sick feeling. The day before, I made some calls, and some former students prayed for me. My sister took me to the bus terminal at 6:30 a.m. I anticipated going there, but I had reservations this time. I thought that if it doesn't work out, it will probably be because of what happened to my friend. I said to myself, "Devil, you are a liar, and the truth isn't in you." I knew that I was going, and I was staying to finish what God had started in my life.

I hugged my sister and told her that I would call her and that I loved her. I thanked her and my brother for accommodating me. I was glad to be moving on, but it was a bad situation that I was going into. I boarded the bus at 7:25 a.m., and I had to put one suitcase on the bottom of the bus. I had a carry on bag with me, and it was a warm day that morning. I had a little breakfast at my sister's house, but I was still hungry that morning. I got off the bus, went back into the bus terminal to get some more food just in case we had a long ride into the next bus depot which is another opportunity to get some food. I prepared for the long journey as I went to get some snacks. I looked at my ticket and my destination. I thought, "Wow. What have I done?" My destinations said from Evansville to Nashville, to Memphis TN, to Dallas, to New Mexico, to Arizona, and then California. I slept most of the way, but I was a very different person halfway there because I was getting closer where I felt God was sending me. I remember getting off and on seven to eight different buses. The buses were clean, nice, and looked like they were almost new.

I was not the same person after learning Bettye's fate. I hoped that after I arrived in California, somebody would tell me something different instead of something that I wanted to hear. I saw many things on my way to California. I saw cows, deer, and all kinds of animals in the day time and at night. I was laughing at the bus driver because he said that we should arrive in Memphis at a certain time. He was wrong because he had an old bus schedule and didn't realize it. I was not trying to get there anytime soon, which is why I took the scenic route to California. I wanted to make sense of what happened to my friend. I wanted the truth. Nothing else but the truth so help me God. I often wondered what she had gone through in those final moments of her life. I hoped that she was okay from all that she went through.

A few things were in question. I was already on the bus for six hours, and all kinds of things were going through my head. I'm going somewhere I have never been. I thought negative about how well they would receive me there. If they didn't receive me, should I stay or go? I thought that if I didn't make it in California for whatever reason that I could go back to Jacksonville and get back with the Potter's House Church. I was so familiar with that ministry that I thought it would be good for me link up with them. They had an on-fire Bishop. He would preach until the cows come home. He didn't take any junk from anybody. He helped a lot of people get their lives together such as homeless people. I hoped that I was coming to do the work of the Lord. I always thought about my son and my daughter. I kept praying for them. I realized that there are many things out of our control, just like Bettye's death was out of my control.

I ate food in Memphis and Texas. I couldn't eat anything else. I had a couple of chicken Burritos, chips, and a large drink. I noticed that it was getting dark and I was thinking as I looked out the window. We were not quite there because we had to stop at 30 to 40 more depots before we were crossed over into California. I slept all through the day and night. I hoped that I could stay up all the way there, but I knew that was impossible. I was very nervous about going to L.A., but not because of what had happened to her. It was because I was going into new territory. I prayed and sometimes cried not knowing what the outcome was going to be. Have you ever been in a situation in life not knowing what's going to happen, or what the end was going to be? I trusted God for everything thus far. I lost hope in people, places and things. My God and my family are my hope. I was going to California by myself.

I had already been through Nashville and Memphis. I woke up on Saturday at 6:00 a.m. as we were passing through Arkansas and it was so warm there. We stopped to get some breakfast on the second day of my long road trip. I will never forget the bus ride. It was quiet, and there were only eight people on the bus. I looked around and said to myself, "Lord, let your will be done." We didn't make it through Oklahoma and Texas until about 10:00 p.m. There were tumbleweed and dirt throughout both states and hot as well.

I was so tired of riding on the bus because I was changing my seats frequently after riding for two days. I tried hard to focus on the task at hand. It was sweltering all day. I talked briefly to this black lady whom I had met in the Arizona bus station. She asked me where I was going. I told her, "I'm on my way to Bible College in California." She looked at me funny. I guess she thought I was lying but I was telling her the truth. She told me that she was moving to Phoenix, Arizona for the second time. I asked her why. She said that she was tired of Ohio and just wanted to move back to Arizona. She told me how nice the city was: good jobs and hot year around. I told her, "If it's for you, it's for you. Let's exchange numbers and stay in touch before we board the bus again and split up. I want to be friends, but I'm not ready for a relationship." A long distance one! I wasn't having it. She was the first person that I had a real conversation with since heading out to the West Coast.

God spoke to me about some situations when I was on the bus. There were some weird people on the bus when we went through those small towns after passing through Flagstaff, Arizona. I had made a choice not to befriend too many people on the way because I didn't want any stray friendships which occur where you meet someone and then are led astray from your purpose in life. After we had to split up, I said goodbye to her, and I shook her hand. She was dropped off in Tucson, Arizona. I had switched many buses by this time. We were not too far from crossing the California State Line. I saw Interstate 5 passing through Tucson. I start feeling good even though I had reservations about my friend Bettye.

I tried to focus on Bettye before I got to my destination. I thought about changing my clothes and showering because I had been on the road for more than 48 hours. On Sunday afternoon, we weren't quite there yet, and I was restless. I ate well, but I thought about my last stop to Los Angeles, California Greyhound bus station. We still had to drive six to seven hours. I wasn't supposed to arrive in L.A. until 9:15 p.m. I couldn't understand why the bus route sometimes drove out of the way. For instance, we had to drive south from Phoenix to Tucson. Then we came back in picking up other people and driving several miles outside of the way. That drove me crazy. I had no choice but to go with the flow. I had to get myself together because we were getting closer.

After we crossed the California State Line, I saw a Palm Springs, California sign. I saw hundreds of white metal windmills. They were huge and stood tall. They were spinning all over the place. I looked on both sides of the bus, and they were seen for miles away. I had mixed feelings, and I was not the same person. Once I saw that we were getting near our destiny, I thought about Bettye being in the morgue because nobody had claimed the body. Even to this day, I don't know what happened to her body. At 5:00 p.m. I ate again, and I realized that California is one long state to drive through.

I saw animals, trees, and all kinds of vegetable fields. The nurseries had the most beautiful flowers I ever saw. I was getting sleepy at 7:00 p.m. as we got into Southern California outside of Pasadena. We had made several other stops before arriving in downtown L.A. I was so stiff and tired once I got off the bus. It was 9:20 p.m. After I got my suitcase from underneath the bus, I had to make a call to the California Ministry Institute. I called them, told them my name, and let them know where I was at. They said, "Okay. We are sending someone to you as soon as possible." I hung up the phone and waited for about 15 to 20 minutes. I looked up and saw a van with the name California Ministry Institute. I was so happy that they came. A man named Walter picked me up. He was funny, and we hit it off right away. I put my things in the van, and he gave me a little tour of L.A. as we headed to the ministry. We were on the 405 Interstate which is busy no matter what time of the day. He told me all kinds of things that were going on in the city of L.A. and the Ministry. I arrived in South Gate, California on September 4, 2007, at 9:45 p.m. I was so glad to be on my own and trusting God for my life.

I saw the place where I was going to be living, it was nice and looked much better than what I left in Jacksonville. I was happy to be here. As I got my belongings out of the Van, we walked to the school from across the street. The closer we got, the better I felt. There was a hand full of students still up. As we were passing through, I introduced myself to some of them. I checked into my dorm. I was signed to a dorm of men who were strong and courageous. They were like the Goon Squad. They were tall, big, well built, smart, funny, and had big hearts. I knew if something went down, we were going to be alright. God knew what I needed. I needed protection from God and those men of God. They joked all the time, and we hit it off from the start. I was so happy to be in with them and at the school. I was feeling everything out for the first few weeks. I met the big group of the 40 to 50 faculty and staff. The ministry had been a huge success for years. I met the Directors, Mr. and Mrs. Montoya, who were of Spanish descent. I met some others as well that ran other departments. This was a huge operation. We had classes on Mondays to Thursdays and tests on Fridays. Our classes were from 9:00 a.m. to 12:00 p.m., lunch from 12:00 p.m. to 1:00 p.m., and raise funds from 2:00 p.m. to 7:00 p.m. Our everyday routine was to go to school in the daytime and fundraise for the rest of the day.

The classes were Church History, Acts/Holy Spirit, Major and Minor Prophets, Old Testament Survey, and New Testament Survey. Monday thru Saturday, I had a full schedule. I would wake up at 6:00 a.m. every morning, pray beside my bed, shower, get dressed, and got ready for devotions in the morning. After the devotions, was praise and thanksgiving. Next, I would get my breakfast. I did this routine faithfully every day for a long time. Once I started something, I couldn't just stop suddenly. It was a nice facility and very peaceful. I would walk around in awe of the complex.

I was in the T.V. room once we had downtime. I met a whole lot of men and women students. I met Cindy, Kim, Nancy, Pamela,

Carol, Lucy, Amy, Mercedes, Angela, and many other female students. Some were from California, Nevada, Arizona, Florida, Utah, Montana, and Washington. This was a great place to be in a co-ed setting. The male students I met were okay as well. I remember some of their names like Brad, Brent, Walter, Perry, Michael, Tony, and so on. I got along with most of them. I was new, and curious about some of them. I wanted to be a friend to many of them. I knew that it wasn't going to work if I wasn't going to be real with them. I figured that I had come this far, and I couldn't be fake about why I was there. I had to introduce myself to the annual students and staff at the new students' party. I told everyone where I was from and why I was there. I was getting off to a good start and chatting with everybody from Mexicans to people from India and Africa. Some of the names I couldn't pronounce.

I realized that God had put me in with a group of people that were my family at this point and time. No matter how I looked at it, this situation was an act of God Almighty. I got along with everybody as if we had known one another for a long time. After all the introductions, we ate dinner. We had all kinds of food and guests. I shook so many hands that I felt like my hand was going to fall off. I liked that we were all under one umbrella. It seemed like we were all on one accord. We had one area where we would all congregate because of some crisis in the ministries if we needed to get some things off our chest. I would stay in my lane. I just listened to whatever they had to say.

A lot was said. People asked, "Who is in charge of our leadership classes?" We had to pick dorm leaders for people who needed to clean up their areas. Some of the students needed home skills. We needed God all the time. The only thing I was in somewhat of a disagreement of was the fact that when I was in Jacksonville some of the classes I took there was supposed to transfer over to California. A faculty member told me the classes were not going to transfer over. I was given no explanation. I thought, "This doesn't make any sense." I guessed it was because it was from a different curriculum. It didn't matter because I was committed to God. I was not clear about everything. As the days went by, I got into the routine of all things. I visited Hollywood on the weekends and went out to eat during our free time.

On October 23, 2007, I had been in California for at least a couple of months. I had been to a few places. One day a crew of 12 students went out on a fundraising outing. They were raising money for the ministry. We had to bring back at least 70% of what we had fundraised for that day. I thought, "Wow, this is very interesting." Some of us brought home 500 to 1,000 dollars in a 5- to 6-hour outing by going door to door. We fundraised in downtown L.A., Compton, Mission Viejo, El Segundo, and Laguna Hills. It was very nice to fundraise in Hollywood because there were regular homes, bungalows, and Mansions. I made around 400 dollars, and I had saved up as much as I could because I was thinking ahead.

After being there for two months, I never did get the full story of what happened to my friend Bettye. I asked the faculty, staff members, and students. I tried to go home by flying back to Evansville. I wanted to show my family that I was doing okay. I wanted to see if my pastor, Mike Kough, could he help me pay the difference if I couldn't cover the cost for the round-trip plane ticket. I wanted to get it by November so that I could go home for Christmas. I checked out the prices, but they were high. Some of the prices were 600 for a round trip ticket. I didn't have that much. It was wishful thinking. I needed to save more money and realized that I wasn't going to make it for Christmas. It seemed like we fundraised every day. I started to save more money than I had previously. I put the next holiday on my list to get a plane ticket to see my family.

I finished out the rest of the year on a high note. In 2007, I went through a lot of personal soul searching and tragedy. To this day, I still don't understand the inner workings of God entirely. Many things I still scratch my head on. I can't figure Him out, He is not to be understood, and His ways are not our ways. I thought about my cousins who were from my dad's family that lived in Compton. For some reason, I didn't want to be involved, but I called so I could tell them that I resided in Southern California. I called my cousin, and she called me back. She said that she was coming to see me, but that didn't happen. I wasn't worried because I knew that God had planted me here for quite a while. If I wanted to see her, I would have done it. I was swamped, and I later found out that she lived in Gardena, California.

I had been all over California, from San Diego to L.A. I saw homes on the mountain tops on cliffs. I had been in earthquakes and tremors. I trusted God and prayed that nothing would happen to us. It was dangerous being out there at times.

There were times we worked in ministry around gang members, thieves, and murderers. It didn't stop us because we knew that God was and still is in control. We fundraised on the Westside, Eastside, Northside, and Southside. I knew that I had to stay prayed up and focused out there. God can use you when you are focused on Him. God can't use us when we are doing what we want to do without His permission. When I went back to my dorm, I would line up God's word with what I was doing and how I was living while I was there. I didn't like all the things that I did and wasn't doing. For instance, we were awakened one morning in our dorms every so often to do bed checks. I thought it was corny, but it made sense. If someone took off how would they know if you follow the rules? We truly held people accountable back then. Now people do what they want. I was amazed that when something happened, we had long meetings quite often. I understood policy, proceedings, and organizations. I always wanted to be fair and balanced. I wanted to be upfront and personal with my friends and students. I trusted them, and they trusted me. I needed love and peace.

On November 9th, 2007, my fellow students and I were invited to go to Saddle Brook Church. Pastor Rick Warren is the head of the church there. We were invited to a Thanksgiving special. I was so excited once we were told that we were going in a couple of weeks. I didn't know where the church was in California. We had seen the calendar for that day and anticipated that day of food and festivities. We continued what our agenda was for our ministry, but I noticed that we were always doing something positive. For the New Year, we had an opportunity to go to Phoenix, Arizona for pastors' school at Phoenix

First Assembly Church. Pastor Tommy Barnett was the pastor there and was hosting Arneus Williams who was the Hall of Fame football player with the St. Louis Cardinals at the time. I met the comedian Sinbad and HairSpray actor Elijah Kelly all in one day at Pastor's School. I was having so much fun. We stayed at Jesus Christ Ministries Arizona in Phoenix, Arizona a whole week. I was so excited because I had found out that Tommy Barnett was the Founder of the Dream Centers across America. He was helping many up and coming ministers and pastors in the United States. Tommy Barnett and his son are the founders of the Dream Centers in Los Angeles, New York, and Phoenix. I was interested in going into these ministries because of the lifestyle I was living. I wanted to be apart of the success rate that I heard about all over the country. I wanted to be apart of a winning team. I didn't understand the ministries competitions. I understood Jesus Christ and the Fruit of the Spirit: love, joy, peace, forbearance, kindness, goodness, gentleness, faithfulness and self-control. I was involved in many complex ministries. I have seen ministries where they had circus ministries and animal ministries.

At the ministry in California, we had to wake up at 6:00 a.m. and shower, and fifty students loaded up in vans. We would get breakfast and go to a Riverside, California car dealership by 8:00 a.m. We washed about 10,000 cars every weekend. I wanted to say no like some of the faculty did on the weekends. I wanted to say no every weekend until I graduated from the California Ministry Institute. There was a mess every weekend because we didn't finish until late in the afternoon or between 2:00 to 3:00 p.m. We had to load and unload the cleaning equipment. Some people were teamed up as couples because that's what they did. However, I teamed up with a group of five or six people out of the 50 people. They gave us instructions on how and what they wanted to be done. Eventually, I was happy to be in this ministry because it taught me how to work together as a team player.

I also had been involved in ministries where they would have you work alone. It is awesome when you can complete a task that is assigned to you. But for teamed up assignments, I always helped people, like one friend of mine named Kyle. He didn't know how to spray wash a car. I showed him how to hold the water sprayer correctly so he wouldn't get the water all over himself and others. I told him to hold it down where you get the access soap off the edges of the cars once it was time to rinse them off. I tried to help many people.

During our break, we ate like kings and queens. The school provided fixed lunches with everything from bologna sandwiches, peanut butter and jelly sandwiches, chips, bottled waters, apples, and oranges. We prepared for the task because some weekends were very hot. Some of the funds that we made off washing the cars every weekend went to towards tuition, room and board, the faculty's salary, and for our personal needs like soap and toiletries. Mostly everyone was a happy student. I didn't see a high turnover rate here. I saw students leaving from Phase 1 and re-entry but not the Bible School. My eyes were opened about how this was a big success. I knew that you have to work together to be a team. When you are working together, and God is your pilot, it's an entirely different story. I began to be more open minded as time went on and less judgmental. I survived the

California myths that people mentioned. I came from a small town and realized why I was here. My only purpose was to do God's Ministry. Nothing else.

Charles Spurgeon identified the first sign of God's call to the ministry as an intense, all-absorbing desire for the work. Those called by God sense a growing compulsion to preach or teach the word and to minister to the people. It's not about us; it's about giving God your all. He loves us all. He wants us to bless others with His word and His songs. We all need to be ministered to. We all need one another more than we think. It's a problem in the churches today where you see things that are going on that is not God's doing. Man has let God down by his way of doing ministry; that is why we see many churches across America closing today due to lack of funds and misfortune. You hardly ever hear about a church closing because God asked them to leave especially when the church is flourishing. Many scandals are going on in churches. I heard stories in California where the pastor was dating someone on the side while being married. There was a gay pastor who was ministering full-time, and the congregation liked him. There was a pastor embezzling money from the church, and he still denied it. Allow God to judge the people. We as Christians need to look to God for answers and not judge people like we are still doing today.

God showed me many things while I was there, and he opened my eyes to why he sent me here in the first place. He wanted me to change my life and my way of thinking. He knew that I was going into unfamiliar territory. These people were from Haiti, Africa, Mexico, Venezuela, Morocco, Philippines, and all over the world. The school that I graduated from had ministries around the globe. We only had about 20% to 25% of our students that were from America. We only had three to four Black or African American men there. I was just happy to be one of them. I felt like I was chosen because God laid His hand on me to get my life together and become fully equipped to serve Him and His people.

I will never forget December 6, 2007. One of the faculty members told a few male students and me that there was a ministry that they started years ago that did natural disaster work for the State of California. They did work, cleaned up, and served the people that needed their services. Richard said that a man called and said that he needed eight men to help him go on disaster relief trips. He would pay us and fly us to wherever we are needed. I was excited because Richard told him yes. He had gotten permission from the Executive Directors. I was so glad that I was chosen out of approximately 100 men on a sign-up list. I was experiencing God's favor. Our first trip was in a van, and we camped out for two weeks at Camp Pendleton. We had to help set up the food services and serve for the Hotshot firefighters that were putting out fires all over that vast land. It was scorching out there, and I saw those men with their gear on. Those guys were very fit. They were ripped with abs, tall, and skinny. They had to be in shape to do their job. We served about 500 men that day. I saw smoke for miles as I took a break. I couldn't imagine putting out hundreds of miles of land fires. I saw guys slumped over from the heat. Some guys threw water on themselves and drank lots of water. I prayed and ministered to some of them. They knew about Jesus Christ but weren't ready to commit or serve Him. For two memorable weeks, I had fun working out there. At night I would go to the tent that I pitched. I was so tired some nights. I would wait until the next morning to take a shower. On the first night, I thought, "This is so different," because we all had to pitch our tents right by the job site.

Lions, tigers, and bears only came out when it's time for food. When they are not hungry, they don't come out. They sleep all day and wake up at around midnight. We already pitched our tents to rest, read God's word, and ate dinner several hours before. We would go to bed and the next morning serve the Hotshots again. We heard some sounds from animals. I saw creepy crawling bugs that I have never seen before. One morning we cooked about 800 pounds of sausage and eggs in a gigantic cooker and fryer. It was the first time I saw something like that. Later that day, we prepared dinner. We went into the meat cooler and saw that we were to fry 1,000 pounds of steaks. I saw so much meat and seasoning, it was crazy. I saw how to make everything from pancakes to chili. I met so many cooks from the company that called us to work for them. They were from all over the country. I met some good people in my life from the ministry. God has been good to me. When we were given instructions to do what we were told, we all made a promise not to mess up because we wanted to be successful. We trusted the Lord. We were obedient to Him and our boss. I was happy because I knew that we had no complaints while we were there, so we were going to be called repeatedly for more jobs. One month later, we went back to Bible School. Everybody asked us how it was working in the disaster area. It was an experience like being somewhere in the desert where it's just you, God, and a few people.

On January 19th, 2008, we got another call about a disaster in Texas. I will never forget that we stayed on the practice field of the Houston Texans NFL team. Richard said they needed us again to serve in Houston, Texas. I told him yes again. Afterward, we flew to Houston for this fun-filled work day. We stayed for two weeks and served the people of the city of Houston. We stayed in a brand-new white trailer with a huge hitch that had an air conditioner, drinks, and food in it. We were treated like stars on this trip because of the way they accommodated us. I asked who the trailers were for and found out that they were for us which was a blessing. We flew out there early in the week on a Tuesday. We didn't go back to L.A. until about two weeks later a Saturday night. It was only about a 2- to 3-hour flight. We prayed for people as we were serving them. We told them that we loved them, and that God was in control. I passed out tracts in my free time. I did lots of hands-on ministries.

God's word says in James 1:22, "Be ye doers of God's word and not hearers." I did what was presented to me because I thought about the experience God was blessing me with. I could have stayed back in school and said, "No. I don't want to do this." I participated because I knew that it was going to make me a better man of God. God opened doors for me that I would be in awe of. I didn't have to ask anyone for anything anymore. I just was chosen to do things on campus. I was going on all the trips that they had for us. I was up for the task, and I knew that it was relief coming at the end of the task. I just trusted the Lord and was obedient to His word. His voice is like no other. He is not a man or a woman. He is God and God all alone.

There is nothing that can change my heart, mind, body, and soul except his relationship with God. I have been through many trials and setbacks. God was with me all the time through thick and thin. He doesn't need us, but we constantly need Him. I truly believe the reason why He calls us home is to spare us from any more agony that we already suffered or been through. He heals us even in death to call us home from pain, torture, and sadness. You can understand God by reading and studying the word and in its entirety. If you don't understand something, purchase a concordance to get wisdom, knowledge, and understanding. God is who we should be worshiping. We worship everything else besides Him today. Now we are paying the price for things that were not supposed to be a part of our lives. People are creating things for us that God despises and should have no place in our lives. God can change whom He wants to change at any moment when He sees fit or when He is ready for that person to get His revelation. His world is different from ours. He is heaven's greatest blessings. He has great things in store for us more than we know. I knew that I would be involved in ministry but never knew in what capacity. I was interested in going all the way as I did for all the sins I committed. I did many of the things that made me scratch my head and say, "Okay. I just did that. No, not me."

I had been at the California Ministry Institute now for about five months. I was so impressed with where the ministry was headed. I was exposed to several different ministries. After lunch one day, all the students had a meeting because we were getting information about changing up the routes for fundraising.

I learned that we were going to Garden Grove, California where the crystal Cathedral was. Seven people headed in a fundraising van.

It was my first time seeing this beautiful church. I thought about what was going on inside once we drove by and took some photos. It was the tallest church structure I had ever seen. I heard that this church had one of the largest musical instruments in the world which is the Hazel Wright Memorial Organ. I drove past that church a couple of times and saw that the city was quite clean and nice. I realized all small cities and towns had their drawbacks. We fundraised all evening until 7:00 p.m. and then went home. We got back at about 8:30 p.m. and counted all the funds. It was a good day because we had collected over 5,000 dollars for the ministries that day. We did it every day for a long time. I was in the ministry on the day Michael Jackson died. I remember seeing a green helicopter flying over my head, and I knew something was wrong. I didn't know who died until we got home from fundraising near Bel Air, California area.

I saw some of the most beautiful homes that I had never seen. There were mansions with well-manicured lawns that had bells and pools. I saw the coastlines and beaches at least three times a week. My friend and I would go to Hollywood to eat free stuff from advertisement companies that were trying to get people to buy their products. I toured Sunset Blvd and Rodeo drive. The Hollywood Walk of Fame was interesting because I saw all the names of past and present stars. I thought about becoming a star so much that one weekend. I went to sign up for an acting studio, and they took pictures of me. I thought, "I'm getting out of here," because I realized that I was in California for ministry not acting. I felt that I needed to be obedient to God. I wanted His permission for acting but never got it. I stayed true to God and myself.

I went out with my friend one day, and he asked, "You want to go to a game." I asked, "What game?" He replied, "The Houston Rockets vs. Los Angeles Lakers." I said, "Yes. Where are the tickets?" He said, "All we have to do is go to Pico Blvd. in downtown L.A. to get the tickets because ticket scalpers will be selling the tickets cheap in the first round because they know the Lakers will beat the Rockets in the 2nd round of the playoffs." I asked, "How do you know that?" He said, "Trust me. Let's go there tonight and get some tickets."

We got ready at 2:00 p.m. and road the rail car all the way downtown. We got off at Pico Blvd. and walked a little way to the Staple Center. We arrived and saw people coming up asking about tickets. People were in the game. We were there early and got lucky about 5:20 p.m. Outside the staple center, a Mexican man sold my friend and I tickets to the 2008 Playoff between the Lakers vs. Rockets for 50 dollars a piece. We were in the nosebleed section. We were calling out to Kobe Bryant and Yao Ming from high up on the bleachers. We received the Lakers T-Shirts because the first 20,000 people got T-Shirts. I remember going to the top of the bleachers as far as I could. I sat next to my friend and an Asian man. The arena was sold out that night. The Asian man's name was Wan. He said that he lived in San Francisco and was born in China. I couldn't believe that I was watching the first of the 2nd playoffs. I saw Kobe and Yao play for the first time, and they played very hard that night. It was a close game. Because I was involved with God's ministries, He allowed me to be apart of some nice things.

A few months later, we went to see ministry concerts. I saw so many ministry concerts, like "Jars of Clay," for the first time in L.A. They played songs that were just very uplifting. I saw Israel Houghton in concert at the Staples Center. I saw many other gospel groups, and I thank God that I was exposed to see these popular musical groups. One evening I went to see the Los Angeles Dodgers vs. Arizona Diamondbacks at the Dodger Stadium. I saw their former manager Don Mattingly win a ballgame that evening. I was happy for him because we are both from Evansville, Indiana. I thought that was cool.

2008 and 2009 were a blast. I wanted to live out there as I was coming down to graduating. I had only about three or four months left before graduation. It came very fast. I was always learning new things and doing whatever I had to do to graduate. There were requirements of how and when we could do our graduation finals, and we were studying like crazy. My class of graduation was 2009, and we had some people that were very good at studying but couldn't preach at all. I realize that some people can teach and preach. Some people are good at administration ministry. I stayed in my lane. I tried to help people, and they were helping me too. I found out that some of the students could write and some couldn't. I saw people panicking and saying that after they graduate, they were going to be done with ministry. It didn't matter if they were quitting today or tomorrow. It didn't matter. I thought about going back home briefly. I knew the day I left Evansville back in 2006 that God had spoken to me and told me that I was going away for good. He blessed me like He can bless anybody else. I never thought that I was special. God caused me to understand that if I put my trust in Him, everything will be alright. I will never forget all that He has done for me.

I was there when the Executive Director passed away from the Riverside California Ministries. He was one of the Regional Directors. Many people were devastated when they heard about his passing. I knew of him, but I didn't know him personally. I met him only one time at a ministry conference. He was a nice man of God. He was responsible for all the bills getting paid and bringing in donations. He hosted many ministry conferences in Carlsbad, Linwood, Riverside, Long Beach, Bakersfield, and other cities or towns. I went to many conferences because they would always talk about God being all-powerful in the Supernatural. They also talked about God being who He is and what we ought to be. I always wanted more of God and less of the world. I had distinguished right from wrong and wrong from right. Some people can be wrong, and they still insist that they are right about the situation. I can tell them the truth about what God's word said, and they argue, fuss, or fight over what they feel is right. I don't get into things like that anymore. I study God's word for myself so way I will not be deceived. In the last days, many will be deceived.

Matthew 24:5 (BLB) says, "For many will come in my name, claiming, I am the Christ, and will deceive many."

I always study and learn about the scriptures because I want to understand their meaning and topics. I love the subject matter, and I love going over everything again. I always had to be ready or else I wouldn't be prepared to move on to the next level of ministries. Some days were better than others. I had a lot to learn. I saw people that acted like they knew it all. I needed to know who God was for myself. I didn't want someone telling me about God. God is more than what the world will ever know. I realized sometimes we must think outside the box, look around us, and see what we are faced with today. Most of the world wants nothing to do with God. Everything revolves around money and fortune. I always say my favorite words, "Thank You, Lord, for housing, food, clothing, and everything."

I always said, "Thank you, Lord, for my family. Lord, lead me where You want me to go even though I didn't know where I was going." I couldn't go anywhere else. I had to obey God because I knew that I would be dead if I didn't. I didn't have a chance. It was not an option to let my ministries go. I wanted to explore more as time was winding down. I saved funds and got my weight under control. We had plenty of good food that was provided for us. I thought about where I was headed after California. God knew where I was going, but I didn't. Sometimes God will make it plain and simple to you. Many times, He will make you wait until He is ready to decide for you. I had made some good friends out of all the places I had been too. California was the best preparation and teaching school that I have ever been a part of. I learned so much there and it was a class act organization. They treated me with love and respect. I was so grateful to God to be a part of an organization that made God number one in their lives. We were all transparent with one another which is something that you don't see anymore. I asked God to give me a new life, and He did it for me. Imagine what He can do for you. If it's in His will, He will do it for you.

For months, I went to school very happy and free from drugs and alcohol. I started to get some nice things. I appreciated the nice clothing and suits, but it was nothing like receiving the Holy Ghost. Sometimes, I was up all night as Jesus Christ talked to me. He let me know that my kids were okay. Since I wasn't there for them at the time, I always thought about them and prayed for them. I love my kids and grandkids. I would give anything for them to be in my life.

While I was in California, I had a few times to fly back home. I went home about three or four times on holidays. When I went home, it was a long flight both ways. Because of going into two different time zones, I had some jet lag. When I made it back to Evansville, I didn't feel the same way I did when I first left home. I was getting annoyed about being there. I asked myself, "Why did I come home? What did I come back?" When I started asking myself questions, it was made clear that God was making moves. I'm glad I listened because He saw something I didn't see. I realized that it's not about creation. It's about the Creator himself. I understood that when God speaks you better listen. I was distracted, and I kept my eyes on Jesus. I needed to get myself prepared for a big graduation ceremony that was looming ahead in a few months.

My graduating class had about twenty graduates in it. Every week, we rehearsed for graduation together. We tried on our cap and gown. We did our class work and fundraising. Early one morning, our Director and his wife asked us a question in the cafeteria. They asked if we wanted to be a part of the city parade that was coming up in the spring of 2009. We all agreed yes and wanted to be a part of it. The whole student body and the graduating class got ready for the parade in the upcoming weeks. We arrived at 8:00 a.m. on a Saturday. We had got up at 6:00 a.m., showered and put on the red ministry shirt and beige shorts. We were given a dress code of what to wear. I got ready for the parade and ate breakfast in the cafeteria which is where everybody would meet before we left somewhere. The cafeteria is where we had our study hall, revivals, or other life-changing events. We also ate breakfast, lunch, and dinner. It was a blast. We were all excited to walk in a televised parade in Southern California representing the California Ministry Institute. I felt so good to be invited by the City of South Gate, California.

I realized that the neighborhood I lived in was 80% Mexican, 10% African American, 5% White, and 5% other nationalities. There were many Mexican gangs in the hood where my school was. They knew who we were and respected us because of what we represented. They never said anything to us because God was in our lives. God kept them from us. He shielded us and kept His angels with us. They were shooting people up all over the city. We were never involved. God had given me a blessed time there. I went out to dinner with some friends at our favorite spot: In-Out Burgers. Anyone who has eaten there says the food is great.

We would see gang members in many places that we went to. I prayed for them when I saw them. I knew that if you are not a part of something that is positive, your life could be in danger. There was a lot of teenage pregnancy among many Black, Spanish, and Latino. Some of the girls didn't know who the father was because they had multiple partners. I felt terrible for them, but I knew there was a ministry for them. Most of the men got them pregnant and left. I knew that was wrong and I felt like I did the same thing to my kids. I was in contact with them periodically. For some reason, I thought more about them than I had previously. I wanted to reunite with them as soon as possible, but it never happened.

I kept the faith in God, kept on doing the right things by God's word, and stayed very positive. I thought about the distance that I was living in between moving away from California after graduation. I thought about where I was going in the future. I prayed that I didn't choose somewhere I want to be but where God wants me to be. I had been through the routine of everything, and I was a little restless at times. I knew that my time was coming to an end. I had met many people as well as locally and internationally ministers, pastors, and bishops from many different churches or Ministries. God blessed me with many friends and acquaintances. Some of them I don't talk to anymore. Some of them I still talk to. What I have learned is that many people will cross paths with you and never show you agape love. I look for that in a person, and if I didn't see it, I would try to see if I can try to get them to display that first. I would say, "God is good. All the time, He is good."

I learned so much there such as when to speak when spoken to, which is a lost art these days as well. We are out of order in many ways. An example was when I was at work when I was in California. I was working to afford some of the things I wanted and needed. I was talking to one of my school mates as he was there waiting for me to get off from work. As I was talking to him, somebody just came up to me telling me that the Jesus I believe in is fake and phony. They said, "He isn't real." I could have gone off and said what I wanted to say. I realized that the enemy could lie to other people and make them feel like they are saying something to make you change your mind from what you believe in. I'm not moved by great men of this world. I'm moved by God's word, His laws, and His great power.

I could have got involved in a personal relationship with a few women in the ministry while I was in California. I wanted to be in a relationship, but it didn't happen because God was in control and has been in control ever since. I had to wait a long time for Him to give me permission. There were only two black girls in my class. The rest of the girls were Mexican, Asian, and White. There were many Mexican males there. Three Black and two White males. I interacted with all of them every day like we were brothers and sisters. Some of them showed their true colors at times.

I got up in the mornings, thanking, and praising God for waking me up. I realized that we make choices every day: some good and bad. I had some bad days, but they were not often. I wasn't depressed. I had gotten bored. I realized my calling was to help people with drug and alcohol or dealing with deliverance. I kept saying, "Use me, Lord. Use me. Use everything up until I come into these ministries." I started living again. I wanted some of my family and friends to witness what God had done for me. I wasn't the same person. I was changed from head to toe; inside and out. I knew that after I left the California Ministry Institute, I would never be the same. I knew that there was nothing that could hold me back now from serving God. I understood who He was and is. People would test me and treat me badly. It didn't work because I had the fear of the Lord in me. Once Holy Spirit comes on you, you are not your own anymore. Other people get tested and tried. They would fail because you must know the word of God for everything to work in your favor. You can't just go off what you think is right. I had to come to grips with reality.

On April 20, 2009, I was ready to graduate from the California Ministry Institute. I was a well-learned minister by now. I not only learned the basics, but I learned the meat and potatoes of the Bible. I learned that sermons are great. Praise and worship are awesome. But you must have a personal relationship with God which is more important to me. The question for everyone should be, "What relationship do you have with the Father?" If you can't answer this question, you need to start over and ask God for whatever it is you are missing from Him. A person who doesn't have a relationship with God is doomed for life. Everybody has a belief system, and they think, say, and do whatever. You have to ask yourself, "What did God put me here in this world to do? Why am I here? Where do we go when we die?" When I started asking myself questions like these, God began speaking to me. I know that He put me in this position today because I listened to Him. I was tired, and I knew that I was on track for a real blessing from the Lord. All I wanted to do was be on God's winning team. I didn't care who was on the team as long as God is on the throne. I realized that far too many times we have people who think they are on God's throne sitting with the Father. I must tell you that there is none other than Jesus Christ on the throne with the Father God. We can't measure up to Him. We are just messengers to Him. We are vessels that are guided by the Lord Jesus Christ.

I went into the cafeteria to study every night when we got back from fundraising. I saw people there that were nervous. The faculty said, "If anyone fails the test to graduate, they will have to do another semester." They talked about it before because it has happened to quite a few people before. There was one guy who was supposed to graduate with us, but all he wanted to do is fundraise and do a little class work. I couldn't understand that part about him. I saw the day that he went back home to San Diego. I asked, "Hey man. What's going on with you?" He said, "I guess it's not for me." He was only interested in chasing girls and did what he could in the classroom because it was required. I saw many students that were there at the beginning and the end. Most of them were there for God, but some were there as demons and evil entities. I stayed away from all those things. I knew who they were, but I never entertained the thought of giving them any praise. God exposed them. Therefore, I continued to praise God.

I talked to my family and friends back home. It was apparent that I wasn't going to stay in California from the fact that the Director said that two places called me: New York and Atlanta.

I didn't have very long to choose to go to either place. I knew that after I graduated, I was going to go home to Evansville for a while maybe two weeks to a month. I decided to go to Atlanta because I wanted to be down South because I never lived in the deep South. I talked to their Director, and he gave me an offer that I couldn't refuse. He offered me my own house, which was free room and board, but the New York Ministries only offered me a room. Both were for teaching classes to other students. After that was established, I called my family and told them where I was going again so they wouldn't have to worry about me anymore. I was always cordial and descent by saying goodbye to everybody.

I packed up and got prepared to leave again. It went by fast this time. I had been all over the state of California. I saw the windmills and how they grow most of America's crops. I saw Mexicans in the fields working. I saw how they built houses and cars. I saw everything that God provided for the ministries. I'm very grateful for all that I learned including trying to go down to Hollywood Blvd.

Once you find out your purpose, pray to God and ask Him for clarity about it. Act on it according to His purpose. It's God's purpose, and we are the ones to carry His purpose out. I took my last few rides around the train to downtown L.A. I went to the mall in Crenshaw. I tried to visit many places as I could for the last time. I wanted to remember California as the best place I had been thus far. I was delighted here.

I packed everything up and cleaned up all my clothes. I said goodbye to many of my minister, pastors, and bishop friends. Many of them had their churches. Some of them had two or three churches. I wasn't where they were, but I knew that there was going to come a day where God was going to use me. I called and talked to my friend Pastor Mike Kough. He was happy for me, but he always told me to move on and continue to serve the Lord. He truly cared for me. He always told me if I needed anything to call him immediately. I never had to call him for anything because God took care of me. I tried to make sure that when I left this school, I would keep in touch with the people there. I eventually did, but many things have changed now. Some of the people are gone, and a couple of them have passed away. I was so honored to be in the Alumnus of this Ministries. One day my wife and I are going to fly out there and see the old gang. I heard that some of the students and faculty are still there.

I had gratitude about how much I learned from the California Ministry Institute. They knew how to praise God. I was very impressed with their Worship. I have been to churches where they played the same old hymns every Sunday. I have been to dead churches. I have been to churches where there were only ten people, and God moved more than the church that had 100 people. I have been to churches where there were awesome praise and worship, but the pastor was not a preacher. I continued to study God's word. Some of them were getting their interpretation of what the scriptures were saying. We as Christians don't need to get into heresies which is dangerous. The word of God will always stand up to all the bull crap that is going on in this world. I had been a hard worker all my life, and I worked hard at everything that I had been involved in. I came to California thinking that there wasn't too much more that I could learn. Well, I learned more than I expected and more. I never did find out what happened to my friend Bettye. I just left it at that.

For a long time, I felt that I wasn't going to make it. God gave me several chances. I used to feel sorry for myself, and now I was cleaned up, turned around, and made a 360-degree turn. I went from darkness into God's marvelous light. It took me some time. I had a heart change about myself and things in my life. God explained to me that I had to be fixed by Him. There was nobody that was going to help me but God because all my life I depended on my parents. After they passed, I immediately went to God instead of looking at everybody else. I knew they weren't going to help me get to where I needed to go. When you are helpless, you know it, and people know it. They will try to take advantage of you. You can't let people know everything about you. I hid a lot of my feelings when I was in California because I was far away from home. I had an accent, and people thought I was from down South. They would ask me, "Where are you from?" I said, "The Midwest." They said, "It sounds like you are from the South." I started to get upset, but I thought about it. Why allow people to get me angry that know very little about me. Let alone they don't even know God.

I made my rounds checking out everybody and told people that I was going home after I graduated for a few weeks. Most of the students I talked to went home. About 75% of the people who graduated before me went home. The people who graduated after me went home as well. I was kind of shocked. Many of the students I went to school with were drug addicts, alcoholics, homeless, and prostitutes. Some of them had problems with their parents because they were living with them. I saw arguments where some of them were here for some other reason. When I first met them, they were the same after one or two years. They didn't change. I asked, "Why did you waste all this time here?" They didn't learn anything. They just wanted to have a piece of paper or the diploma on graduation day. I knew I was going to change once I found out that I could no longer depend on me anymore to continue in sin. I asked God to fulfill all my needs because I wanted to have a better life. I wanted to be free-spirited in the right way, to be loved, to be successful, have peace, and be free. I wanted God, and He delivered me from myself.

On May 5, 2009, I graduated from the California Ministry Institute along with my other classmates. I was so happy on that day. I prepared myself for a long journey. It took a while to sink in that I had graduated from there. I remember waking up that morning, and it was a surreal feeling. I awakened that morning and prayed on the side of the bed. I said, "Lord. Thank you for this day, oh God." I looked over, and another student that was in my dorm got his stuff packed up and ready as well. He was graduating with me. We looked at each other and cried because we came all the way to the end. He was continuing his ministry.

I was so glad to be going home. I made reservations for my flight home two weeks before I was to leave from the ministry. I set up my flight from L.A. to Evansville for May 6, 2009, at 8:45 a.m. I will never forget that flight. I put on my cap and gown that morning after I ate breakfast and talked to people. I was happy for everybody. I missed some of them still to this day. Our ceremony was at 1:00 p.m. After lunch, we went through our ceremony notes on what we were going to say and our one last walk through. It was only like 21 graduates out of maybe 100 to 150 people. It seemed like every month new people were coming in. They had to sign a commitment letter. I signed one before and it said that as a student you had to uphold rules and regulations. There were about 500 or more people in the auditorium at my graduation. I was nervous as I was watched everybody receive their diploma. Then it came time for me to receive mines. I was glad to have graduated from Bible College. I smiled from ear to ear.

I was going around after we all said what we had to say. I said, "It has been a long journey for me. Thank God for the journey. I started from a small town in Indiana. I was on drugs and alcohol for quite a long time because I used the substances for coping with my problems. I had been in an accident that almost cost me my life. I was paralyzed from head to toe. If it weren't for the healing and deliverance from God, I wouldn't be standing up here today. I thank God for His mercy and grace." People were crying and clapping.

I found out that when you tell your story, tell the truth, for we Worship God in Spirit and Truth. I want people to understand that this could and has happened to someone else. I realized that God is the ultimate healer and provider. He can do anything at any time. The graduation ceremony lasted for two hours, and we went on past 3:00 p.m. There was a lot said among the staff, students, and graduates. I prepared to leave the next day. I went out that night in L.A. for the last time. I went to Hollywood Blvd. I went up and down the Hollywood Walk of Fame and many other places. I had said my goodbyes to everybody that I possibly could until the next morning. It was my time to leave and move on.

I had saved some funds along the way for traveling back home. I prepared for whatever God had in store for me because He taught me how to move out of the way. He also taught me how to stay in my lane as far as what He wanted me to do. I can't do what other people want from me. You must have discernment for that gift. God gave me many challenges and many blessings. I am so grateful for everything that I have learned. You never go backward in life. You move forward and tell God about your struggles. Stand firm on His word. Don't get caught up with people, places, and things. Get caught up in the things of God. Read His word daily. I still do. Tell God you need Him more daily. He will deliver you all from sin and damnation.

Psalm62:8 (NASB) says, "Trust in him at all times, O people: Pour out your heart before him: God is a refuge for us. Selah."

The graduation ceremony was over, and I headed home to Evansville, Indiana. I thought, "I'm going home. I don't want to, but I have to." I knew that this was the greatest thing that ever happened to me. I packed up my belongings as usual, and I had three suitcases headed to the van. I got up at 7:00 a.m., and it was very hot. I ate very little breakfast because I had to catch a morning flight. L.A.X. Airport was quite a long way from the

School. We loaded up the van and took off on Interstate 5. The driver was a new student named Lance who I had met briefly. He had been there for only two months. He was a good person who had lost his mother to breast cancer. He didn't get along with his dad. He told me about what he went through. He had a rough life. I told him to trust God, and all our hope is in Him. He dropped me off at 8:20 a.m. I had to rush and get to the gate that I was departing out of. I hugged him and said, "Take care."

I rushed to my area, made it to the counter, and loaded up everything. I was on the plane by 9:00 a.m. I looked at my ticket and my destinations. I was flying from L.A. to Chicago. Then from Chicago to Evansville. I slept on both flights and ate very little food. I didn't arrive in Evansville until 4:00 p.m. because I had a layover for three hours. My brother picked me up, and he helped me load up my things in his car. I was so glad to see him. I reflected on what I had left behind, and it was the best two years of my life. I will never forget what I have been through. I wouldn't trade this experience for anything in this world. God gets all the credit because I was the one who was in need and the need was met. I didn't go anywhere this time. I was at home for a couple of weeks. I got prepared for a ministry teaching job. I came to realize that God was in control of my entire life.

I went by to see my friends at Potter's Wheel Church and volunteered every week until I left to go to Atlanta, Georgia. I talked to Pastor Mike Kough and Pastor Mike Ballard. I was happy to see them. They were still helping people in the community, feeding them, and clothing the needy. I told them about the experience that I had in California. They were good listeners and said, "We knew that you were going to make it out there because we saw progress in your life every time, we saw you when you came home to visit." I was shocked that they would call and check up on me. I guess they didn't want me to know. I knew that the power of God was in me. I was a changed man forever.

My family came to my brother's house to see me. I didn't want to party anymore, so I just stayed home. I went out in the daytime to see people, but by 6 o'clock, I was in the house watching T.V. with my brother. I looked at the photos I took throughout my journey. I was a different person and took my beliefs about Jesus Christ very seriously. I wasn't going to let family or friends stop me from serving God. I meant that and I still feel the same way now. I went over to my sister's house because she invited me to dinner. We chatted. I had brought a picture over to her of Sinbad whom I met in Phoenix while I was in Bible College. I told my sister that she could have the photo.

I was so happy to see all my family. After a week, I felt out of place, like I was missing something. I knew what it was. I was missing my kids, and I arranged to see my daughter. I was so happy to see my daughter. I hugged her and told her how much I loved her. I needed to see her before I left. My son was in Indianapolis, so I couldn't see him. He knew I loved him and missed him. God was putting everything back together as I knew He would. I talked to my nephews and nieces. They said that they could see a change in me. I said, "Thank God for the change." I went over into my old stomping grounds one day and saw the same guys were still there. I remember partying with them. I remember all the things I use to do. I no longer did it anymore. I'm still friends with them, but the difference is I don't do what they do anymore. I knew that if God changed me, He could change them. Someone said to me, "They have to want it."

CHAPTER 11

Jesus Christ Ministries/ Atlanta, GA

I was still in Evansville sorting out my clothing and speaking to my family about what I was going to do with my life. My friends were excited for me when I told them I was moving to Atlanta. I was skeptical at first because of the stories about what was going on there. I learned that you must see for yourself. I looked at them and said, "Lord help me and help them." I prayed all day long about this move because I wasn't feeling it. However, I was obedient and learned that you might choose the place you think God has put you at because He gives us free will and choice. I had decided to go to Atlanta and found out that God had chosen somewhere else for me altogether.

    I was only a few days out from leaving for the ministries in Georgia. I had to come with a different mindset this time. I talked on the phone to the Directors, Mr. and Mrs. Johnson. They explained that I would be living in an old-style Victorian Mansion. I would be teaching classes to about twenty students. They told me what my daily schedule would be like. The first thing that they told me was that I would get a nice huge room to sleep in. I would get paid a $50.00 a week stipend. I was to teach their curriculum about Jesus Christ and his disciples. I told them that I would be there on June 2, 2009.

    I left my brother's house to get some breakfast. He took me to the bus station, so I could leave for Georgia. It was sunny and humid that day. I was happy to leave because God told me it was time to go. He gave me the signs again. I was getting restless and anxious about being there. I knew that if I had been there any longer than I should have been, I probably would have a relapse. I shortened my load this time. I left at 10:00 a.m. He dropped me off there, and I waited for an 11:00 a.m. bus pickup. I was there early for a reason. I wanted to make this trip. I had only two suitcases. I gave my brother a few clothing items, and I left a lot of things with him because I didn't want to be carrying unwanted stuff with me. I accumulated many things from every ministry that I was involved in. I was no longer worried about material things, and I wanted to be comfortable. I love God and wanted to serve Him in whatever kind of capacity that He would allow me to. I had a destination ticket, 11:00 a.m. to 9:00 p.m., from Evansville to the Atlanta Bus station. I had told the directors that I would be calling them upon arrival.

It was an okay ride except for the air conditioning on the bus not being cold enough. It was terrible that day because people were complaining when we got to Nashville, Tennessee. I couldn't believe what was happening myself. I told myself that I would not be on the bus for more than a couple of hours and it was true. I was so happy to be near my destination. The only problem is the little tiny small towns you go through before you end up at the major hub. I saw people on this weird bus ride. Some people were drunk and acting crazy. Another man went to the bathroom and stayed in there too long. When he came out, the bathroom smelled of cigarette smoke. I thought, "Man, people are out of control these days." I saw a couple sit next to each other just making love, kissing, and hugging. I thought, "You all need to go get a room when you reach your destination." I realized that there is a ministry at airports, train stations, bus stations, restaurants, etc. People are hurting everywhere.

I went from Evansville to small bus depots in Kentucky, Tennessee, and Georgia. I had a long ride, and it was okay but very exhausting. I called my friend to tell him I was okay because the bus had stopped near Chattanooga, TN to get some food for us. It was about 4 p.m., and we still had a 4-hour ride left. It started to rain after we left from eating at a nearby store. I got a sandwich, chips, and a drink. I ate and almost fell asleep. I had eaten too fast. As we were passing by some mountains, I heard somebody say, "Look! That is the Great Smoky Mountains!" as I was trying to sleep. I looked up and was looking at the Smoky

Mountains. I saw this big steep ridge on the side of the bus. I anticipated this trip would be my last one in a while. I'd had enough. I imagined how the Atlanta ministry would look as I was on the bus resting. I tried to visualize the ministries and how it was structurally set up. Once again, I was wrong because our thoughts are not like God's. Our ways are not like His ways either. I couldn't wait to get there and see the blessings of God. I had hoped for the best.

I got to Atlanta at 9:15 p.m. and I wasn't too happy about the trip in the end. Once I got off the bus, I waited for the bus driver to open the hatch at the bottom. He took his time because he had to use the bathroom. That was when I called my people to come and pick me up. They didn't answer the phone. I kept on calling until I got somebody. I finally got a staff member named Raymond who was the driver staying at the house. He came to pick me up, and I was so happy to see him. The bus terminal in Atlanta was busy and did not feel safe. I was there waiting for over 30 to 45 minutes before he came to get me. I didn't realize that the Ministry wasn't nearby.

The Ministry was in Stone Mountain which is in a rural area. I saw the van approach the building, and I knew it was him because of the writing on the van. He parked the van, and I stood there. I waited for him to get out of the van. He got out, and we introduced ourselves. I put my suitcases in the van. He told me where he was from and where he has been. He talked to me about his family and friends. He was a very nice man. He offered me dinner, and he talked to me about how God has blessed him and his family. He was using drugs because he had lost his grandma who raised him when he was a boy. His mother had to work hard because she had no help financially. They were poor because he had no father living in his house. I told him about the problems that I had. I told him about the addiction that I had to drugs and alcohol. I was lacking the education at first. We talked about many things that night on the way to the Ministries until he told me that we were almost there.

As we approached the house at night, I couldn't tell how it looked because it was dark outside. The house was powder blue and a huge mansion. My eyes got huge, and I said, "Lord!" I realized when the house was explained to me, it wasn't explained clearly. I unloaded my belongings, and he took me to my room. I thanked the Lord for my room and board. I thanked Him for helping me get to the Atlanta ministry safely. Whatever God wanted me to do here was going to be brief. I saw it coming because this was a pit stop ministry. This ministry was getting me prepared for the ministries in New York. I met a few people that night. A few students were watching T.V. I shook their hands briefly and went to my bed. I made a couple of phone calls to family and friends. I told Raymond thank you and goodnight. I went back into my room and stripped down to my underwear. All I thought about is going to bed and my kids. I prayed for them. I was in bed by 11:30 p.m. I went to sleep quickly because the mansion had central air.

The next morning, I woke up in a lovely beautiful home. I was shocked because this home in the daytime was the most beautiful home that I had ever lived. It had wood and marble finishing inside and outside. I ate breakfast in awe. I was introduced that morning to all the rest of the students and faculty. This ministry wasn't anything like California Ministry Institute, but it was a well-oiled machine. I looked at the classroom and the job schedule. I was happy that they had structure and a decent curriculum. Most of all it was God in charge of this place because I saw His hand upon it. It wasn't for me; it wasn't for the faculty. This ministry was for these young men with life-controlling issues. After breakfast, I was shown around the entire house. The home had about ten bedrooms. We weren't allowed to take photos of this home. I signed confidentiality and many other contractual agreements. I was ready to serve. Then I got a call that the directors were coming at 5:00 p.m. to meet with me in their office. They had a house somewhere else, and they owned other homes as well. I proceeded to sit in on some classes until they wanted me to teach. I went all over the house and was in the biggest kitchen that I had ever seen.

The first full day was a blast. I met twenty students that day and getting to know them was so inspirational. There were only three African American students there, and the rest were White. I learned a lot from one of the students named Phillip. He had been on the streets of Atlanta ever since he was 21 years of age and he was 28 at the time. He told me how he had got tired of being out on the streets and was on crack for quite a long time. He finally wanted to get help. There were people in there that had nowhere to go. People abandoned them because they were not happy with their families. They told stories about eating food from dumpsters, sleeping all over Atlanta in ditches and abandoned houses. Some of them slept in community parks and shelters. There were students there with mental illness. We all needed prayer because they gave me hope to cope with some of the things I was going through.

I asked them a lot of questions because I was curious and somewhat skeptical. I asked them what made them do some of the things they did? It was always a tragedy. For instance, their grandmother who was the one who raised them passed away. There was also a lack of funds in the home. Someone lost a best friend that was close to them. It was always something that triggered them. I was there to be a "Messenger of Hope "to them. I had to be very honest and listen to them about everything that they were going through. I finally went to take a shower at 4:15 p.m. to get prepared for the meeting with my directors. I waited in my room and took a quick nap. I got a call, and they arrived in 20 minutes. I dressed quickly, and I went to the office. I met them for the first time. I stood up and introduced myself. Immediately I knew that I was there for a moment because God let me know that I was going to be a temporary fit with them. I saw it in their eyes that they wanted me. I saw that something wasn't right with them. I felt an evil presence from Mr. Johnson and his wife went along with whatever he was doing. I had a gut feeling that they were doing some underhanded things. They had an aura about them that was arrogant and contrary.

Anyway, I stayed the course as long as I could. I did the schedule and curriculum as ordered. I start teaching classes about two weeks after I arrived. I wanted more than what I was doing because the schedule wasn't flexible. It never changed, and it never fluctuated. I wanted to do other things until one day we got a work order. We were doing our regular schedule, and

I received an order to pick five boys to clean up a cemetery in Atlanta after classes were over. The cemetery had a lot of leaves and branches that needed to be cleaned up. It was an all-day job that required five men with several plastic bags, rakes, cleaning gear, and gloves. We made preparations and provisions for the job. Another staff member and I assisted them in getting the job done. I wasn't thrilled about supervising them at the cemetery. I learned that no matter what the job was, we had to work as a team to get the job done.

We went there on a Tuesday morning to do the job but couldn't finish because it was more work than we expected. The job consisted of us putting mulch in certain areas of the cemetery. We had to clean up the broken branches first. The cemetery was about two miles long. It was one of the largest I had ever seen. It was hot outside, and we all probably drank a gallon of water. We ate some bologna sandwiches, chips, and water. Some of us drank juice. We worked from about 9:30 a.m. until 6:00 p.m. We had an hour drive back home. When we got home, we were so tired. We came back the next day to finish it off. That didn't happen either. We went on Tuesday, Wednesday, Thursday, and Friday. They wanted us to cut their grass in addition to all the stuff we did that week. In four days with five men, we made about $1,500 for the ministry. I will never forget this experience. It wasn't my, the students, or the ministry funds. It was God's funds. That is why I was obedient and committed to this ministry. After we completed all that we could that week, we start getting other work orders. We moved this man and woman. They wanted four guys to move them into a three-bedroom home. We got that done in one day for $500 for

6 hours. I oversaw the move without picking up much of anything. I realized that I could help them navigate the move as far as putting things where they needed to go. I was good at things like that. I was obedient and persistent. I wanted to please God. One Sunday morning we went to church. We all got dressed that morning, ate breakfast, and loaded up the van. We were about 30 miles outside of our vicinity. I looked up and said to myself, "Sometimes there is no need to ask questions. Just pray and ask for traveling mercies." We went to a church where it was a mixed congregation. I was there with the students, and we were in the presence of some awesome worship leaders. The people were so good at worshiping God that the services lasted for about two to three hours. The anointing was there, and the leadership was okay.

I went to a couple of different churches and said, "There is something always missing." I just wanted to be involved in a Bible-believing church. In Atlanta, there are several hundred churches available for bishops, pastors, ministers, etc. I asked God to help me. Whether I was in church or not, I just wanted to be in right relationship with the Father. I had to wait on God for His signs and wonders.

One time the Directors called me in their office on a different occasion and asked me if I was willing to teach classes in another house. I told them if it was in God's will then I would. It wasn't in His will because God had another plan for me. They asked the question a couple more times and offered me my own home that I had to share it with some new students. They moved me into the home all by myself and wanted me to wait for at least a month or two before they could get some new students. It was confusing. I would wake up to nothing but the house and me. He promised me the job once they had more students. It was a bad sign to me that they didn't have their stuff together. I waited on this to happen, and it never did. They called themselves promoting and helping me, but they disappointed me. I was on the verge of leaving. Their goal was to open two houses. I would teach a classroom, and another staff member would teach classes in the old House. I had been there for almost two months, and I thought, "No way." I felt I wasn't treated right by this ministry. I knew that it wasn't for me after he had moved me over to a much smaller and different home. I had problems sleeping there. I thought, "How are you going to deal with this situation?" I dealt with it according to the will of God. I was in that house for quite some time until I told the director that I didn't want to stay there anymore. Afterward, they shut the house down, and I moved back in with my old buddies. I was so glad to be back in the house where I started. They came by to see me again and checked up on me. They had students watching me, and there was hardly anything there.

Looking back on that episode, I was not going to be somewhere that I wasn't happy or not needed. I was going to obey God anyway. I realized that I was on borrowed time. Once I moved back into my old place, I helped them prepare meals, helped with homework, and helped with cleaning up the entire house. The work order wasn't good. They never told me what they do. They allowed me to learn all I could with them. I was never the same after this place. Looks are deceiving. I started to tell them that I wanted to go home.

Some places you will be there for a season and some places you will be there for years. It's according to God. I wasn't there for four months. They were organized, but they had no vision. They bought more houses all the time because the director loved to purchase homes. If it were left up to him, all the houses he bought would go to ministries.

All I had was hope when I was there. Hope is the key. I asked for a meeting with the Johnson's because I wanted to be transferred if all possible to the New York Ministries. I waited for them to respond and they took their time. I finally got a meeting, and I told them that things weren't working out. They asked, "Why?" I told them that I didn't see myself getting anywhere fast. He said that he was going to call the director in New York and get back with me. I was so happy that he called New York for me. The next day all I did was help them cook and clean all day. I wanted to do more than what I was doing when I first got there.

I listened to God, and I listened to God's people. I will always look to my Heavenly Father for direction. When one door is shut, another door opens. I knew it was over for me because all the signs were there. Some ministries last a season. Other ministries last a few months to a couple of years. There are other ministries that last forever. I have also seen ministries that never get off the ground because of unbelief. God wants to use all of us for His glory. I couldn't just sit around and continue to do this kind of ministry. There was no more growth in this kind of ministry. I found out that if your ministry isn't growing in God, then there is something wrong with your vision. By this time, I had been a part of many successful ministries. I can tell you that God is in those ministries because you can't run a ministry just off money and raw talent. You must have the Holy Spirit and the right people that are sold all the way out to God. You must have God's vision to take them higher in Him.

A suggestion in taking people higher in God would be doing a study of the Old Testament and then mapping the Red Sea out in the Bible. Study what happened in B.C. or A.D. Afterward do a study of the geographical area the next year if you want to explore and see what happened. You can get 20 to 40 people together and see if they want to go on a trip to Jerusalem or wherever the destination calls for. Then proceed from there. Some people get more of a revelation and or visual from seeing everything in person. I love thinking about what it was like in those days. Now, of course, we do know that times have changed, but God is still God. No one can take His place.

Georgia was the only place where I felt out of place the most. There was the hidden sin that I was around in the ministry which was so hurtful and painful. I was glad that it didn't take me that long to catch on to what was going on. There were faculty members still getting high away from the ministries. I thought, "I wonder when they are going to call me back and let me know the deal."

After the summer was over, I was grateful to get a call on August 19, 2009. I spoke on the phone to the ministry people in New York. They said that they were going to give me a chance and that I had to come straight from Atlanta on September 8, 2009. I told my students that I was leaving because I had bonded with some of them. I called home and told them the same thing. I also told them that I wasn't going to be coming home any time soon. I had to do this for myself because I didn't want them to worry about me. I knew God was on my side. I also had to believe in myself. I had more confidence in what was right and wrong by God's word. I had a change of heart and revelations about many things. I wanted to have a better life and lifestyle. I needed a better thought process. I needed a whole new life, and God gave me what I asked for. It takes time and guts to move on as I did. Many times, I wanted to give up. I fought it for days because giving up wasn't an option. It takes a lot of work to grow in God. The funny thing is some people think that if they're in church all is well. You can't hide in church ministry. It doesn't matter whether you sit in the front, the back, on the pulpit, or in the outer courts. God has an assignment for everyone. All assignments are not from God unless He gives you one. Some assignments are given by the people of God and not God himself.

I was always skeptical with the Georgia Ministry. When I was given the assignment, it was not given by the Lord Jesus Christ. The director was trying to create ministries in these properties he owned by putting students in the houses. I questioned many things they did. I observed what was going on. Then I lined God's word up to what the ministries were about. I prayed for this Ministry. Many churches and ministries are open because of the money the congregation is giving in tithes and offerings. God wants us to rely on Him and trust Him for everything. He doesn't want us to be concerned about how much other people give and the ones who can't give. That's why it's better to give than receive. He wants us to love and trust him. He does not want us to get caught up in ministries. He said in His word that, "Heaven and earth will pass away, but His word will remain the same." There is a blessing in reading God's word.

CHAPTER 12

Jesus Christ Ministries/New York City

At approximately 1:00 p.m. on September 8, 2009, I departed from Jesus Christ Atlanta Ministries to start a new journey in ministry. I knew that everything wasn't going to go well. I trusted the Lord for everything that I had already been through. I had a flight from Atlanta-Hartsfield to New York LaGuardia Airports. My departure was at 3:00 p.m., and I said goodbye to everyone the night before. It was a somber goodbye, and it seemed like no one cared. They just weren't happy at this ministry. I realized that when a ministry is run like this, there is a problem from the top down. The director was hardly there.

When he was there, people wished he wouldn't come because he barely held any meetings. He checked on his business. God is not to be ran like a business. That is why many churches all over the country are closing. God comes first, not the business. We are supposed to be the messengers for God and help people turn their lives around for Him.

I asked Raymond to help me get my suitcases together. He helped me, and I thanked him for that. He also drove me to the airport. I was so happy and relieved of my stress. Things come out when you are moving on. Raymond told me that nobody stays there long because all the director would talk about is getting more students to make more money. He told me several other things as we drove to my destiny. He said the more students you get, the more donations they would get from different churches. Plus, they could sell more images of crosses and many other things. Many churches and ministries are out of order today. The only thing you can do is pray to God for the leaders to stop the madness.

I got there at 1:30 p.m. to check in my luggage. I was in terminal 8 Delta Airlines and waited upstairs until 2:45 p.m. They started calling first class, zone one, zone two, and zone three. I realized that I was zone four and that was near the back of the plane. I thought, "Oh well. I'm going to sleep on this three-hour flight." I was in my zone at this point and time because once I boarded the plane, I never looked back. We backed up, and I saw the flagger behind us. He waved to the pilot to turn out, and once the pilot started down the runway, he sped up. I heard the engines roaring outside of the plane. I always love that sound because it reminded me of thunder, lightning, and Jesus Christ's power. I slept some, and I had a little snack from the airline stewardess. I was never the same after arriving in New York City.

It wasn't my first time here. I came here for the first time in 1981. I played on the AAU Basketball team, but this time I wasn't here for basketball. I was here to serve God and to serve Him well. God made me understand that very well. I was on the plane sleeping and by 6:15 p.m., I arrived at LaGuardia Airport. It seemed like we were only in the air for an hour. That hour was actually three hours and 15 minutes. It was still light outside my window. I stood up once we landed and I didn't talk to anyone coming or going. I was in my own world. Sometimes it's better to be quiet and say nothing at all to people you don't know. A person's body language tells a story. I had to wait until most people got off the plane because I was near the back. I went up front slowly and walked down to baggage claim. I picked up my things and went near the entrance to check if someone had my name on a sign in front of them that read "New York Ministries here to pick up Jerome Meriweather." That is what Director Wilkes said to me on the phone. I didn't see that, and I waited for almost two hours before someone picked me up. I waited downstairs and made several phone calls to family and friends. Then I made calls back to the people who were supposed to pick me up. They said that someone was on the way. I went back to the baggage claim area and sat. I asked God to take over my life and transform me into His light. I finally saw a New York Ministry Institute van pull up with a man in it by the name of Pastor Jared. He was a tall white male who had a wife. He had no kids and was from Missouri. We shook hands, and he helped me with my stuff. I was not going to talk to him about what happened in Georgia. All I told him was it didn't work out, and that was it. If there was anything else that needed to be dealt with, I would deal with it later. I was determined to stay, possibly get married, and get a job. It was a long 30-minute ride back to Brooklyn from Queens.

I arrived at the New York Ministry at 7:20 p.m. I met some young students that night watching T.V. The day I arrived was the day I became a real man of God. I was there to help the students, and I was sold out for God. This ministry had a very diverse types of people from all over the world. People I met were from Africa, Asia, Pakistan, England, China, and Israel. I met people from across the globe. Brooklyn has a very diverse class of people from everywhere as well. It is not the same. I went out to several different places with my friends that I met in the Ministries.

I had to be very open to them about my life and my past. I told them that my dad was a pastor and I grew up in the Midwest. I had a good life growing up with my parents and family. We were transparent with each other. My eyes lit up every day as I taught because God opened doors for me that I thought wouldn't be open. I realized that immediately because He can do whatever He wants when He wants. Over the next couple of days, I unpacked my clothes and got my apartment together. I had to keep myself prayed up and be serious about serving God. I couldn't represent Him sometimes or some days, but I had to be sold completely out for Him. I said to myself, "It's time to learn the city and learn about the people of Brooklyn all over the five boroughs."

I had to buy myself some clothes from there so I could look like a New Yorker. I still had a country accent and had to get used to the new lifestyle. I was glad to be out of Evansville. It was a thing of the past, but it will always be home. I needed to get it all out of my system. It was such a big change for me. I learned that most people that were born here are not so friendly. It was different for me and some things until this day I still don't understand, such as why some people can be so mean and heartless. I wanted to be different, but I had to be myself. I changed for Jesus Christ, my family and myself.

I didn't have too many friends because I found out that when you change your life for God, many people leave you. I left for a good reason. They left because I was no longer participating in their drug and alcohol activities. I was so free from bondage. I had to smile and do what I always did. I prayed and continued to put God first. For everyone to succeed, we all need God. It was time for my life to be changed forever. I saw my life being over. God flashed my life before me, and I heard His voice say, "Move on and out of where you are now." I was engulfed in God. I knew what He taught me was more than all that I was taught in Bible institutions and churches. I always felt like I needed to be on point with what He taught me. I asked God to show me the hidden things. I wanted to be spiritually inclined to God's word. He taught me how to live. He also taught me how to be successful in ways I never imagined.

People need to wake up and see that there is a Hell and Heaven. Just look at the world now. God is so powerful and real. God is waiting for us all to come together. It is plain to see that violence was never God's plan. People are dying in the streets; mainly African American men. People are fighting for fame and fortune. Kids are raising kids. Men and women are shacking up for sex. People are cheating on their taxes. People are leaving their children with their grandparents who are way too old to help them. Why is their homelessness in the richest country in the world? Legalized drugs such as opiates and weed are killing more poor people. There is racism. Animals are abused for their hide, tusk, or other things. People are asking where God is in all of this? He is right there just like Sodom and Gomorrah. We all will be held accountable and responsible for our actions. I will not live my life as if I don't see anything happening. Some of us are so silent and stiff-necked because it's not happening to someone in your family. A day will come when God will call our attention to something to hold all of us accountable. We all must act to all the things that are happening in our lives.

Brooklyn is one of the fastest growing cities in America. It is growing in apartment buildings and real estate. When I moved there, I got to see all the buildings going up all over the city. The city is still growing and very expensive. God is the ultimate provider and healer of everything. I didn't see any churches being built. Many of the churches I saw were for sale. The Black churches were mostly storefront, and the Catholic churches were huge, gothic and mythical in New York City. Manhattan, Brooklyn, Queens, Bronx and Staten Island are the places that are supposed to be less expensive. However, they are becoming more expensive. People are turning their houses into apartments. I saw many homeless shelters with over one million people homeless in New York City. There are many ministries there like anywhere else. I was glad God chose me to come to New York to minister to people. It was easy to look at the bad and the good about things we see going on.

I needed to be around people that knew what was going on here. I met a friend by the name of Donald who showed me all around New York City. We went shopping, rode the E, A, J, C, B, D, and R trains. We rode a train one day out to Brooklyn. I said, "What are we doing on this train?" We rode out to Far Rockaway. There is a train that the break releases once it runs over the water in the tracks that we crossed. I thought we were in the water.

I was in the Bronx with him one day, and this woman tempted me. She was a demon and tried her best to get me in her house so I could throw my ministry and life away. I said no way and told my friend we should go. I left her standing outside when she told me that she gets high because she lost her son. She had a look on her face that said I hate myself. I prayed for her and I went by to see her a couple of times. Nothing happened between us. I was so glad to be strong enough not to mess around with her.

I had connections with the New York School of the Bible at Calvary Baptist Church in Manhattan. I had taken some courses like Koine Greek and New Testament Survey. My friend told me about the classes so signed up through Bowery Mission. I saw 100 people enroll in classes when I went there to enroll one morning. I was living in Ft. Greene, Brooklyn. It was so different that I embraced it. I went to Bed-Stuy, Brownsville, and Crown Heights. Trust me, it is a whole new world. It is a free education on how you can live or get an education like a college degree and move to higher ground with God.

I saw people standing on street corners and people laying on the ground in the winter time. I saw liquor stores on every street corner. There was a church and a funeral home on every other street corner. We need those things, but it serves its purpose when we need it.

I never questioned God because He has given us His word that He would never leave or forsake us. I said to myself that I want my church to be called, "The Potter's Wheel Worship Center." I want all nationalities in my church. Jesus Christ is the potter who mends us and puts us back together. I'm the clay or the dirt that He forms to His liking, and I become obedient to Him. Then I go into the pot, and God allows Jesus Christ to water it. God makes it grow. I become the minister that obeys God and His teachings. I sleep, eat, and breathe God. At some point, we as Christians must fall in love with the Father, Son, and Holy Spirit. We have fallen in love with the world. It was satisfying at first but who do you call on when the person you are in love with hurts you in so many ways? Do you call on when your wife or kids when they hurt you? Do you call on your son, daughter, brother, or sister that hurt you? Do you call on your pastor or your best friend when they hurt you? Do you call on your mom, dad or co-worker when they hurt you? Call on Jesus Christ. Holler and cry out, "Jesus."

I asked God to give me clarity and direction. I always asked Him to create in me a clean heart and renew a right spirit within me. I started to see beyond the madness. People allow Satan to come in their lives through negative thinking and even looking at someone in an unnatural way through lust and perversion. I prayed for myself and for people at the churches that I was affiliated with constantly.

I spent many days at school on the weekends. I was tired and bored. I was familiar with New York City after five to six months of being there. I had to reinvent myself by applying for different jobs. I have experienced being a part of organizations. I knew one day that I would be a minister of a church that I was apart of instead of just teaching classes. I didn't know when I was going to be an ordained minister. I started seeing that some people were in my life for a season. Some people were in my life for a couple of years, and they just disappeared. Some things are meant to be, and some things aren't. God is meant for me. Every once and while I called home to Evansville to let my family know that I was still alive.

My friend Donald was always taking me to Pennsylvania with the church mission at the Bowery. We were going on singing men's retreats. Every time we sang, we would get a donation. I met many friends there. I thought, "If I ever leave the Brooklyn Ministries, I will go to Bowery." God will let you know when your time is up. I eventually did leave. Jesus Christ Ministries told me to come to the office one morning. They asked, "What are your plans for the future?" I found out once they start asking you that, they are going in a different direction. I ended up moving to Manhattan. It's God who you should be keeping your eyes on. We are His messengers, and some of us are giving people mixed messages that God is all about having nice things. God is more than food on our table, clothes on our back, money in our pockets, cars, houses, vacations, and jewelry.

I saw jealousy and lost people in my classes. I taught young Black and Puerto Rican men, as well as many White men the word of God in all these ministries. Heaven will have some of everybody from all over the world. We all need to get it together, do God's work, and stop bickering about who gets what and who is the H.N.I.C. I want God to put me where he wants me and travel the world doing humanitarian work for the Lord. The United States is the wealthiest country in the world. Everybody is coming to mystery Babylon because all the wealth is here, and this is not the place where God will begin or end us. Just like the Roman Empire, the United States will fall because money can't keep you in this life. God is so powerful and always setting us up for His coming. Sin, poverty, racism, voting, jobs, finances, marriages, families, churches, health, domestic relationships, and foreign relations are calls to action.

I believe we need a serious call to action for the hatred in this country. We need a call to action on jails and prisons. Ryker's Island and many other solitary confinement institutions are unfit to live in. Inmates of all races, creeds, and colors are dying and being mistreated daily. From my own experiences, many of our Black men are lost and need God totally in their lives from a spiritual and mental standpoint. Their lives are ruined because of their environment and the way they think which affords a dead end.

God can take you from Prison to the Palace. Joseph's story goes much deeper than just what he went through with Potiphar's wife. His brothers thought he was the weakest link. They sold him into slavery. One thing many people don't understand about Joseph was that his family didn't know who he was since he had been away for a while. God was on him and all inside of his whole countenance. I know I can relate to Joseph story. I was the so-called weak link out of all my brothers. God had a greater plan for my life that I didn't even know existed. I always had a curious personality and was very ambitious. I took notes in my head, wrote information down in my head, and recorded until I could get it all down on paper. God is my greatest source of power anyone can have. This is what I have learned since I moved to New York. I moved to the Bowery in Manhattan once I left Brooklyn.

After January 12th the following year, I was terminated from my contract of educating students at Brooklyn. It was a private ministry institution and a different environment. I hated moving because I had always made friends and had some nice things. I had been in New York City from September to December and in Brooklyn teaching classes at the end of 2010. When I said goodbye to the people in Brooklyn, I was okay with it because they had a lot of financial troubles. I was told they were barely staying open. The founder was there for 40 years. When he left, he left the Ministry in good shape. It seems it went down after he left. I said, "Lord I must move on in my journey."

I was in a transition period and still heavily involved in ministries all over New York. It was another famous ministry institution from way back in the day. One of the most powerful presidents came to do a speech there one day. They have had countless celebrities visit. I had a nice bunk bed, and I thought, "Man what a facility!" I met several men that were in there with me. I had to tell them why I was there. They had no clue why they were there except for there was nowhere to go. I was listening to them, and they were just glad to have a place to stay and three meals every night.

Some of us are not where others are at in their walk with the Lord. I respected them for their honesty. My ears were open, and I was interested in their conversations. They told me how they grew up, and after I heard their stories, I had no excuses. A man said that his daddy left the house when he was five years old and the impact that it had. The other guy said he was sexually molested, and he couldn't stand his mother's boyfriend for doing it to him. They struggled all the time on food stamps and slept with relatives some nights. People thought that was funny. I told them that only with God could they change. Many people try to talk to them about 'rags to riches' stories. I told them how God could clean them up and turn their whole life around. Our foundation is Him. Sometimes you must meet people where they are. Scriptures are great and have a profound place in our daily lives. Sometimes we must listen and say nothing at all or give positive feedback. I understood some of their problems. I had my own, and I made comparisons to what they were going through. Some of our situations are just silly mistakes and doing dumb stuff such as dropping out of high school. I thought about dropping out, but I graduated. I wanted to tell the other 60 men to pray and ask God for forgiveness because some of the men came out of bad marriages where they never forgave themselves or their ex-wives. Some of the men came out of very low-income families where the father had a third-grade education and never made it out of the ghetto. Their relatives brought food over, and they did extra work on the side to make ends meet.

There were times where I wanted to give up and throw in the towel because of honest mistakes and watching fools do foolish things. I care just because others don't. I love and care about myself. I just needed a push from time to time. I never gave myself any credit for whatever God has done for me. I never understood how someone could take credit for what God is doing in their lives. Who gave you the job to get the food on the table? How did you get the job to buy a car, house, and clothing? It's all the Lord's blessings. God deserves the glory and honor for blessing us all every day.

They had praise and worship there at night, and in the day, we went to school and had devotions. We worked on the kitchen detail from time to time. Sometimes the clean up was very nasty and messy. The mission faculty was throwing donated food away every day, so they had a special team inspecting the food. It was nasty pouring large amounts of milk down a drain. There was a sour smell. There were large amounts of bread that was thrown away. I saw so much food and clothing being discarded. One can only imagine.

I had to be ready to go the extra mile and do all I could for this ministry because I was a student again. I realized that when your roles change, you still must remain humble and stay ready to learn always. I had a friend named Neil who was a good teacher and expositor. He knew the word but was always ready to go to the next level. I was in his class. He was very vocal about teaching and preaching God's word. He was open about his strong faith in God. I could always listen to him teach. He made it plain and simple. I could talk to him about many things. He taught us about how God can forgive us, how God can be very cunning, and how God can be a huge mystery. God listens to us through His redemptive power.

I had been all over Manhattan once I moved uptown. I went to Harlem to see how it was there and saw a whole lot of ministry opportunities. I would be in Pastor Neil's class, and then I would go out to look at church locations. I went inside and visited the churches to see how they set up their worship. Some churches worship Jesus and not Jesus Christ. Jesus was a Jew. Christians are not Jews. I saw so many things being done in churches. Some of the things that are being taught and done are not of God. I think we must be careful about how we believe the church today should be run. My church will be on the cutting edge of what Jesus Christ taught, topics that line up with the word of God.

For some reason, I knew that I wasn't going to be here for very long because of what I was doing in the classes. I was helping everyone that I could help at the time. Have you ever helped people so much that it finally dawned on you that it was time to help yourself? I had to get my life together. One day one of my old friends from Jacksonville Ministries called me. He asked me if I wanted to come to his Ministry in Dallas, Texas to teach some classes. I told David that I would think about it and I would get back to him on it and if I did come, he would have to fly me to Dallas.

A couple of weeks went by, and at the time I was transitioning out of the men's Mission into another place for disciples. I moved out because the staff member called and made the necessary arrangements for me. Meanwhile, I kept the vision that God had for my family and me. I always thought God called me and chose me to carry the mantle for my family, friends, and enemies. At this point, I had no choice because I had no reason to turn back. All I could do was keep my eyes on the prize. I didn't need any direction from anyone but God. It was strange because He gave me a crash course on life skills, how the world works, how people think, how people move, how people move when they use God to their advantage, and how to treat people from all walks of life. I learned many things throughout these ministries that I was involved in. Most of them were run like a business. Jesus Christ was present at the beginning of the services, and all is well. He wasn't there throughout the services. God must be in the services constantly.

When something happens to me, I stopped blaming God and others. I tried to figure out why things happened to me in the first place. God will not give you so much that you can't bear. Don't get discouraged and lose your mind. Pray to the Master who has the Master plan. I knew then that I was on to something. He had given me the blueprint on life.

Two great commandments are seen in the following scriptures. Matthew 22:36-39 (NIV) says, "Teacher, which is the Greatest: Love the Lord your God with all your heart and with all your soul and with all your mind. Love your neighbor as yourself."

I moved out of the mission and went into a transitional housing unit where I saw men who were just what I would call dead to the world. They were useless. Once I moved all my things in there, I felt terrible. I felt like I was going from good to bad to worse. I was going along to get along at this point and time. Sometimes I felt so bad that I wanted to take off, scream and cry out to God. I couldn't act like what I was going through at this time in my life. I wanted to call home several times, and I couldn't bring myself to do it because God was showing me this is what his people look like. Nobody cared for them. In a sense, this is what He was saying to me: nobody cared for me, but my family and Him. I had to care for myself and His people. The unit I moved into had a one-bedroom apartment in it. I only paid 200 dollars a month for it. The reason why my rent was low is that I had favor from God. I was no longer teaching at this point. I was not feeling this place because I begin to see that they were letting any and every kind of men in this transitional shelter.

CHAPTER 13

Jesus Christ Ministries/Dallas, TX

On November 4, 2011, my friend David called me again. I prayed about it and ended up telling him that I was coming because of the situation I was in. It was very cold outside that year in New York. I was living in the Lower East Side of Manhattan. I was given a tour of Thompson Park. I had been all over Manhattan that year. I visited old sites where the mafia had started when they first came to New York. I went to all kinds of professional basketball, baseball, and football games. I went to Broadway shows. I thought that my time was up in New York. I discovered later that I should never have left because I had returned to continue my life becoming a Minister.

November 23 was my brother Tim's birthday. I flew from New York to Dallas. That day it was not only cold, but it was snowing. The snow was hitting the plane as I was boarding it. I was tired of going from one place to another because I realized that going all over the place in ministry is not stable. I had to make a choice, and I asked God to help me find a resting place where I could have a permanent ministry home. While I was on the plane, I thought about all kinds of things. Once the plane took off in the air, I was so glad to be on another ministry journey. I was by myself and wanted to be stable. I knew that God could do all things which strengthens me. I had never been to Dallas before.

I told God, "Okay. I made a choice this time." I know that when we make our own choice to leave, God will do us all as He did to Jonah. We might not get swallowed up by the whale but somehow or someway God will put us back where we belong. He could have sent me back to Evansville, but He didn't. He could have closed all the ministries down on me. He could have sealed my fate. We seal our fate by the things we say and do. I needed to get somewhere, lay low, and hear the voice of God again. I was always in chaos ministries where something was always happening.

I wasn't talking to people in my family. I was just doing my thing. I had a choice to make, and I hoped that the ministry that I was headed to wasn't like that. All I could think about was stability. I left New York that day at about 11:00 a.m. from LaGuardia Airport and I was not that happy. I flew from New York City to Chicago and had a short flight to St. Louis, MO. I left St. Louis Lambert Airport at 6:30 p.m. It was still snowing that day. I had to pray on this flight because I was by myself and the wind was hitting the plane so hard. There was a lot of turbulence that night. I landed in Dallas at 8:45 p.m. It was one of the worst flights that I have ever been on.

I got off the plane and got my suitcases. I went down to the bottom parking lot where people were picked up. I saw a van that said Jesus Christ Texas Ministries. A guy named Robbie picked me up. He was a tall white man and seemed to be okay. He helped me with my things. I was glad to be starting over, but God made it clear to me that this wasn't the place for me once we got here. That night was a long night because I flew into Dallas Love Airport. The roads were barely visible because of the weather conditions. We drove for 30 to 40 minutes. By the time I got to the ministries, I was tired, and everyone was asleep. I said good night to Robbie, and I just put my suitcases in my room.

I had a hard time sleeping that night. I was in a frenzy from the start. I was a paid teacher and stayed on campus with the students. I said to myself, "What have I gotten myself into?" I went into my room that night, and it was a cold weird feeling. I prayed to God to watch over me. I don't know what happened years ago in the town I was in or before I arrived. It was a weird feeling in the house I was staying in on campus. The next morning, I awakened to bright lights in my room. The room was huge and wide open. I had put all my things away that morning. Afterward, I took a shower and went out front to see if anyone was getting breakfast at the campus cafeteria.

After going into the cafeteria, I saw ten students that I had met that morning. I introduced myself to them and sat down with them. We ate eggs, bacon, biscuits, coffee, and orange juice that were quite delicious. I was full as I talked with the students. I was trying to get to know them.

A short while later as I was interacting with them, I was summoned into the office to visit with my good friend who was running the ministries. He had called me earlier to say that He was looking forward to meeting again in about an hour. He said he would be in the office briefly today. I was so happy to hear from David. I just wanted to start helping the students and do what God had sent me there to do. There were only eight students that were white. Three were Mexican men. There was only one black student in the class. I was so happy to meet them because I felt it was an honor to be teaching God's word to them. I knew that the word of God being taught to them would extend through them to their families. I would see them interact with their families after teaching at the end of the week. I would see the look on their families' faces. I would see the smiles. I also would see the good days and the bad days that they were having. I encouraged them to study God's word and grow. The legacy I wanted to leave them is for them to have Jesus Christ as their number one in their lives daily, read, eat, and sleep with the Bible. I just wanted them to get the maximum benefits for what God wants for their lives.

I cared about them and missed them. Steve is the only student that stay in touch with me. He got his life together, and he lives in San Antonio, Texas. He watched and listened to me teach the class. I realized while I was teaching that I may not touch all their lives with God's word. I might touch only one out of the twelve or fourteen students. God deserves all the credit for all He has done in their lives. He uses us as messengers to line up His Kingdom.

Everything went well for the first few months. The curriculum was a good schedule. We got up at 6:00 a.m., showered, brushed our teeth, and put on our clothing and shoes. Next, we would get on our knees and pray to God, Jesus Christ, and the Holy Spirit all at one time. Then we would do devotions at 6:30 a.m. and be in the cafeteria for breakfast at 7:00 a.m. Afterward, we would go to have a morning clean-up detail which consists of all the students getting their rooms inspected. After everything was okay and we gave them a good report, I would tell them to get prepared for class at 9:00 a.m. There were only a few students who were always trying to buck the system. Some of them didn't want to make their beds. Some of them would hide food under their beds in case they wanted a snack at night. Some just wanted to disrespect the process of serving God. I was committed to God and my assignment.

After meeting with David and some other staff members in the office, I realized that we were meeting to discuss what we could do to help the students advance and grow in God. I was just listening at first, but I could tell that they weren't used to me.

I had a different approach to God's word than they did. I didn't understand how they would try to tell me to do things their way and maybe another way will work in the class. I realized that there wasn't anything wrong with the way I was teaching. I taught the materials that they have presented and given to me. I believe what they didn't like was the effectiveness of the way I taught the classes. Most of the students liked me. I liked most of the faculty until some students started having problems with them. I believe in confronting a problem from Matthew 18 scriptures. The disciples came to Jesus and asked, "Who is the greatest in the Kingdom of Heaven?"

The Bible says, "He called a little child to him and placed the child among them. And he said: Truly I tell you, unless you change and become like little children, you will never enter the Kingdom of heaven. Therefore, whoever takes the lowly position of this child is the greatest in the Kingdom of Heaven. And whoever welcomes one such child in my name welcomes me." The rest of Matthew 18 talks about causing the little ones to stumble. Some of the faculty members were trying their best to make me stumble, and I stayed the course. I prayed for them even though I went through some stuff with them. I trusted in the Lord and finally told myself that I'm staying. I would let God and myself down if I had done what they wanted. Sometimes when you up against opposition, stay in your lane and allow God to expose the problem itself.

I was finally left alone and just kept on teaching. I knew my Lord and Savior because I wasn't always like this. God began to work with my heart, my mind and everything else. I no longer felt the need to fight physically anymore. I looked at them and laughed at what the scheme was from time to time. Once I had a student mess with me about how I taught. He wanted someone else to teach him. If I was so bad, then why hasn't the Executive Director said a word to me?

I just felt bad for the faculty member that didn't like me. This person asked me questions. Where are you from? Was anybody in your family in ministry? I told him that my dad was a minister in Haiti and in Evansville, Indiana before he passed away. He acted shocked. I told him, "I was grateful to have had a father who served God. My mother served God too. They had their church and were missionaries." I may have given him information that he didn't want to hear, but I told him the truth. People don't like the truth. I had to look at a man who was not getting it in his mind what was the truth. Other students, faculty, and staff members asked me the same questions. I just moved on from all the drama that he tried to cause in my life.

I had fun teaching classes for about four months. I had got used to being there. God was tugging on my heart one day. I thought about joining the Dallas Missionary schools, but I realized that my assignment was not done. I truly believe that God was giving me a glimpse of what He was showing me soon. One time I wanted to leave because I didn't want to become a monk like some faculty members who were sitting around the campus on a day off. I wanted to have a life outside and inside the ministries. I did just that. I went to ball games and out to eat dinner with some ministry friends that I met at other churches. We would go to different churches every week. None of the churches were Black churches. That's when I didn't understand the territorial part of many churches and their congregations. Today it still goes on where many denominations, their pastor's and their churches don't fellowship because of their beliefs. I wonder what God is saying about that. One morning I woke up to load up the van with 30 carved wooden crosses for sale. I questioned selling them because of the commandment that says, "Thou shalt have no graven images of God," which still apply to this day. I felt so bad and wanted out of this ministry. I didn't tell them but felt like it was wrong. I wasn't comfortable with it, but I knew that it was their main source of income to keep the ministries going. They were selling fast, and people were buying them every week. We were making those crosses in the activities room with a rotary saw and carving tools.

There were more positive things that came out of this ministry. When I visited other ministries, I could tell when God was there, and when He wasn't there. People were doing their own thing and using God's word to call themselves Christians which is a dangerous road to be on. What does it profit a man to gain the whole world and lose his soul? This means a lot to me. I want to continue to serve God wholeheartedly. We get caught up in things that God don't want us to be a part of. We are only doing it because either it makes us look good or want to be a part of a culture that we think God approves of. I stay to myself to this day because I don't want to be out of the will of God. People that you interact with in church don't always have your best interest. Do their actions line up with God's word? Whatever you do when you're young catches up to you when you get older. For example, if you drink, eat, or smoke too much, and do a lot of drugs, when you get older those bad habits can lead to kidney failure, liver damage, heart disease, cancer, and diabetes. Too many sexual partners can lead to HIV and Hepatitis C. I saw stories of too many celebrities who have died of this list of causes and effect. Don't think it can't happen to you because none of us are excluded from sin. The body is a temple and if we don't care about it, who will? I realized that it was time for me to change when I was here because I knew that I wasn't going to be here that long. God had me stop and bless the students. Down the road, I will be on another assignment. I did the best I could although I fell short sometimes because I wanted to please God so much. We can get in the way of God and what He wants from us. I was tempted many times.

Matthew 6:13 (ASV) says, "And bring us not into temptation, but deliver us from the evil one."

Luke 4:13 (ASV) says, "And when the devil had completed every temptation, he departed from him for a season."

1 Corinthians 10:13 says, "There hath no temptation taken you but such as man can bear: but God is faithful, who will not suffer you to be tempted above that ye are able: but will with the temptation make also the way of escape, that ye may be able to endure it."

James 1:12 says, "Blessed is the man that endureth temptation; for when he hath been approved, he shall receive the crown of life, which the Lord promised to them that love him."

These are the powerful scriptures that I like to read when the enemy is tempting me. I pray first then I start reading these because they comfort me. I'm always under some attack, and I don't waver. I feel bad for the attacker because I don't give up that easy. The Assistant Executive Director, Freddy, was always negative. I knew he didn't like me, and I understood that I wasn't from Texas. He went to David behind my back and told him to get rid of me. There was also a young staff member that didn't like me. I knew that they were trying to set me up and it didn't work because I let God fight my battles. They tried to get me to argue with them. They tried to use the students and some other people against me. God told me to be still, and I was still. They would leave me alone for a couple of days and then start again. I hardly ever said a word to them because God said, "Teach the classes and be positive. I got you!" God was still blessing me because He allowed me to teach and still be a part of the ministry during the turmoil that they have created. The creator God showed up.

CHAPTER 14

Jesus Christ Ministries/Houston, Texas

I stayed at this ministry in Dallas for about four to five months. On March 16, 2012, I got ready to move to another ministry in Houston, Texas. I talked to David, and he had told me that everything was going to be okay. He called me a couple of days later and said he had spoken to the Executive Director in Houston. He said that he had an open position for me. I told him, "I'm going to pray about it." He went on to tell me that there was an old man there who had been teaching there for a long time named Ernest. He was 71 years old and getting prepared for retirement. He told me that they needed someone so Ernest can teach me what he taught the students and how I could be his successor. I knew that I was going because the phone call had already been made. I agreed with David to move on. It was one of the best decisions I made since I have been in ministry. You see when you are truly anointed, God will cover you and bring you into total submission. I was glad He had done that to me. I packed my clothes and moved on. It was the first time that I didn't say goodbye to any of them except for a special needs friend that I had met at a church that I had been too. I said goodbye to a young white student named Steve. The rest of them was just there waiting to finish up their time.

I had done my time. The difference is I'm serving God, and they were masking because they didn't want to change. I left on an early Saturday morning. I was happy. Freddy, the Assistant Executive Director, drove me halfway to Houston. I hardly said two words to him. After we drove over a hundred miles that morning, we made the swap. Kevin came to pick me up. I got my belongings out of the van, and it was one of the best feelings I had ever had in my life. I said goodbye to Freddy, and he said see you. God can allow you to see things in people that you may have never seen before. When things go south, stand firm on the word of God. Don't give up. Don't back down. Had I given in to the enemy, I know that I wouldn't be where I'm at today.

So many people hate for no reason. I asked people that were in our group why they would hate someone so bad? Nobody had a thing to say. People know why they hate. It is ingrained in some people, and they hate because they want to. I know it's sad because what might not affect me may affect you or vice versa.

After we got down the road, I saw this as a new start. We made the swap at 2:00 p.m. Kevin and I stopped to get something to eat. We arrived in Houston, Texas at 4:00 p.m. We pulled up to a couple of houses and a school that was much bigger than the school I had left. They had a little pond, and I wanted to go fishing. It was okay, but I saw myself going back to New York. I told myself, "I'm going to make the best of it." I met some of the students there, and it was a much smaller number of students. I only saw seven students. They gave me my room in an apartment and a stipend every week. I called my family to let them know where I was especially after all the stuff I was going through. I looked at the part I played. I asked God to allow me to make peace with myself and with other people when things like this happen. I learned that many things are out of our control. When I introduced myself to them, I realized I was very tired of these types of ministries. I wanted something more stable and better than what I was used to. I wanted to be a pastor and have my church. I wanted to be a minister. I wanted to be ministered to. I wanted to do greater works for the Lord. I knew that I had made a mistake moving to Dallas.

I felt like Jonah because I wasn't supposed to leave New York. I thought Dallas was going to be my land of milk and honey, but it is New York City. I had to live with the wrong decision I made, so I was masking in Houston. I really didn't want to be there because of what I had experienced. I thought, "Man if I could leave the ministry in Dallas and join T.D. Jakes ministry." They didn't want to go to those churches. They wanted to go where the teachings were people in training. I understood that but we needed substance. We didn't need milk all the time. I wanted 'meat and spit out the bone' ministry. When I got to Houston, I wanted to go to Joel Osteen's church.

When I was doing ministry in Houston, I would be on a cleaning detail with the students. I was there cutting grass and helping them understand scripture. They just wanted to get rid of me. I was so happy to not be in their midst anymore. I knew that I wasn't wanted there. I kept on serving God. Brian, the Executive Director in Houston, wasn't the best director in Texas. He was the last resort before someone got sent back where they came from. Once I got there all he did was have people, some students and staff watch me. It was so sad to be in the company of people who claim to be God's people but then have so many demons using them.

I could never understand them to this day. Even though we go through some things, it is God's battle, not ours. I just remained obedient to God which results in a reward. I never was furious at them because if I had done what they wanted me to do, my ministry wouldn't be successful today. I forgave them and asked for forgiveness from God. I said some things inwardly about them that I shouldn't have said. I believe we make excuses for some stuff that we say to ourselves and others. When you are in that situation, do what God's word says. When the enemy puts a mountain in your way, God will help you move it. That is why I praise God and honor Him every day. I was never the same once I knew that God would show up after being mistreated. Some ministry leaders don't even know that they're treating some of their colleagues and faculty bad. It affects everybody that is involved in the ministry as well.

A couple of weeks after I unpacked, I thought, "Why did I leave New York City?" I was in Houston physically, but mentally I was in New York. I was going through the motions waiting for the opportunity to move back there. I put my heart and soul into helping the students. I didn't know if they wanted me there for backup or what they wanted me to do. I was never told my role when I arrived. Over the phone when I spoke to them, they wanted me to clean and other things. When the classrooms were not clean, I had to clean them up for the students. I had to do many things when the people in ministry were not doing what they were supposed to do.

Don't gripe, be the change agent. I usually say, "Teamwork makes the dream work." Be the example, not the problem. God will see to it that you will be able to do exceedingly above far more than what you would have done on your own. I have learned to put others before me. That is a gift. You must stay in prayer and read the Bible so God can give you your blessings. It is no secret to what God can do. It was never about race, color, and creed with me. It was always about God's love because He said in His word that love is greater than faith and hope. I was always a gentle soul, and never a mean-spirited person. I reflected on my life, and I was 42 years old. I was in over my head. I looked back on how I was involved in several different ministries before I arrived in Houston. I came to understand that this was just a pit stop to slow me down, reflect on God, get myself together, and get ready to move back to New York. For weeks, I was angry because I would wake up in the mornings not doing anything. I was sitting there, and the teaching job I was promised was never in the cards. They tried to destroy me by not giving me any students to teach. They only gave me work details in their dorms. For example, I had to tell them when to clean up. I had to tell them when it was time to sell crosses. I was the enforcer. I knew that wasn't God's plan for my life which was so unfortunate. We had a meeting about it after I had been there for a month. I didn't even see this as a ministry. I saw it as a place of business. That's the way they ran it. I questioned sometimes why I was still there until I heard a voice that said it's time to go. I should have left the day and gone back to N.Y.C.

There was a student there by the name of Darrell. He was an addict and tried to stop his drug and alcohol abuse. I felt sorry for him because he was trying to know God. He was there way before I arrived. He told me some things that went on, and I didn't ignore them. I just watched, listened, and learned. When things are not right, God might put you there to clean things up. Sometimes it's not good to leave. When God tells you to go, you better go when the writings on the wall. Out of all the ministries I had been a part of, this one didn't have that many students. They hardly taught God's word. It was done only in the classroom. They didn't go to church or do bible study that much.

I had to call my family back home and some of my friends that I had met in other ministries. I told tell them that I didn't ever want them to go through what I had gone through in Dallas and Houston. It was enough to make you walk away from God. It took its toll on me. I made calls back to New York to see if I could come back and stay in the mission there in Manhattan. They said that if I arrived at a specific date and time, I could come. I was skeptical because the guy I spoke to was not sure if he could get me in or not. I just prayed to God because the last thing I wanted to do was go back to Evansville. God told me that if I went back home to live, I would not last long. I was scared at this point. He made it plain and simple to me.

I knew I was moving back to New York. I had saved several hundred dollars because I didn't spend any money. The food was free, and I had a lot of nice clothes. I talked with the Executive Director Brian to see where his head was. He told me that they had no plans of hiring me for the position because the old guy was getting a regular salary to teach the whole curriculum. They didn't want to pay me what he was making because I was new, and I didn't have that much experience like Ernest did. I was livid. Why didn't they tell me the day they brought me there? Instead, they allowed me to sit around and do nothing for almost three months. That's when I was fed up, and I was gone. I asked one of the staff members to get ready to drive me to the bus station tomorrow because I planned on leaving. I was in my room and thought about being used, abused, and always conforming in several different ministries.

I don't know, but God knew what was going on. I've had some awesome things happen to me in ministry. There were times that I never thought that I would make it because of the way ministries today are presented and how the money gets in the way of tithes and offerings. If you have enough money, you are treated better. Some ministries treated us like we were slaves. When I was in Cleveland, there was a time when fifty people were on a bus, and we couldn't shower. I don't know how but one of the faculty members asked a parks and recreation personnel worker if we could take showers in a recreation park that was indoors. It wasn't the best place for us. I reflected on some days and I felt that I made one of the biggest mistakes of my life. On June 24, 2012, I left the Houston ministries. I was done with these kinds of ministries. I told the Director I was leaving, and he said okay. I told him that I needed to get my belongings together and that I was going to get a bus ticket back to Evansville, but I was actually going back to New York. They took me to the bus station at about 6:00 p.m. and there was a motel right across the street. After they had dropped me off, I thought whatever is going to happen will happen at this point. I had been off drugs and alcohol for quite a while, but I relapsed that night. I just gave up, and I was tired. I had no one to blame.

I went to the counter at the bus station and found out the time was the Greyhound was coming from Dallas to New York. I looked at the price, and it was $150.00 one way. It wasn't on the schedule for that evening. I told myself, "I'm going on to get myself a motel for the night." The motel had a pool, and the rooms were 50 dollars a night. I made the mistake of staying for almost a week. When I checked in the motel, I went right back out to get some beer, wine, and cigarettes. Once I got back in the motel, I started drinking and smoking. I decided I was going to look for other things and something told me to sit still even though I had already relapsed that evening. I felt so sorry that I didn't want to go back to New York. I went back out the door to get something to eat, and all I could find was fast food. I got me a couple of burgers and fries. It was a blessing and a curse. I smoked weed and snorted some coke. I called for a couple of friends to wire me some more money, and they gave it to me. After four days, I thought, "It's time for me to get out of here." There was a girl in her early 20's that I had met on the second night I stayed at the motel. She watched me get in the pool. She knocked on my door acting like she was looking for someone, but I knew that game. I had a few hundred dollars left, and I finally purchased my ticket to get out of Houston.

I had made the mistake of getting high and relapsing. I felt low. I justified what I was doing because of something that I didn't like. I felt like I wasn't supposed to be going through this. I knew it was my fault because I should never have come here in the first place under these circumstances. That night as it was getting late, I sat in my motel. I thought, "What have I done? It's time to go!" I made the arrangements the next morning to get up, check out, and pay for my bus ticket back to New York City. On June 29th, 2012, I was headed to New York City. It was the craziest situation that I had ever been in my life. I got breakfast that morning and checked out of the motel relieved. I said to myself, "I'm not telling anybody anything." I got on the bus at 10:00 a.m. and it was a two-day bus trip. I felt terrible, but I was glad that I dodged a bullet because the girl tried to get me to have sex with her. I resisted because I felt like she was trying to set me up. I should never have allowed her to come into my room. I was not going to play that game because I was riddled with guilt that night. I got myself together because I said to myself, "I'm going to get myself some help when I get back to

New York." I was tired and hungry on the bus. I wanted to call my family, but under these circumstances, I thought, "No way."

In Tomball, TX, it dawned on me to call the guy at the mission because I never returned the call. I was so sleepy calling back to the mission. He said that he was going to try to have a place for me when I get there. I looked at my bus ticket, and I was crossing into five states before I got into New York City in 48 hrs. I went through Louisiana, Georgia, South Carolina, North Carolina, Pennsylvania, and New Jersey.

All I thought about was getting back into the Bowery re-entry program because of the relapse that I had in Texas. I had to take care of that before I could move forward in my ministry. I was scared because I didn't know how to express myself about what happened. I know that I have used alcohol and drugs. I was not feeling well about it. I felt like I was going to be punished by God. I thought that my ministry was over. I felt like nobody cared so just do myself a favor. I thought, "You are never going to be nothing so pack it in. Give up and not continue to do the work of the Lord." I realized it was Satan himself talking to me. When I finally got to Pennsylvania, it hit me that I had to call the Bowery Mission to see if I could get accepted because I was "homeless" at this point. I didn't have anywhere to go. I slept most of the way and did not talk to anyone during the whole trip. I ate some food, got back in my seat, and felt self-pity. I was playing the victim until I remembered what God's word said. A righteous man falls seven times. I was trying to justify what I had done until God told me that it's time that I own up to my responsibilities and quit making excuses. I made to Brooklyn at about 6:15 pm on a Monday.

I had got myself a metro card and went back to the Bowery. I slept on the pews that night until they gave me a bed. It went for almost a week, and I realized that they weren't going to help me anymore. I got up enough nerve and went to a men's shelter in Manhattan. I checked in there because they wanted my I.D. I gave it to them, and I checked in the shelter that afternoon. I saw some shady things that the men were doing that the first week. For instance, a guy goes to shower, and another guy was looking out stealing some of the guy's things that he needed while he was in the shower. It was going on periodically. I knew that if they were doing it to him, they could very well do it to me. I was ready to throw in the towel.

I stayed for maybe another week and then I just started to make phone calls trying to get to somewhere better than where I was. I thought about my life being at stake, my kids, my family, and all kinds of crazy things except giving up. One morning awoke and set out to go into Queens because Manhattan was too bad at the time. I got on the E Train because I wasn't successful making phone calls during the week. I got on the 6 Bus and rode around Jamaica and Queens, New York. I saw some young men and young ladies standing outside around noon. I was thinking I ought to see what is going on over here. I got off at the bus stop and prayed to God.

CHAPTER 15

J-C Rehab/ Jamaica, New York

I approached the people that I saw. I heard them speak and some of them were cursing. I saw some of them smoking cigarettes. Some of them were standoffish and very aloof until I asked them a question. I asked, "What is this?" This guy told me that it was a drug rehabilitation program and it was residential. I thought, "Yes! Yes! Thank You, Lord." I played it off and acted like I wasn't going to check in. I just wanted to go inside and talk to a staff worker. I wanted to get the help that I needed. I went inside and spoke to Mr. Beninham. He told me that I could check in that day and that it was a year-long program. I asked, "What do I need?" He told me I needed an Identification card, social security card, etc. I said, "I will get my things in a shelter. It was awful there. How is this place?" He said, "It's not a shelter. We help homeless people. We help out drug and alcoholics, etc." I told him that I would be back late in the afternoon because I had to make a few stops along the way before I return. I had to go to Manhattan to pick up my clothing, and I returned to J-CAP at around 3:30 p.m. I was admitted into the residential program on July 14, 2012. I was so happy, and I never looked back. I was relieved of my hurt and pain now because I knew Jesus Christ brought and led me to this place.

After I checked on that day, people stared at me. We didn't know each other. This program is like a hospital and a place where you can get your life together. I was in pain. I cried like a baby once I knew that this was where God brought me to settle down. I needed to make some sense of what I was doing wrong in my life. I wanted to change for myself and wanted a new life with Jesus Christ. I knew that I had to start all over again. I was very upset the first few nights that I was there. I needed to turn my life completely around. Can you imagine being apart of something your whole life and have to start over getting to know who Jesus Christ is?

One morning, I woke up to three other men in a room that I didn't even know. I was terrified because of their backgrounds and conversations. They were not going in the direction I was going in. We were in the classes together. We also ate breakfast, lunch, and dinner together. We even played pickup basketball games in the gym. I cared about them. I just didn't let them know it. In our spare time, we studied our homework together, and we shared some of our innermost secrets.

I called my family and friends to tell them that I was in a much better situation this time and I was going to contact them periodically before I went home. I knew that I was going to get my entire life together this time. Some staff members there really cared about me. Every time I asked for something, they helped me. Ladonna always wanted me to think outside of the box. She asked me what brought me there. I told her I was involved in a ministry in Texas and something happened that shouldn't have happened. I looked at the parts I played in every situation up until this point. I never blamed anyone but myself. I knew what my position was the whole time. I can't believe it, but I stood strong despite not having anyone in my family around me. I had no moral support. God was dealing with me. I had to sit down and wait on God for about two or three months before he sent some people to help me on my journey that He had paved for me. I was tired of my past. I was only concerned about my future because I couldn't do anything about what I had already done. I had to let go and allow God to work on the inside out. I fought for so many years and lost many battles trying to do it on my own. I finally said, "Here I am Lord." When I got up in the morning, I prayed to God. He just let me be me without strings attached. I socialized and talked about meeting people right where they were.

I was out of my league. This place was off the chain. There were at least 150 to 200 people in rehab every day. I observed their different personalities and backgrounds. It was painful that I was in this place. I prayed for God to deliver me from many things. I needed deliverance from drugs and alcohol. I wanted freedom from God Almighty. You know when God steps in your life and takes over, all we must do is trust His process not our own. I had one bad decision after another. Only God could clean it up.

We should look at ourselves in the mirror and face our enemies head-on with God's power. I committed to staying clean and sober. I committed to serving God for the rest of my life. It was out of my control at this point because I had given my whole life to the Lord. I'm no longer in control. He is in control of my life. I made many mistakes, and I was at J-CAP because God made this my destination. My mistakes were behind me and in front of me is a bright future with the Lord on my side.

It still feels good to be clean. My body feels rejuvenated in the flesh and the spirit. I was always intrigued by the way some of the students were acting once they started getting cleaned up. It dawned on me that they were cleaned up by the power of God just like me. The staff and the faculty helped me tremendously. They not only waited on me hand and foot, but they helped me realize my dream of becoming a man of God because they taught all of us life skills. They taught me to give up an addiction that you must implement positive reinforcement training. For you to let go of your addictions, you must have the word of God, study your bad habits, and try to figure out why you do what you did. Once you do that, then God will begin to heal you and allow you to take steps to rectify your problems. I was delighted to have been a part of a group that showed love and, for the most part, had a lot of gratitude. It was meant for me to come here and I made quite a few friends. We stay in touch even today. Some of the students have passed away, and some of them are still using drugs. I pray for them.

Being at J-CAP gave me the time and structure I needed. The facility that I stayed in was spotless. We had a curriculum that was so strict that I was glad to have a structure like this. We ate breakfast by 7:00 a.m., lunch at 11:30 a.m., and dinner at 5:30 p.m. I would always wind down by 9:00 p.m. I realized that I needed some quiet time because of multiple things that I was going through. I had not seen my son and daughter in several years. My family and I weren't on good speaking terms. The only time we would come together was a wake or funeral. I'm a firm believer that we are supposed to tell people we love them and show an act of love or kindness while they are living not when they pass away. It is hard to get through to stubborn people and people who think they know it all. It is hard for people to let go of grudges. They can be mad at you for so long and don't even remember why they are mad at you. It is easy to forgive. Just let go of the past. God will take care of the rest.

The mean streak I once had is now gone because I gave my life to the Lord. He has made me a gentle giant. If you walk around angry at the world, it can get you in a lot of trouble. No one wants to be around you. Your family members will exclude you from family events. Your spouse or girlfriend or boyfriend will end the relationship. The job and co-workers will exclude their relationship with you. You won't have the job for long. You must ask yourself where God fit in all these situations. The bottom line is if you don't take control of your anger, it can turn into mental illness. Some people feel like they don't have a problem and won't seek proper help. The help is that Jesus Christ can heal anyone from mental illness. You must seek professional help as well. Then you must find out what God will have you to do in His ministries. He will reveal it to you. Don't feel bad if you know that you have a problem. Get the professional help that you need to deal with the past. Even deacons, ministers, reverends, pastors, and bishops are professional help. Praying, fasting, and using anointing oil to hear God results in healing from God. Our problem is that we must wait on God. He helps those who help themselves.

The sad thing is when a person knows better, for whatever reason, they turn a blind eye to what God is doing in their life. They get blinded by their proud ways and forget where they come from just because they were ordained in the church. They put on this mask when they get there. Outside of the church, they are doing the opposite of what the bible says: drinking, smoking, partying, sex abuse, etc. Men and women that are in high positions need to allow God to always be in front of their decision making because if you do that, you will be at peace knowing that God decided for you not that you agreed because of a personal vendetta. People get jealous because I'm a leader and not a follower. I had people always coming against me throughout my entire life. I had people at J-C Rehab that didn't like me, and I knew why. I was different, and I always will be. What's in the darkness shall come to the light and all things will be revealed in due time.

James 1:2 (ASV) says, "Count it all joy, my brethren, when ye fall into manifold temptations."

Luke 2:10 (ASV) says, "And the angels said unto them, be not afraid, for behold I bring you good tidings of great joy which shall be to all the people."

Philippians 4:4 says, "Rejoice in the Lord always, again I will say rejoice."

I was there in all the chaos at the rehab and still rejoicing in the Lord. One day, I met a couple named Ernest and Norma Bailey-Payne that came to J-C Rehab. They were very kind to me. They saw something in me, and they knew that they could mold me. They took me under their wing and helped me. They are my spiritual parents. I'm so glad that they came into my life. They let me meet their families and friends at the church. The day I met them was so unexpected. They came in the building on a Tuesday and said to other students and me that they were trying to get a choir together and a bible study group started in the church. God sent them to me because He knew that I needed guidance. I was the only one from J-C Rehab that advanced in the church. Everyone else from J-C Rehab disappeared from the church. I was so shocked because my prayers had been answered. I wanted to go to church.

I got acquainted with the rehab and the people there. I had only been there by this time for only two months. I had to adjust to my schedule, the chores, and the curriculum. Once I had that in check, I knew I was in heaven. In other words, I made time to pray and go to church on Sunday. I started to attend church every Sunday with my spiritual parents. Also, I went to bible study on Thursday nights from 7:00 to 9:00 p.m. I was so excited, and

I ended up joining the church a couple of months later. Nineteen other students and I went to church faithfully every week for months.

This was a learning experience for me. Don't be hard-headed because you must listen to what God is saying to you. When God tells you not to do something, and you do it anyway, you will say, "I should have listened to the Lord." Satan will lead you astray and have you thinking that you don't have a chance to get your life together. I serve a faithful God who is just to forgive us of our sins. He will fight your battles for you. "Vengeance is mine, " saith the Lord. I was at the top of my routine and following what was right in the eyes of the Lord. I still count on the word of God because if you take your eyes off Him, things happen to us. For several days, I thought God must love me more than I could have imagined. I was given favor to do many things like speak at bible study classes. I was getting ready for something big. I wanted to teach at the church, and I got the opportunity to do that. Next, I prepared to do an initial sermon. I wanted to do it in God's timing, so I wasn't in a rush. For months, I was studying and preparing. I was so afraid about how well I was going to do. I asked God to prepare me.

I fasted and asked God for directions. I told myself that it was a great honor to serve God. I called my family and told them that I joined the church. I was always optimistic about my calling and had been praying about a sermon. I asked the Lord to help me figure it out. He gave me so much wisdom, knowledge, and understanding of His word. I was able to discern what He was speaking to me about. Many distractions and voices were ringing in my head. I blocked them out every day until I could hear what the Great Lord God was telling me to preach. He wanted me to be "real" with Him and myself to show the congregation that He was in charge.

It took me quite a while before I had settled down. God gave me a word to preach and I started working on it, studying, and dissecting what He wanted me to say to His people. I sat down and looked at my life and saw how far He had brought me. I had a lot of sleepless nights toiling and seeking His face. I desired better things and wanted a better life. I was ready to go to the next level. I embraced the calling because I knew that those that endure with Jesus Christ wins the race. There was no quitting in me. God gave me tons of strength.

I saw the beginning, and He told me to preach about the parable of the lost son (Luke 15:11-32). I studied these scriptures from October 2012 until I had my initial sermon. Meanwhile, I met my future wife Ramona Ellis on Monday, October 13th. We met while we were working and I came in smiling like I always do. She told me to sign the sign-in book. After I signed in, she looked at the sign-in book to see what my last name was. When I exited the building, I turned around, and she said goodbye. The next day she was on lunch when I met up with her. I asked her for her number on the elevator, and she said, "Follow me." I followed her off the elevator. She wrote down her number and gave me a bagel. We talked on the phone all week, and I wondered what took her so long to call me after work. I finally reached her at 9:00 p.m. Over the phone, we made plans to go on a date. She had to take her eight-hour class at 32 BJ. I texted her throughout the entire class.

After class, we met on 14th St. Union Square in Manhattan. We went to the One World Trade Center. We just did some window shopping. We made our way to the South Street Sea Port. We ate at Johnny Rockets, then we went upstairs and sat in front of the water at Pier 17. It started raining like crazy and we waited until it stopped. It was so romantic, and we kissed one another under the moonlight shining over the water. We held hands all the way to the train station. I dropped her off at her sister's house and then I went home. I called her to make sure she was safely home.

The following weekend Ramona told me that she was moving. I was moving out of the J-C re-entry program that was established to allow me to get a job which I already had. It also allowed me to find housing. I moved out into a shared apartment with three other people on Selover Road in Queens. When people are jealous of you, they will sabotage anything you have. I had gotten off from work, came home, and noticed that bleach was sprayed on my brand-new suits. People don't like to see you advance in anything especially the church. When I asked what happened they said, "I don't know who did that." We were living together and going to the same church. God spoke to me, "They did worse to me than what they did to you." I was hurt by it and told my girlfriend about it. She told me to let it Go. Eventually, I did. I continued to go to work and do Bible study at the house. I worked on my sermon and rehearsed it repeatedly. I realized that God had given me a new life, brand new girlfriend, job, church, family, and friends. I never would have imagined that I would end up on the pulpit serving God, preaching, and teaching.

    I had my pitfalls, ups, and downs. God always kept me focused on what He wanted me to do. Everything that I had accomplished was God and Him alone. I knew I couldn't do it by myself. I fell short so many times. It was ridiculous for me to take the glory and honor from God. He is my all and all. "Lord God, I will bow down to You Forever. I will be forever grateful for what You have done in my life," I'd pray. There were times that I would ask for forgiveness because I felt a sense of entitlement. My father was a pastor, and I felt I deserved the best that God had for me. I realized that my father's calling is different from my calling. Everybody's calling is different. I wanted to express myself everywhere I went. I had to tone it down. We should never forget where we come from. Someone is always watching you whether you believe it or not. God is watching you more than anything.

    My routine on Monday was to pray in the mornings then get breakfast. I went to work, and once I got off work, I called my girlfriend. Sometimes, we talked all night. On Tuesdays, we had a bible study at my house. I did it faithfully and was very open to learning more about God. On October 22, 2012, my girlfriend and I rode out Hurricane Sandy. It was a great experience for us. My girlfriend lived on the 15th floor in a huge apartment building. We looked outside and felt the buildings swaying back and forth. It was crazy to see the storm and witness things flying all over the place. I never saw so much devastation in my life. Once it was over, I saw people's homes and cars tossed around like rag dolls.

Moving back to New York changed my life. I often wondered why I would end one Christian ministry and began another one. It wasn't like I quit or gave up on God. I was going through some changes and trying to find myself in God. I had nothing to justify my faults. I quit blaming others once I was given a new mantle to carry in God. I reverenced the Lord. I loved and respected others. When God gives you a new life, you feel spiritually blessed. I can't think of any other time when I was very glad to be in God's arms and very protected. It was like a big weight was off my shoulders. I was at NJBC and was in awe of what I was doing there. I felt like God had given me a new lease on life. I had in mind to do fundraising ministry but also wanted to do deliverance ministry. I had so many things in my head because I was doing outreach ministry as well. I had done pastor's school ministries in Arizona. God allowed me to see that the ministries that I was involved in had taken me to a new level.

The way ministry was done at NJBC was totally different. I had to prepare myself for a higher calling of excellence in ministries. There were some people, places, things, family and friends that I had to let go. The ignorance of the negative aspect of living the truth from a lie will cost you your life. For example, thinking it's okay to get high and work. Eventually, you don't want to go in to work like that. It will cost you your job. I was done with some of the guys I was hanging out with back home and abroad. You must free yourself from toxic relationships from people on the job and people from the church. Just free yourself to God.

He will open doors that no man can shut. He will close doors that no man can enter. He wants to bless so many of us. Some of us are so blessed we can't see past the blessings God gave us because we think that is all we must do. He gave us the anointing to operate out of our God-given gifts and talents.

I had always been a hard worker and someone who had overachieved all my life. When I committed my life to something, I would always question the purpose of why I was doing what I was doing. I fought at the beginning of my life because I thought I was going to die. Now I'm in the middle of my life. I have a long journey ahead of me, and I want God to take me to higher levels of ministry. I want Him to use me for His purposes. I needed this time and place to move upward. I never looked at the glass half full.

When I started something, I would finish it. I never really felt comfortable not serving God. When I began to self-serve, I became cautious about certain things. I just wanted not to have any problems that I couldn't handle or deal with. I work very hard to be where I'm at today even though I'm not satisfied with what God has done for me. I'm thankful, but there is more. I know it is because I feel it and I can see it. He won't let you see everything right away, but there are things in the spiritual realm that He is allowing me to see. I'm amazed at the discernment He has blessed me with. My Lord and Saviour Jesus Christ told me everything was going to be alright. I had to be willing to let go negative thoughts, train myself how to be more helpful to others, how to be more of a giver, and to a leader. I wanted to be more like Jesus. I had done all I could in a sinful nature.

The things that I didn't do, I didn't want to do anything at all anymore. I had come to a place in my heart where I didn't want to live a certain way anymore. I shut a part of my life down for good because I wanted to be free. I don't go to clubs anymore. I don't sleep with other women anymore. In other words, I don't live a sinful way at all anymore. God has given me the fear of the Lord and reverence to Him. I didn't think that I was going to get on that level. But today I'm on that level. Life is short. Friends come, and friends go, but no one can ever replace God.

CHAPTER 16

My New Home

I was still thinking about writing my sermon and studying for it. I wrote it out five or six times before I rewrote it again. Finally, I said, "I'm not going to pressure myself because I'm still in my infancy of becoming a minister." I would call my girlfriend and ask her if she would go to church with me. She would agree. I was so happy that she would come with me and she stayed all day. I thanked her for being so kind to me. I felt she was going to be there for me. I didn't know to what capacity. I discovered that she was just what God gave me. We were going out to dinner several times after church. I was always amazed at how she could keep me laughing and crying at the same time. She taught me how to listen. I listened to her situation, her life on how she grew up, her health, and what bothers her. I said to her, "You are mine." She communicated with me almost every day. I called her all the time to ask if she needed anything. I was checking up on her. Outside of my church friends, my girlfriend was the first lady to tell me that I was a leader and God had a higher calling on my life. I knew without a shadow of a doubt that God could use all I had been through. What I was running from was being in the accident years ago. It caused me to be bitter and angry with God.

I knew that He brought me out to fulfill His ministries for His glory. One day I want God to say to me, "Well done thy good and faithful servant." I took God for granted, and He gave me several chances. I thought I was never going to get on this level. I must admit, I wanted to give up on God many times when I first started in ministry. I wanted to throw in the towel because I knew that obedience is better than sacrifice. I would rather fight people than fight God because our arms are too short to box with God. He can do things that will get your attention, then have you carry His mission out. He can make you forget all the things you want to do for yourself. These things happened to me. It was like I had been washed, cleansed by the blood, and living water. I was hanging on to some things, but I ask Him to break up my bad habits and feelings about some issues that I had.

I don't like people who sit there, and they know they have problems. They sit in church all day on Sunday and never say anything until church is over. They could have gone to the altar for prayer and asked a minister, reverend, or pastor to pray for them. I invited my friends to church that I was living with. They had gotten to the point to where they didn't want to come to church. They started acting like the people who were in the program. I just kept doing Bible study and stayed home because I saw things more of a distraction than anything.

God is more faithful than anyone is for you. I accepted God back into my life because I knew I wasn't going to live no other way but His way. Letting God in your life is easy, but it's hard to give God your life. I have been there and done that. I gave him my life because that is the choice I made. I didn't do it for my family, pastor, and friends for any other reason. I gave my life to the Lord God Almighty out of fear that turned into love. The Bible says, "Perfect love cast out fear." I wasn't lost or homeless anymore. I didn't do things anymore without thinking things through. I was very cautious. I watched out for who could be in my circle.

I had been born again and sanctified by the blood of Jesus Christ. I stand on the promises of God. All the sicknesses and all my health problems are in God's hands. I had my share, and I asked God to heal me. I asked Him to bless me financially. I asked Him to rid me of people trying to get over. The spirits that are manifested today is God giving us the vision to take our people to the next level and be victorious in what Thus saith the Lord. I understand that you must carry out what He wants done. If we say that we love the Lord and can't carry out His mission, then who are we? I never understood sitting at home when the church is open, and no one is hardly there. Some of the people don't know why they are there. Some are there because they are tired of God beating their butts up. Some people are in church making the church their gossiping post. Some are protecting their interest. Some are there because they are lonely. In other words, they probably couldn't tell you anything about the Bible except what they have known for years. God has made me versatile with His word. It is no secret that God has brought me a mighty long way. He has also given me His power to stay relevant to what is going on in the world and what is to come.

I was reorganizing and reinventing my life. I was trying to live right by the word of God. I found out that I was beating myself up when I made a mistake from time to time. We all make mistakes. The problem is that some of us make a mistake and never address why we make mistakes. I couldn't understand why I did some of the things I did. That's when I knew I was in over my head. I kept making more mistakes while making matters worse for myself and others. The things we do affect others. What is dangerous is that there are people in your life every day that affect what you do daily; your job, the church, marriage, and friendships.

I sat in my apartment trying to figure out God. We can never figure Him out. He is too much for us. I went to work, came home, and studied for my sermon. I was nervous, and I wanted to back out of it. Sometimes I thought I was not worthy of His calling. I believe nobody is worthy of this calling. I studied the entire book of Luke. It was amazing when I read Luke 15:11-32. "And he said, A certain man had two sons: And the younger of them said to the father, Father, give me the portion of goods that falleth to me. And he divided unto them his living. And not many days after the younger son gathered all together, and took his journey into a far country, and there wasted his substance with riotous living. And when he had spent all, there arose a mighty famine in that land: and he began to be in want." When the son began to eat like the pigs, he said, "God what have I done?" The Bible says he joined them as a citizen of that country, and he went into the fields to feed the swine. After eating with the pigs, he came to himself. He said, "Father, I have sinned against Heaven, and I sinned against you." After his father forgave him, his father brought the best robe, put a ring on him, and put shoes on his feet. His father requested fatted calf to be killed and eaten. The elder brother was nearby because he heard music and dancing. He called out servants and asked what these things meant. What it meant was his brother had returned home. He wasn't injured or wasn't sick. The eldest son was angry and said, "All these years I serve you, and this is what I get? A slap in the face! Neither have I transgressed." The father tells his eldest son to be glad for his brother, for his brother was dead and is alive again: and was lost and is found. The moral of the story is that we make mistakes in our lives. I studied that for days upon nights until I finally came up with the sermon that stuck out with me.

I had studied for at least three to four months. When God gets His way, greater things will happen to us. I was in my room feeling great because I knew that I was ready and willing to serve God. I was never the same when I would get off from work, and on the weekends, I would practice, "What thus sayeth the Lord." I called home telling my family and friends about it. I was humbled and very glad to be going up on the pulpit to preach God's word. I was never the same after proclaiming God to be the head of my life. I thought that I need to be the head, not the tale.

I was preaching to the people about riotous living and when we receive our inheritance, God has to be in it. If He is not in your everyday life, you will make mistakes like the "Prodigal Son." He had lowered himself to a lowly standard eating the husk of what the pigs were eating. He partied all day and all night until his money was gone. He had no money for food, clothing, or a home. He said that he wasn't worthy of being called his father's son. I was in that situation where I was blessed with the blessings of my father and just messed everything up. I was so mad at myself when I was in the accident. I partied every day because I wanted to give up. I was going to quit everything I was doing because I didn't know what God was doing in my life. I knew after doing a lot of research and studying, I was going to get many sermons out of the Bible. I wanted to write and rewrite what I had already written. So, I wrote it again and it was seven pages of the sermon. I just went over it again practicing what I was going to say. I was excited and a little scared too. I managed to clean up some extra wording by concluding with what God has done in my life and what He said He was going to do. I need to get my thoughts and God's word in order. I waited for God to show me who I was as a preacher because I knew that I couldn't be like anyone else. It's God and me against the world when I'm on the pulpit.

CHAPTER 17

My Initial Sermon - Prodigal Son

A week before I had given my initial sermon on a Tuesday afternoon, a co-worker of mine and I were working together that day. He called me to ask me to meet him someplace after I had done my job. He told me and explained to me how to get there. I wrote down the train I had to catch and made sure I had the correct address. It was on the west side of Manhattan. I got there, and he showed me what he had to do. I asked him, "What was this?" He didn't know what it was either. I called it a contraption. It was this funny looking piece of a projector. It had some legs on it, and it was a top-heavy piece of equipment. We picked it up out of his car and put it on some wheels. We rolled it across and down the street on the sidewalk. We were at the other end of the street getting ready to turn the corner, and the contraption slid off the wheels. It hit me in the face causing me much pain. I fell hurting my face and my back. I had blood all on my face, and it was swollen. I made it to the hospital, and I was in so much pain that day. I kept it to myself. It happened so fast all I could do is go on with the sermon as planned. I worked everything out with the doctor. He tried to tell me to take it easy and all this kind of stuff. I had different thoughts. I was in pain and thought about when I was in the car wreck. I thought that the wreck was much worse than what I went through on that day. I prayed to God as I was going to see the doctor twice a week. I continued to go to church while getting back rubs, acupuncture and getting extensive rehab from my injuries during the week.

I felt like someone took a baseball bat, busted me in the face and back with several times. I didn't want to go to rehab, but I had to go because I had a limp for a while and back spasm after the fall. I called my girlfriend that night and told her what had happened. I was ready to go back to work, but my doctor kept on giving me rehab and some medication for back pain. I had scars inside my mouth that required stitches. The doctor wanted to keep me. I asked him to send me home. He said, "Let's take some x-rays first." I didn't get out of the hospital until that night at 8:15 p.m. I went home, slept and rested. I had sharp pains in my back. One day the doctor called me to ask me about my back, and I told him that I was still in pain. He had given me strong medication before, but I didn't want it anymore because it made me sleep a lot. He asked me if I wanted to have back surgery. I told him that I don't want to do that because I felt like it was not going to be in my best interest to have it done. He explained to me some things about back surgeries. I was already getting shots in my back. I felt like that was enough. The only thing about the cortisone shot is that it wears off in about an hour. I did not want to take any chances and thought the surgery wouldn't be good. It was a big decision that I had to make sooner rather than later. It seemed like when it rained or got cold outside the pain would flare up. I knew the summer was coming because it hardly hurt at all. It was always between October to late March. My doctor and I had a good friendship. One morning I had an appointment with him. When I got there, he said, "How are you?" I said, "I feel terrible." He said, "Okay. What's bothering you?" I told him that the pain was in my legs now. He said, "It would be good if you would lose some weight. You probably would feel a little better." I didn't take offense to him. I listened and changed my diet little by little. I wasn't happy about it at first because I struggled with my weight in the past. I asked God to help me with my weight problem. It was food intake, but it is also hereditary because my dad stood 6'3 and weighed about 400 pounds. I was a big strong man of God.

I knew that I was in for a big change in my life. My doctor told me that he goes to the Brooklyn Nets games. He had tickets for my friends, me, or if I wanted to take someone from church with me to the games. I was shocked because he had seasons passes that cost about $3,000 to $5,000 annually depending on where your seating arrangements are. He gave me three tickets on three different occasions. I took my girlfriend for the first and second time. I took a friend of mine the third time. There were all-inclusive food and beverages were free. We could eat anything we wanted. So much for my diet that night. He didn't have to do it.

On March 17, 2013, I had the opportunity to be an ordained minister on God's sacred desk and preach God's word. I was so glad and honored to be apart of NJBC. It was around 3 o'clock, and I had anticipated preaching my sermon. The pastor gave me instructions on how to preach a timely sermon. It was a full congregation that day and it was a cold day as well. I started sweating, and I had to go into a room at the church. I prayed and meditated before I went out there. I took deep breaths and asked God to speak through me. I was virtually unknown currently. I thought, "What an honor." I knew that all the preparation was about God. I looked at my God and my spiritual parents Mr.& Mrs. Payne. I told them that I was ready to go, and, on that day, I was never the same. I knew that the anointing of God is upon me. I went behind the pulpit and got on my knees and prayed, "Oh God. Please help me with my initial sermon. Lord, I need thee. I pray that the words that come out of my mouth be acceptable in your sight, my strength, and my redeemer." I got up and sat down. I looked out in the crowd and was honored to be a child of God. I was ready to be a licensed minister at this great church. I preached the sermon "The Prodigal Son." I felt the entire sermon, and it was for me. I talked about many things. I know for a fact that this sermon changed my life. It wasn't right for a boy in Jewish customs to ask his father for his inheritance this early in his young age. The Bible says that the father divided his inheritance between him and his brother. It didn't say what his other brother did with his inheritance. Still, the older brother got mad at the younger brother because he was treated like a king. The younger brother was given a robe, some shoes, and a ring. The eldest brother was upset because he said he never did anything wrong. That's how we are when we judge people and try to justify how we feel. I was so happy to be concluding my sermon.

I preached for twenty to twenty-five minutes. I ended my sermon and then I was voted on that day. I sat down, and several people voted for me: my girlfriend, Mr.& Mrs. Payne, and some people that I didn't even know. I was tickled to death. I smiled as if I had just won the lottery or something. I just knew that after I was voted on, all was in my favor. I gave my testimony and benediction that day. I was mesmerized by God and the congregation. I thanked Bishop Rice and Executive Minister Sondra Browne for allowing me the opportunity to preach God's word. It made me realize that God can change anybody's life. I talked to people, and I told them what happened to me in my childhood. I told them about a lot of things that happened to me. I said that the only thing that kept me alive was God because of the nature of how and when things happened to me. I wasn't prepared for all these things. I relied on my family and friends to deal with all the things that happened to me. Sometimes, God would take me off somewhere, relax my nerves to minister to me. Other than that, I would go to work and church. I wasn't your average person that sat in the house. I will always be grateful because of what God has done for me. He opened and closed doors. Most of all God put me on notice of what was going on and how He connects with people according to His word. People are giving up and committing suicide. Many terrorist acts and terror plots are going on. Police are killing our black men. Black on black crimes are being committed. People are struggling with putting food on their tables. I saw so many things happening that year. I was glad that God was dealing with me on that level. I was preparing for many sermons. I just wanted to be used by God. I have been a minister now for over five years.

Many people go through their trials and tribulations. They don't fully understand what it takes to give their life to the Lord. I learned that God will do for you what no one else can do. The Holy Spirit has been good to me. He has protected and shielded me from devilish people that tried to harm me. They decided to put up barriers to block my blessings. The Lord leads me around the barriers. He gave me a clear path to righteousness. He also allowed me to open my eyes and see who my real friends are. I am shocked that God revealed to me that people in ministry aren't your friends at church. My real friends are people who love me unconditionally and don't judge me. Beware of someone who has known you for a while and suddenly don't talk to you anymore. It's like they just fell off the face of the earth, but they are still at the church. God told me to just fall back and watch them. You can't be all things to all people. God has put me in a position to help the lost, homeless, drunk, drug addict, prostitute, and the person who has life-controlling problems. I know my calling is for the person who was in a car accident and God healed them either through death or through learning how to walk or talk again. God has called me to many things. I ran for a while and came to my senses. I was way out there because I had lost my way with God.

I had left God, but He didn't leave me. It always amazes me when people say that God left them in the wilderness. I know they left God, but He didn't leave them. It usually happens when things don't go our way. We feel isolated and feel like no cares. We usually give up and turn our backs on everybody. I have been there and done that too many times. I realize that Jesus Christ has given me my wings back. I failed many times and have been successful at many opportunities. God is the ultimate Provider and the ultimate Healer. God is the Saviour. There were things going on that I couldn't control. I had to leave Evansville. I know that I wouldn't have made it thus far. I was on a collision course to hell. Some people don't get that far in life. They can't think that far ahead, much less acknowledging the fact that He exists.

I was truly thankful to my Lord God because I had been given many chances to get my life back in order. I was out of order for many years. I knew that my time was running out. I told God that I would go wherever He wanted me to go, and I would do whatever He wanted me to do. Be careful what you ask for because He gave me what I asked, but I had to work for it. You can't do ministry sitting on the sidelines. He taught me how to stay in my lane. He anointed and chose me to do many of His works. I'm forever grateful. His ministries consist of helps: developing young men to do the right thing, stay in school, get an education, get a degree in college, get a good job or start a business, get married, and take care of their families. Those are the earmarks of the young African American men. Having some good friendships along the way would be wise. We all need someone we can talk to or confide in. It's easy for me to speak to God. I need friends in my life as well. I have a few friends that I can talk to at any given time. I value the word of God any day over my family and friends. It has given me a brand-new way of living and thinking.

I was never the same person once I changed my mind, heart, and every fiber in my body. There are things that I just no longer do anymore. There are places that I won't go anymore. There are people that I won't even go anywhere with anymore. This wasn't something that was just taught to me. I know that God exists because I listened to myself. I would be back home in a whole heap of trouble. It was like He flashed all these things passed my eyes. It was like He flashed my life before me and what the end was going to be. I was ready for the change in ministries because I had been in ministry for a long time with my father. I had been in other ministries for quite some time as well. It was time for me to be on my own in ministry.

I found out that everybody is not going to like you. Many people are not going to accept you fully into their cliques. God isn't in many ministries. They are just people investing their time and being open to whatever is in them that they want to talk about. I have been through some tough times while being involved in ministry. Nothing was greater than joining NJWC. I knew that God had set me up for a good training church so He can launch my ministry.

CHAPTER 18

The Wedding

Towards the end of 2014 and the first quarter of 2015, my girlfriend and I were planning a wedding. We were walking down 14th St. in Manhattan. Someone put three brand new wicker baskets on the curve. Sitting inside one of the baskets was a wedding planner binder. That wedding planner binder helped us plan our entire wedding. We saw the materials sitting out there, and we didn't know if it was trash or something. Someone had just discarded it, and we didn't even know who these people were. The bill from the discarded papers from this wedding was $25,000. I told my girlfriend that we didn't have that kind of money. It was an invoice of all the things you would need to plan a wedding and more. The binder helped us make the wedding list for the guest and family.

It also helped us line up all the wedding party. It gave us a timeline of when we should pay for all the materials we needed. We went to Anton's in Queens. We had a discussion with the wedding planner there. We came back a few weeks later with the first deposit. My girlfriend began creating party favors, bouquets, and boutonnieres. My girlfriend and her wedding party went to David's Bridal Shop to pick out the dresses and shoes for the bridal party. They were fuchsia pink. The groomsmen boutonnieres, bow ties, and handkerchiefs were the fuchsia pink. The suits and shoes were all white. Ramona went to a website and found two beautiful wedding dresses at a discounted price. We went to Zales Jewelry website and purchased the three rings. A few weeks later Ramona's rings came first to the Green Acres mall store. I took her engagement ring and got down on one knee at the store and asked her to marry me. We had the store clerk film it. She said yes. I stood up and kissed her. While all these great things were going on, I was still going to see the doctor twice a week. I knew God was changing our lives. We allowed God to come in our lives entirely at this point. We started taking trips together.

Our first trip together was in Miami, Florida. We were supposed to catch the Carnival Cruise Ship, but we missed it because of a plane delay. The airlines gave us two days in a hotel room on the west side of Miami. It was quiet, not near the beach, and we had nothing to do. We enjoyed our time together. Ramona had already planned to take us to a South Beach Florida hotel where there are more attractions and restaurants. We went to the Clevelander restaurant, ate, and listened to music. Next door to the restaurant was the Versace's Mansion. Ocean Drive had restaurants, shops, and hotels. The beach was steps away from it all. We went to the beach, and the water was aqua blue. Ramona refused to get in the water to swim. She waded in the water. I thought, "Wade in the water, wade in the water children, wade in the water, God's gonna trouble the water."

One night when we were walking down Ocean Drive, a man rode up in this car that looks like a golf cart with advertisements on it. He asked Ramona and me if we wanted a free ride. We said sure because we were tired as we were on our way back to our hotel over ten blocks away. We asked him if he could take us to Walgreens on the way. He said yes and waited for us outside then took us back to our hotel. We gave him a donation after he had dropped us off. The hotel was very nice and clean. The room we stayed in was huge and right near the beach. We could look out the window and see the beautiful water and the sunset every night.

The next day we went to Bayside on the bus to eat and do some window shopping. We were looking for bargains and souvenirs as we were having fun. We finally sat down to eat some seafood, rice, and peas. We talked and just had an awesome vacation. There were all kinds of bags, t-shirts, and key chains that were advertising Miami. At the end of the vacation, we wished we could stay longer because we were having a ball. We caught the plane back to New York early the next day. It was a three-hour flight that was quick by our estimation. We were so tired when we got off the plane at J.F.K. All we could think about is getting home, resting, and the fun we had together. While we were in Miami, we would look to see if we could find a church to visit just in case we returned. We could fellowship with the congregation. I thought about that when we had made it home. This was in the summer, and it was hot down in Miami that year. We thought about all the memories that were caught in our minds. We started talking about when we were going to take our next vacation. We had to save for our wedding, so our next vacation was our honeymoon. We both continued to go to work and go to church every Sunday. We did go on weekend vacations to Connecticut for a couple of days.

On September 12, 2015, we had our wedding at 10:00 a.m. at N.J.W.C. We stayed in a hotel overnight, and I had to go to the church early that morning so my wife could get her wedding party together. I waited downstairs in the hotel lobby for the limo driver to pick me up. I waited for about 20 minutes. At about 8:15 a.m., I looked outside and saw a limo pull up. I knew it was for me. I went outside to get in the car. The limo driver and I said hello to one another. I told him the address of the church. He drove me to the church in what was about a five-minute ride over. Once we arrived there, I got out of the car and went into the church. I talked to some of the staff and groomsmen at the church. I was so excited when I got to see all the arrangements and love that was there for us. We know that God has been with us throughout everything that my girlfriend and I have been through. I knew that God was in our relationship because He formed it. I wasn't with anybody for at least a few years before I met her.

Back at the hotel, Ramona began to get ready for "The Wedding." She waited for her friends to arrive to help her get dressed. She gave them their bouquets, jewelry, and mini crowns. My wife's crown was large with swinging rhinestones. Her dress was all white with a long train with lace and sequence. Her shoes were silver. Her vale was sheer white. All the flowers were fuchsia and white. She began her journey with her bridal party to the church in the limo. When she arrived, her girlfriends got out, and Ramona stayed in the limo. Two of the bridesmaids had to rehearse because they didn't make it to the rehearsal.

I went around with the groomsmen as they arrived and told them along the way, with the wedding coordinators, where we were supposed to be and how we were to stand. It was time to get everybody into position. The bridesmaids were lining up in the hallways. Mr. Payne was on the right side of the doors. The bridesmaids were on the left side leading to the pew. The music started to play. I marched in first and took my position next to the pastor. The bridesmaids and groomsmen marched in after me. They separated, and the groomsmen lined up behind me on the right side. The bridesmaids lined up on the left side waiting on my fiancé. It was a pivotal moment when I saw my fiancé and Mr. Payne took the position as the father of the bride.

I started crying once I saw how beautiful Ramona was at that moment. She walked down the aisle holding Mr. Payne's arm, and I looked at her. She was stunning. She arrived at the altar with Mr. Payne. Bishop Rice officiated our wedding and the ceremony. Bishop Rice said, "Who gives this bride to the groom?" Mr. Payne answered, "I do." Then he walked my soon-to-be bride to me. We both held hands and faced one another. We looked into each other's eyes, and I felt so great about our marriage. I was still crying. She wiped my tears from my cheeks and said, "Everything will be okay. I love you, baby." Bishop Rice pronounced us man and wife. I kissed her multiple times. Everybody stood up and gave a big standing ovation.

We were so grateful and honored by God. Rev. Browne and Rev. Newberry assisted Bishop Rice in marrying my wife and me. We had marriage counseling at the church. I understood that Jesus Christ is the head and we are His people. We ought to act like it and do all that we can to help the church out in many ways. After the marriage ceremony, we took our pictures in front of the church. We all went to Anton's for the reception. We went to our private suite upstairs and ate some hors d'oeuvres. My wife then changed into her second wedding dress. She hired an assistant that came along with the venue. We marched into the banquet hall where everyone was already seated at their tables. We danced into the room where our wedding party was on the dance floor waiting for us. We sat down and ate some appetizers before we had our dinner. Everyone came to our table to greet us. It was time for our first dance. We did the tango dance. It was beautiful. Then we went around the room, greeted and took photos with everyone. We got cards and gifts that day. In return, we gave them party favors.

We had chicken, rice, vegetables, and salad. We also sang songs to one another. Ramona sang "For the Lover in You" by Shalamar, and I sang "My Girl" by the Temptations. We had a ball that day, and we started our photo album. We looked back on that day. We would do it all over again. We were ready to live our new lives as husband and wife. The next few days we were ready to go on our honeymoon to the Bahamas. We prepared for our flight and our destination for a week at sea on a cruise from Miami to the Bahamas.

Jerome and Ramona on their wedding day.

September 12 , 2015

CHAPTER 19

Honeymoon

We flew to Miami Florida on September 13, 2015, a day after our wedding. Upon arrival, we stayed at the Casa Grande hotel in Miami Beach on Ocean Drive. We checked in at 1:00 p.m., and we were so excited because we had gotten a suite that was so nice. It was a blessing. We put our belongings up and took a nap. We had some jet lag. We woke up and got some groceries from CVS around the corner. The next day we were going to Bayside to board our cruise. We didn't stay out too late. We just got some food and drinks because we had a stove and refrigerator in our room. The rest of the day we walked around close by the hotel site seeing. We took photos, looked around at different restaurants, and did some window shopping. I was very intrigued about Miami Beach because there were hardly any churches in sight. I knew what kind of atmosphere that my wife and I were in. It was a party town. We were passing the time. However, it was interesting and fun.

We watched T.V. and ate dinner that night because we had to get prepared for an early checkout in the morning. We had to get on the cruise ship and make it on time. I was very serious about this because of what happened to us the last time we were in Miami.

We got up that morning, showered, got breakfast, packed our belongings, and called a cab to take us to our destination. We got to the Norwegian Cruise ship about 1:30 p.m. and boarded. We stood in line for about 20 minutes and waited in the U.S. Customs area. We checked in that area and went into the top of the cruise ship area. It was a beautiful boat. I knew that once we checked in, we would get something to eat first. My wife and I went on the tenth floor to a place called "Bar-B-Que Steaks and Chicken on the Grill." There were turkey burgers, ribs, hot dogs, hamburgers, shrimp, and all kinds of salads. We ate just enough because it was early in the day. The boat hadn't left the Miami port yet. We enjoyed every day that we were there. We ministered to two women on the third day. I did a lot of thinking and relaxing on our vacation. It was one of the best days of our lives. The staff played the song, "Watch Me Ne Ne." We were on the outside top deck that evening, and people were in the pool all through the day.

The first night we had to do the fire drill procedures just in case an accident occurred. They told us what to do and what not to do if a disaster happened. Later, as we walked around the boat, I thought about the pool. I wanted to get in, but all I could do is fantasize about it. All I could see were 50 to 100 people inside and on the outside surrounding the pool. I said, "Honey look at this. There is no way we will get into the pool today." She said, "Maybe." As we sailed for the Bahamas, we were very excited to get out of New York City for a few days. We needed this for our sanity. I told her that we should try to do all that we could do before it's time to go back home. We went throughout the boat dancing. We went to a nice dinner date that night. We went to the Atlantis Hotel. It was like you see on T.V., but in person it is different. We rode throughout the city of Nassau. We saw dolphins jumping in and out of the water. We saw men and women training to jump out of the water near the hotel. We paid a driver to drive us throughout the city. We saw Baptist and Catholic Churches all over there. I saw many churches that were nicely built, and they had plenty of members there. As we went through the towns, we saw poor and rich people. My wife and I learned that it was a democratic city. We were shown houses where the celebrities lived. I collected money because it is a different type of currency than the U.S. dollar. We had to be back at a certain time to board our cruise ship.

We were back on the cruise ship at about 5:30 p.m. My wife and I were so tired. We got a ride back from all the sightseeing that day once we docked there overnight. I went back to the room and went for a sleeping binge for a few hours. My wife slept right next to me. We both were very tired. We woke up at 10:00 p.m. and immediately got ourselves together to get something to eat. We got dressed and went back on the 10th and 11th floor. We noticed that the boat was moving. I looked overboard, and it was dark as the water splashed up against the hull of the ship. I thought, "Wow this boat has a lot of weight to it?" I saw the boat slicing through the water. The ship probably weighed about several hundred tons. I thought about what it was like on Noah's Ark. I know that there was no comparison. What I thought about was the boat's design and all the rivets that they used to build the boat. I wondered if they used rivets at all to build Noah's Ark. I knew that the whole time we were there, we were protected by God. It seemed like every day was a new day.

The next morning, we showered, prayed to God, and planned new things that day. We looked at the program that they gave us. They had a bunch of dancers and entertainers on the ship doing different types of dances. They had Vegas-style cabaret dancers, Broadway shows, and themes every night. It was something new. We went and sat in on them. We were impressed with the organizing of the shows. It was a comedian there that was a long time Hollywood figure back in the day. He told us how he became a comedian by making people laugh. He said that he was a natural at it. He played in several movies.

We played bingo on the second day. That evening we ate lobster tails and butter with some crab legs for a nice lunch special. We ate some wholesome seafood that was fresh. We drank tea. After we had eaten our lunch special instead of going back to our room, my wife and I went up to the deck where the pool and all the other activities were taking place. I saw five children playing basketball on the deck. They were passing the ball back and forth. The boys were tall and looked about 11 or 12 years old. A lot of things were going on that day, and we had the chance to take photos. We saw that they had casinos on the cruise ship so people who wanted to gamble could do that. I told my wife, "Let's keep it moving." They had a newlywed game that we watched for about an hour in the theater. I liked going from show to show with my wife. It was very interesting. I underestimated what the cruise ship was going to be like because I had never been on a cruise until I met my wife. It was something new to me and different because I have never been on the ocean on a cruise line or international waters. It was an adventure for me.

My wife has been on quite a few cruise ships before she met me. She knew what was going to place before we had got on the ship. Sometimes when we go places, we can judge before we experience it because we see what the commercials show us when they advertise for vacations. We also go by what people tell us not realizing that everybody is different when we go to our destinations when on vacations. I was having a great time with my spouse. Even after the third and fourth day we still enjoyed ourselves. We hung out on the deck constantly and on the fourth day, I was able to take my plunge into the pool. We had gotten up early that morning, and as soon as we had got some grapes, juice, and water, I looked up and saw no one in the pool. I told my wife, "I'm going to get my trunks. You get your bathing suit." We ate a little bit before we changed our clothes. It was very hot that morning as usual. We got into the pool, and it was salt water. We floated all over the pool. We met some people who went into the pool after us. Their names were Karen and Mike Duncan from Florida. They asked us where we were from. We told them New York. They said that this was their 24th cruise.

We thought they are addicted to cruises. They asked me what I did for a living. I told him that I was a Public Safety Officer and a minister. They looked shocked and felt blessed talking to a minister. They were two Christian retirees.

Mike told us that he was a retired insurance salesman. Karen was a retired school teacher. They were much older than my wife and me, but they were so friendly to us. Their age didn't matter. The next thing we knew, more and more people came as the morning progressed. They were kids and babies with their parents with floating devices. They were splashing water, laughing, and jumping around in the pool and on the outside of the pool. We decided to get out of the pool and dry off hoping that we could get back in the pool later that day.

We went to get us a full course meal for breakfast. We had omelets, sausage, cheese, turkey sausage, bacon, oatmeal, grits, fruit bar, pancakes, waffles, cereal, milk, juices, coffee, tea, toast, bagels, and muffins. We went back to the room, laid down, and took a nap until it was time to go to lunch at 12:30 p.m. We went to the deck, and they were grilling beef and turkey burgers and steaks. The smoke was smelling good. We sat up on the floor and relaxed as they were playing all kinds of music. As my wife and I were looking left to right, were saw about 400 to 500 people on the entire deck. We were having lots of fun. We ended up taking a nap on the deck as we were on the deck for about four hours straight. My beautiful wife woke me up and asked me to go back to our room to rest. After we rested, we looked at the itinerary to see what was happening on the boat. A man dressed as Michael Jackson was at the theater that evening. We went to see him dance. He danced just like Michael, and he tried to sing like him. We were laughing our tails off. We were only a few days from wrapping up our vacation. Our next stop before we ended our vacation was the Great Stirrup Cay, Bahamas. The following day we arrived. We had already been on our vacation for five days.

We were smitten over the island there. We woke up to a beautiful sunrise glistening over the horizon. We went to get breakfast before we got off the boat. There was a warm island breeze that morning that bent the palm tree leaves as the wind flowed through them. You could smell the sea water in the air. The island was very tropical and very hot. While we were docked out at sea, we saw smaller boats coming towards our ship to take us to the dock because they didn't want to destroy the coral reefs. We all got on small boats which could only hold 50 to 100 people. The boats kept picking up and dropping off people to and from the cruise ship. The surf was rocky, but we made it safely to the island. We all got off the boat, found some beach chairs, and sat in front of the water. Norwegian Cruise Line gave us a Bar-B-Que on the beach that day. My wife and I jumped in the Atlantic Ocean and started swimming on the island. It was one of the best times of my life. We waited until the food was ready because we noticed that many of the people were getting out of the water and drying off. They started heading towards the food. One thing that I was not too happy about was no one prayed over the meal before they served it. By the time we got there, they had to grill more burgers. It was a long line of about 200 hundred people. Once we got up there to get the food, we had corn on the cob, shrimp, seafood and salad. We drink cold iced tea. The entire meal was excellent.

We noticed that people were going back to the main boat and we got on the small boat to go back to the cruise ship. The boat was called the Norway II. We had traveled about 2 miles to get back to our ship. We were both beat and very tired. I said to my sweetheart that the memories of going there were fond. I thought about some of the things that we saw over in Nassau like the photos that my wife had taken of me standing on the shores of the beach there. We saw a huge hotel that was being built that my wife took a photo of. I told her the next time we went back there we were going to stay at the Atlantis Hotel and the Ba Ha Mar Hotel. It was a huge hotel. We saw it as we were sightseeing. We also saw Bethel Baptist Church and took photos of it. It was a beautiful all white building that had a well-manicured lawn.

There were lots of memories as we were into the night thinking about our last day as we were passing through Freeport, Bahamas. We noticed that there was hardly anything to do there except shopping a little while we were docked for about two hours before heading back to the port of Miami. It was a quick ride back because before we knew it, we were back in Miami the next morning. We showered and ate breakfast before we got to the Miami Airport. God blessed our honeymoon.

The honeymoon was over. We got our luggage and said goodbye to some people we had met while we were eating breakfast. We were coming down the ramp off the boat, saw a cab, and waved him down to catch our flight on time because our flight was scheduled for 2:00 p.m. We had got off the ship at 10:00

a.m. We just wanted to be there early so we could make our flight. The cab driver had put our things in his trunk, and we were headed to the airport. It only took about 20 minutes for him and 12 dollars to get there. I just gave him 15 dollars and said, "Keep the change." We got out, got our belongings, and we went to the Delta Airlines gate to get our boarding passes. We got upstairs to our zone and looked at our passes. We saw that we were in Zone 3 at Gate 8. We just waited for one to two hours before we boarded our plane.

We flew out of Miami at 2:24 p.m. My wife took photos of Miami as we were lifting to the top before the plane smoothed out. We looked back and said, "Thank you, Lord." We prayed for our safe return. We prayed every day the whole time we were there because we saw many poor people. Every time we bought something like a t-shirt or sandals, many people wanted us to buy their goods from them. It was a great experience we had in the Bahamas. We will never forget why we were there, and who made it possible. We made it to the J.F.K. Airport at 5:30 p.m. My wife was tired. I was beat and had jet lag from never getting up not one time to use the bathroom. I stayed in the same position throughout the flight.

We got home and put our things up. My wife had three more days off from work before she had to report back to work. We got groceries and just enjoyed each other's company. I returned to my doctor and informed him that I was back home from vacation. He asked to see me a couple of days later because he wanted to tell me of my options to have back surgery or continue to have back lumbar treatments every two weeks. The end of 2015 and the beginning of 2016, my wife and I made vows to lose weight and eat healthy meals. We also made a point to serve God more and to do more for the Kingdom of God.

We thought about joining the Evangelism Ministry. I asked God to give us a sign or to let us know when he was ready for us to join. Then I went on a youth trip to Maryland with some youth ministry friends from Brooklyn. I went on all kinds of ministries excursions. I met a friend who was always telling my wife and me about the baseball games he could get us tickets for. The next thing you know my wife and I were going to the Hampton's with him. We went to a gala with him. I asked him why he was giving us all these opportunities. He said that he has been going to these gala's for years. I think that it was new to us but old to him. Nevertheless, it was never ending fun once we got home. We had gotten back into the routine of life. My wife went back to work, and I knew that I was going back to work as well because I knew that being on disability wasn't an option.

After we got settled a few months later, I spoke to my doctor about my back situation. I was taking pain medication, and I just prayed to God about my options on having surgery. I was terrified at first, so my doctor told me to get second or third opinions. He scheduled me to see a well-known surgeon in the Bronx. I went to him a couple of weeks later, and he reported that I had spondylitis in my back. He said it is a form of arthritis. I was shocked to see his report. I waited for about another month and decided I wanted to get the L5-S1 Lumbar Back Surgery. He said that he was going to get me prepared for that in nearly a year or so because he had to get approved through the board. He also had to find a doctor to perform the surgery. He just wanted me to continue to do what I have been doing before I was to have the surgery. I didn't want to be in pain anymore. I was tired of having back spasm and not sleeping because of the pain. I would never wish any of these things on anyone. I told myself after I had surgery that I would go work out and try to stay in shape. I still had a long way to go before I could turn that corner. I trusted in the Lord. I talked to my family and friends. Some said, "No don't get it done. It will make your back worse." Some said, "What if you get the procedure done and it doesn't work out?" I learned that in everything there are risks. I had faith in God as I continued to go through treatments.

CHAPTER 20

My Back Surgery

On October 14, 2016, at 6:30 a.m., I had L5-S1 back surgery on my lower back. I was glad to have it done. I was already thinking about recovery. My wife was at work, and I told her not to worry about me because I'm in God's hands now. My mind was made up. There was no fear. I was not even contemplating. I was at peace with God. I told my wife to come and see me after she got off from work. That's what she did. I was asleep when she arrived. I opened my eyes and there she was. She looked at me with a smile on her face. I really didn't feel that much pain when I first got up. It was only when I started trying to move around when I felt some discomfort. I stayed in the hospital for one day and came home the following day.

I remember getting in the wheelchair, and the nurse taking me downstairs to catch my cab. I was so glad to be going home because I never liked hospitals or, for that matter, overnight stays. I was so happy to start my recovery from surgery. I had crutches and a cane. I used both and would take my pain medication from time to time. It was hard sitting around for three months and not going to church. It was hard not being able to go anywhere because it was late October and I wanted to go as I please and couldn't. It was a different kind of an experience. I hope that people understand that when you do have a surgery like this, there are many things to consider. First, being out of work for a good while is something to think about. Secondly, the surgery might not go as planned. Thirdly, you have periodic check-ups with your surgeon. Fourthly, the medication that the surgeon prescribes to you. The medication had me sleeping a lot. I was very unhappy with the way I was living as far as when I could return to work and get a good clean bill of health.

I called my family and told my sister Kathy that I had fusion back surgery. She told me to get proper rest, eat soup and salad, read the newspaper, and get plenty of rest. My brother Greg told me to pray to God and ask for wisdom, knowledge, and understanding on why you are going through what you are going through. I wasn't ready for the healing part of my situation, so I had no choice but to settle down. God made me understand that He is my boss. Everything was okay except there was some unfinished business like I was thinking about my son Jerome Jr., my daughter Katelyn, and my grandkids. I always had God and my wife. They are at the top of my priority list. I reflected on my life, and said, "Lord, Lord, God. Thank you."

As time went by, in late November and December, I was given the okay to join Accessoride. It's an organization that helps the elderly, handicapped, and disabled get around through there transportation service. I called them to get set up because I had received a letter saying that I was approved to their services. I set up the doctor appointments. You had to call them in advance so they could come by to pick you up. They were hardly ever on time. It was a disaster at times because I waited outside for a long time in the cold weather. Sometimes I went back inside the house. I was grateful to have the services.

I didn't go to church because I was healing and the people at my church were there for my wife and me. Sometimes I'd look up and someone would be knocking on my door with an Edible Arrangements fruit basket. It was a nice donation to me and my wife. I was so happy because sometimes you think that people are not thinking about you. But they are, and you must acknowledge them by thanking them. My wife and I didn't go back to church until February or March of 2017. I had gone through lots of pain medicine from creams to pills. I always kept my eyes on God. I think that sometimes we get caught up into the situation and not see God's miracles working for us. I don't care if it's cancer. If it's prostate cancer, breast cancer, skin cancer, diabetes, or a stroke, God will be there in your healing process. Even if you were born with birth defects or have autism, God is there providing everything we need. He takes care of his children.

I knew that I was going to be okay. I would make one of my few visits to see my doctor. I went to see him for the 14th time, and he gave me a clean bill of health to return to church and work. I did a lot of soul searching while I was at home. I learned that it's in God's timing that things come together in our lives. You can't rush anything. He must approve everything you do. We must remember as Christians that God is all we need. We need our families and friends, but God has the only "blueprint" for life. He is the only way for all of us. Any other way is where we question God and make our biggest mistakes. I understood that when we are questioned about something, it's the enemy trying to throw us off. Evil spirits give negative energy to people. The Holy Spirit gives positive energy to people. To keep the "HOLY SPIRIT" on you, pray and stay in the word of God. Stay in your lane, and the Lord Jesus Christ will protect you.

I have seen people all over the place in ministry. I know where God wants me to be. Some things aren't comfortable. Most situations are great once He gives you an assignment. Don't be out of place with what He wants from you. Man doesn't validate you. God does. He created you to be what He wanted you to be for His glory. I had a hard time understanding that because I tried to be like my father not realizing that he was passing me "The Message" before he passed away. God gets the "GLORY" we get the "Blessings from God." God didn't put you on the earth to follow people. You follow Him because He will lead you to the "PROMISED LAND." He makes no mistakes. All the stuff that is going on in the world today is not of God. Man has turned his back on God for selfish reasons to cater to themselves. I thought about all these things as I was sitting at home. It's okay to have homes and cars and somethings serve their purpose. For instance, if I owned many homes, I could think of many people in my family that I could help: my son, my daughter, my grandkids, my brothers, my sisters, and other family members. If you have a property and income producing properties without helping somebody out who is homeless and knowing that God made you wealthy, it is selfish. God is not pleased with the things that are going on today. When people become selfish, they want to be greedy and keep it all for themselves. They will not help the less fortunate. We still live in a "me, myself, and I," world. It's all about my family and me. My parents always taught me the following things have no place in the church: cliques in the church, self-gratification, manipulation, jealousy, envy, backbiting, and sorcery.

Times and people have changed. I can't go without saying and telling the truth. God used my church that I attend every Sunday. It's an "ANGEL" of the house. It helped me realize that generations will come through the church with power and conviction of Jesus Christ. God plans for all of us is to carry His word from generation to generation and to build His Kingdom forever. If anyone is there for any other reason, shame on them. Even if you have a mustard seed size of faith in God, He will bless you.

I knew that God had put me in this church to grow. I was ready to go forward once I saw that the name change came along while I was there. God was doing a "NEW THING" in the church. Many people didn't like what was going on because they weren't ready for change. People were questioning if it was from God or man. God does things to advance His Kingdom. I realized that many of us weren't on board. I saw what was going on when it was a Baptist Church. God was getting rid of the tare and sifting the wheat. When God wants you to go, be obedient to His calling, and He will see you through. Don't look back and go forward to your blessing from God. God will put you where He wants to put you.

Some of the greatest men of God preached from the pulpit. Some don't preach at all, but they are great orators. I have watched and seen it all. Some of the ministers and pastors don't even know what they are doing. That is why I'm continuing my theological education today. God put me with a powerful group of people. I have learned something from all of them. I learned that everybody brings something different to the table. If someone needs to be helped along the way, help them. Don't push anyone away because God wants them there. If you were the one to cause your brother or sister to stumble, that is not good. God has done for me what I couldn't do for myself. I have seen Him bless others in so many different unimaginable ways. There are so many reasons to serve God. My number one reason is that I never had someone take a broken body like mines and repair it. He repaired many other things to get my attention. Oh yes. He got my heart, soul, and mind. He has given me power that I have never had. He also got my attention about the abuse of His power. It's not our power to begin with. It's His power to allow us to conquer His glory for Him. There is nothing that I have done that has got me where I'm at today. Because of Him directing me to the source. I want people to know that when we do grow in the Lord, childish things are truly put away. God doesn't need false prophets. He wants us to grow.

1 Samuel 2:26 (NIV) says, "And the boy Samuel continued to grow in stature and in favor with Lord and with people."

2 Peter 3:18 (NIV) says, "But grow in the grace and knowledge of our Lord and Savior Jesus Christ. To him be glory both now and forever! Amen."

"JEHOVAH RAPHA"

God had healed me from myself. I tried to do it my way, and I never dreamed of the speedy recovery that He gave me. I was amazed that my doctor allowed me to go back to work on April 9, 2018. I was so glad to get back to work on the 9:00 a.m. to 5:00 p.m. schedule. I work more hours now than I ever did. I had been cooped up for too long. I was rusty going back to work.

The Parable of the Mustard Seed is one of the shorter parables of Jesus Christ which appears only in Mark 4:26-29. It is a parable about growth in the Kingdom of God. It follows the parable of the sower and the lamp under a bushel. It precedes the Parable of the Mustard Seed.

Mark 4:26-29 (ESV) says, "And he said, 'The Kingdom of God is as if a man should scatter seed on the ground. He sleeps and rises night and day, and the seed sprouts and grows: he knows not how. The earth produces by itself, first the blade, then the ear, then the full grain in the ear. But when the grain is ripe, at once he puts in the sickle, because the harvest has come."

Even when the farmer sleeps, the Kingdom of God is still growing. Its growth is due to God, not man. It follows its timetable. Apostle Paul describes the growth of the church in Corinth in a similar way. Reading the story of the Apostle Paul was a good thing for me. He persecuted people. He had an encounter with the Lord on the way to the Damascus road. He spent three years in Arabia and returned to preach about Jesus Christ, or the Messiah, on the way back to Damascus. Apostle Paul described the early church in Acts 13 and 14. We see three movements:

1. Church leadership shifting from Peter to Paul.
2. The target group for evangelism shifting from primarily Jewish to Gentile.
3. The move from a rural focus to an urban focus.

Paul and Barnabas visited six cities on this missionary journey.

1. Rely on the "Holy Spirit."
2. Evangelize through your most natural relationships.
3. Stay "Flexible" in your approach.
4. "Deepen" your spiritual roots.
5. Don't bend to "Resistance" to the Gospel.

God's approach is the best way to evangelize. We must remember that He will move us into areas where we will need Him to guide us, instead of leaning on our own understanding. That will keep us out of the way of opposition and strife. You will be challenged. All I ever wanted to do is grow in God and heal from the wounds of the past, whether it was spiritual, mental, physical, and emotional. I wanted God to fix my situation. It's easy to look at someone else and say what they did wrong. We need to look to God to help us with our own problems. How was I able to stay on top of things with God? I read His word and assessed my life. I don't care what I'm going through, I look to the Bible for all my answers. In the past, I was doing my own thing. Not anymore, Jesus Christ leads the way all the time. I see some of the churches that are open for business today. Some of them are standing on one leg with a few members. All it takes is for one or two members to leave and they will shut down.

Some of the churches that are still standing have false prophets there. They won't last because they are preaching half-truth and do minimal teaching about God's word. The women that are walking around in short dresses looking for their "Boaz" end up with a street gangsta and wonder why it didn't work out. Men in the churches looking for a wife will find out she's had everybody in the streets before she came to God. Only God can change their lives around. The foundation must be God and only God. Allow God to do His work as He did for me. He will do it for all of us.

Through all my hurts, pains and misfortunes, I have come to realize that it is not me who is control of my life. Romans 7:14-20 (NIV) says, "We know that the law is spiritual: but I am unspiritual, sold as a slave to sin. I do not understand what I do. For what I want to do I do not do, but what I hate I do. And if I do what I do not want to do, I agree that the law is good. As it is, it is no longer I myself who do it, but it is sin living in me. For I know that good itself don't dwell in me., that is, in my sinful nature. For I have the desire to do what is good, but I cannot carry it out. For I do not do the good, I want to do, but the evil I do not want to do, it is no longer I who do it. But it is in sin living in me that does it."

Paul says that we are slaves to sin. There were times where I wanted to give up because I was in the house tired of going through this healing in my back. I doubted at first, and some interesting things were going through my head. I was thinking about all the things that I had been through thus far. I thought it was all over as far me not having too many problems. I thought that I had already been through enough. I was wrong. I had issues with my family early on in my life. God took care of that. He got us all back together again. We lost our beautiful sister Doris "Jean" Hodge, and it pulled us together. Life is short, and God makes no mistakes when He calls us home. She is not with us, and she is glad that she is in the arms of our Lord Jesus Christ. God healed me from the accident I was in at an early age in my life. I didn't understand why it happened, but God knows why. Many things happened to me. My daughter is back in my life. God did that. Her mother tried to get in touch with me on several occasions by calling me a couple of days after my daughter's birthday. I was shocked because I thought that she was not on speaking terms with me. I thought wrong. God can do what He wants to do at any given day and time.

I recall the doctor showing me the screws that were going to be in my back with hinges attached to them before I had the surgery. I looked at the contraption and said to myself, "This cost

$100,000?" Because I did the research on this type of surgery, I knew what to expect. Also, I knew what they used to perform this surgery and its purpose. The recovery time was six months to a year. I realize today that it was more psychological than physical. I needed to understand that God had His hand in my healing. When it is cold outside, I have pain still to this day, but it's not bad at all in the summertime. I'm grateful and pleased with what God has done for me. I no longer take any more pain medication. I feel good, and I don't go to see the doctor anymore. I work full time or 40 to 50 hours a week. My wife and my cat, Syrus, keep me company. I talk to my son, daughter, and grandkids weekly. During the holidays, all I can think about are my grandparents, mother, and father. The legacy that I was left with was to carry the family for generations. Today, I carry the mantle because God knew that I had it in me. My sister Kathy has been called to minister, and she asked me to help her. I will help her no matter what. She needs God's help. He will give her the message to preach to His people. I just want her to bless God with "Thus Saith the Lord."

I realized when I did my initial sermon, it was all about what I went through. It was all my fault and what I did was take ownership of my sins. I realized then I could have done some things differently. This was the route that I had to go because of my sinful nature. God redeemed me and made me whole again. I could no longer be something I'm not anymore. I'm free from bondage. I'm whole again and will serve the Lord no matter what for the rest of my life. I have been through things that most people don't come through and have survived all the things that have been thrown my way. Without a shadow of a doubt,

God has been with me. I wonder what I would do without having Jesus Christ in my life. Being a sinner is easy. I have sinned practically all my life. He has forgiven me for all of it. I'm talking about willful sin. I didn't care about who you were or where I was at. I did it and was always guilty of sin. It felt good, but awful feeling once I was done. The after effects were horrible. I paid the price for all that I did. Some things I did I will never talk about because it is between God and me. It's personal, and it won't change a thing that God has already done in my life. I have been all over the world, and I can say that God is all over the planet. He is in places where "sin" is constantly present like in churches and homes.

CHAPTER 21

Relationships

My relationship with my mother was awesome as well. I used to call her "Hunny." I would say, "Sweetheart where do you want me to go for you today?" when she would ask me to do something or go somewhere for her. We had a good relationship. It was biblical, personal, and loving. Both of my parents loved the Lord and were devoted to God. I truly thank them for a treasure trove of information and what it means to serve God. I saw them at their very best, and when they were ill. I wanted to help them automatically. She was a great cook and an awesome listener. She would correct me from time to time. She loved her family and friends. One thing I noticed about her was she kept her friends close and her enemies even closer. She knew when people weren't right, but she kept on serving the Lord. I will never forget that once she told me that God is all she knows, and she wasn't lying. I watched her get on her knees every night for hours before she went to bed. I still have that image in my mind today. Somebody prayed for me, and they prayed for you. I remember the day she started playing the piano in our house. My dad bought it for her, and she had no piano lessons. She played by ear, and I said, "Wow. She sounds professional!" I thought she was something special and she was our praise and worship leader. She not only served in our church, but my mother played the organ and piano in several churches. I watched her teach my sisters and my brothers how to cook. It was always something to eat on the stove in the morning, afternoon, and at night. Those were the days I will never get back. The memories are all I have now. I saw my mother in my wife: the mannerisms, motherly touch, and candor. I felt that the first time I met her, but I didn't say anything.

The respect I had for my parents will always be number one in my entire life because they set the tone for what life should be like with Jesus Christ on my side. We had our ups, downs, and misunderstandings. It didn't last long because the love that they displayed was greater than the problem itself. I would give anything to have them back. It would be selfish and silly to be acting as though they were just normal people. They were truly ahead of their time. They both brought something different to their ministries. She was a praise and worship leader. My dad was a pastor, humanitarian, and missionary. They both were very open to going wherever God wanted them to go. They flew places when I was a kid and would be gone for weeks. They had fun in the early '80s. I wanted to be just like them.

The best relationship I ever had was with my daddy. He had a direct attitude that was flawless. You see there are men and there are boys. He treated me with love and respect when I was a little boy. I rode in his truck with him. He shared just about everything he had with me. I couldn't for the life of me understand why I was a daddy's boy. But I know now, he was teaching me how to be a man. It was father and son bonding. He talked about not having sex too soon unless you are married. I didn't listen. Oh, I did it anyway. He talked to me about cars, money, God, fighting and how to defend myself. God was the number one in my father's life. I had my first beer with my dad. I was drawn to him because of what he stood for. He never waived his right to serve God. Despite all the things he was going through, I never heard him say nothing wrong about God. He would always say, "Trust in Lord Son." That will forever stay with me.

Even when things are going bad, He will make a way to your blessings. If you think about God when you're in the middle of a bad situation, pray about it and imagine that a year from now things will not be the same. They will get better. I know our emotions get the best of us. Sometimes it's hard to be happy all the time, but the Lord will give us peace. We must meditate on God's word and relax. Take a moment and close your eyes for 10 or 15 minutes. Think about waves in the ocean crashing against the sand on the beach. Think about the birds in the sky flying high chirping as they go by. Think about the gentle breeze brushing against your face. As you lay there taking it all in, you'll realize this is God's creation.

Imagine what heaven is like. I never imagined the impact that God had on my dad's life. He handed it down to me when he became a minister. I fell in love with God and him when I was a kid. I opened the church with him. Wherever my dad was, I was there with him for the most part. He taught me how to treat and deal with people. We don't always deal with people from a biblical perspective. We always deal with people from our carnal ways that keep us bound by the enemy. He loves to see us in conflict with one another. My dad taught me to stay "sucker" free and be a no-nonsense Man of God.

One day we were working all day, and he asked, "Do you want to go out to eat?" I said, "No," because I wanted to get home. I couldn't fool him. He knew everything about me more than I knew about myself. He would always pay me for the work I did. He knew when I was seeing a girl, when I was drinking, when I was lying, when I was running the streets, or when I was not myself. He was studying me. People were not hating on me and telling on me. He knew more about who I was with and where I was going daily. Even in death, he knew that I was going to be a minister. He knew it before he passed away. He told one of my older brothers and me to take care of our mother. I remember when he preached his last sermon. He was dripping in sweat. He had a cold and still preached. He wasn't feeling well that Sunday morning. He could have backed out. He was the best preacher that I ever saw. He took care of ten kids and countless families in the communities. They don't make them like that anymore. He fed them and clothed people's children. He took on the role of father for young men and boys who had no direction. It's hard for me not to be able to see him. He did it because God gave my daddy a huge missionary mantle to carry into Haiti as well. He served in Haiti for at least ten years before he passed away.

People are retiring from work and are just doing whatever they want to do with their time. My father devoted his time to God first, then to his family and lastly to others. This is how it should always be. Building relationships are always what we should be doing. We should try to help people's needs get met. Sometimes we tend to take advantage of people's weakness. When they don't want to deal with you, there's a reason for that. Maybe you can be overbearing, or they have an autocratic spirit on them. I didn't see that with him. Many Christians are self-serving. We need to stop hooking ourselves up and start helping others that need help. But then yet we always help the ones that don't need the help or recognition. I have been observing the fact that Jesus Christ word cuts like a two-edged sword. I must admit I was stiff-necked at one time. When we refuse to honor God and love Him, we are just like the children of Israel and what they did to God. They were God's chosen people. We are Gentiles, and we are His people. He wants us to love one another and not get caught up in being high minded among our peers. That is why Prophet Jeremiah is called the weeping prophet because he preached for 40 years in Jerusalem.

God makes no mistakes. My family is a true testament to what God can do. Once my son called me and asked me some questions about something personal. He was happy that I could help him. I told him, "Don't thank me." I deserve no credit for anything because God will direct your path. I just want him to know that I'm with him. I just pray that God will settle him down. He has a lot of potential, and I'm going to see that the Lord directs his family and their ministries will go forth. I pray for their lives to be full of blessings in honoring and serving the Lord. I pray that my grandchildren serve the Lord and their grandchildren after them for generations to come. I asked God to have them continue his legacy well after I fly away. I just want the best for them. It's easy for younger people to mask God because they are still are trying to figure things out. I had one foot in and one foot out thinking that I will get there when I get there. I realized that God waits for no one. He will accept you the way you are. My son has the desire, I have the power of God, and my daughter has the energy to serve God. She is so young and vibrant. I want all our relationships to be one with God.

I focused on what God was speaking to me through my parents. My grandmother Alma was the one in control of my dad's calling to the ministry. She had an impact on him. I knew it when I was a kid. Whatever she did, he did it either with her or for her. I had first-hand experience when she would call and say she needed something. I would run down the street headed to her house. I think it devastated him when she moved away to Indianapolis with my aunt because he couldn't see her like he wanted to. It must have had an impact on him. I learned that you can have someone in your life that you love even though they are away; they are there in your heart and mind because you no longer have access to them. It can take an emotional effect on you when dealing with life. You don't want the abandonment feeling to come back again from another person. People tend to protect themselves by putting up a wall. To break down that wall they must trust you with their heart.

My relationship with my son was rocky in the early days when he was born on March 31, 1991. I was in his life, but his mother and I weren't getting along. I blame myself because I was doing things that weren't right. I was partying and not thinking about my son or his mother. I was in my own world until several years later when I saw him raising his kids and doing all he could to raise his babies. I'm proud of him. He has all the traits of me and more. He told me some things that were going on while I was gone. I tried to get back in his life.

There is nothing like God setting you up and giving you the green light to advance His Kingdom with trust and self-control. I had to tell my boy the good things I did, but I put it all on the table so he would know what his father was all about before I became a minister. I didn't want no one to tell him lies about me. I told him myself. I wanted to be honest with him, and it was simple. It happened with a phone call, and we spoke about life. It was a man to man conversation. I told him how sorry I was for not being in his life and whatever I could do to mend the situation I will from this day forward. We talked about many other things, and it was one of the best times we had in a conversation. He didn't blame me, and I didn't blame his mother or anyone else. It's time that we as men quit blaming others. Stand up and fight the good fight that the great Lord and Saviour Jesus Christ has given us power from His Father to do.

We are the head and not the tale. I can say that my son has a relationship with Jesus Christ. He has his family in church and serving God. He has a full-time job. He is taking care of his family and has transportation for them to go where they need to go. My son and I finally met face to face a few years ago. We got to know one another again. He made me realize in so many ways that we are alike, and it scares me. When I see him, I see myself in him. He is a lighter version of me. My daughter is a lighter complexion also. My children and my grandchildren look and act like me. My kids know about God, and they will come to know who Jesus Christ is while I'm alive or dead. The Christ that lives in me, I give charge to God for my family. I'm blown away that God's Word is real, and it never fails us. My family's name "The Meriweathers" will always be in the Lambs Book of Life for generations to come as long as we all continue to serve the Lord Forever.

My daughter was born on October 29, 2002. When she was born, I was so happy to have had a baby girl as beautiful as she was. She has my face, nose, mouth, and head. Our relationship was a little suspect as far as getting to know one another because of the lifestyle I was living early on in my life. I have been in her life off and on. Two days after her birthday in 2018, her mother contacted me. She told me that my daughter wanted to speak to me. I got a hold of her and called her a couple of days later. We chatted briefly, and we re-established our relationship. I know it's the saving Grace of God that put us back together. I have been praying for a long time to make amends to my baby girl.

Men as fathers have to be there for their daughters because they need to know how a man is supposed to treat them. This will be an excellent example for them by getting the truth from their Father. I'm glad that God has given me the opportunity to be back in her life because I need her just as much as she needs me. I live quite far away from her. There are no needs for excuses. She asked what my favorite colors are and what do I like to do in my off time. She told me that she wanted to go to college and graduate with a dermatologist degree. She's only 16 and is doing great in high school. I told her that I'm proud of her. She is a very beautiful young lady. She knows that I'm a minister. I want her to be herself when it comes to serving Jesus Christ. I want her to know that to trust in God is to have faith, hope, and love. Those ingredients are key to becoming a servant of God.

She will soon be a grown woman. I want her to be blessed with a God-fearing husband and God-fearing children. I want all the things that my father taught me about God. She deserves the best that God has for her. I wish my daughter the best that the Lord Jesus Christ has for her. I wonder why sometimes things turn out the way they do. I know that it wasn't me who put our relationship back together. Every time I tried to contact her or her mother, I never got through after making several attempts. Don't give up because God will forgive you of your sins. He did it for me, and He continues to show me that He is in control. I said, "Lord thank You," with tears running down my face. I said it repeatedly. I asked God to allow us to reunite face to face so we could go places and have a real relationship now and in the future. I'm truly proud of her. The last time I saw her, I was coming back from California. My brother Gary had driven me over to see her. She was chunky like me. She is tall for her size, and she has a beautiful smile. I. She was only like nine or ten years old at the time. We spoke briefly, and I told her I loved her. That wasn't enough. I know she probably questioned my love for her then. I knew that I was going to be in her life. I truly supported her when she was first born. Then I fell off and stopped helping her because I was trying to get my life together. Later in 2017, I gave her all the support that she needed. I had to help her because her mother raised her on her own. She deserved all the financial help that she needs. I don't blame her mother or anyone else. I want to say, "Lord. Thank You for Your love, mercy, and grace. You have blessed me with a beautiful family." I would never have dreamed that they would be so good to me. I know they truly love me because God has shown me that they do in so many ways. I love my children. My goal is to never let them out of my sight. I pick up the phone and call them to say hello. If they need me for anything, I am there for them. If they need to talk to me because they are going through something, they can call me.

I'm getting older and wiser. My heart goes out to them because of all the things that are going on now in the world. When I was coming up in the late '60s, it was not like this. People can put on an act like all is well. I have been there before. It's like you must smile to keep from crying by putting on a front because you don't want anyone to see your weaknesses. You don't want them to see your pain. It's too great, and it holds you hostage. You don't even know that the devil wants you to be confused and off balance. It's all designed so you won't have a voice. He wants to kill, steal, or destroy our lives. It's his job to sell you a dream. I couldn't live like that anymore. I looked at myself one day just like the cowboys and Indian did in the western shows I watched. At the end when they were at war, they threw the white flag up. I start singing one of my favorite hymns. "I surrender all.

I surrender all. All to be my blessed Saviour. I surrender all to Jesus Christ. Amen."

My youngest brother Timothy was my closest friend when we were younger. We played basketball together at our local community center. We played in the snow and rain. We also played football and baseball in the open lot. We played all day on weekends. I remember when we were playing, we saw a whole funeral procession of cars going down the street. It was like a slow-motion camera that took pictures of this scene. I will never forget it. It was my Aunt Lois' funeral. She was always coming to the house. One day, her husband came over and told my mother that she was sick. My mom went over to her house. My Aunt Lois was laying in the bed with headaches and high blood pressure. I saw her from time to time when she would come over to the house on Division Street. She was one beautiful person on the outside and the inside. She wasn't all that spiritual. She knew how to love in her words and action. I truly miss the bond we had.

Timothy loved to box, and he likes to play sports as I did. He played more defense, and he liked to dunk the ball. We would get into it over games because of the competition we had. I wanted him to be better than me in everything. Why? Because I cared about him. I knew he was going to excel in life, and he did. Boxing was his favorite sport until he was hit in the face a few times and he had a different viewpoint after that encounter. I remember him going into the ring for one of his fights. I wanted him to win all his fights, but sometimes you might have a skilled fighter. Some of the fighters were street fighters instead of trained fighters. I saw it all. My brother quickly started asking me about basketball. He was just tired of boxing. I told him that I would hook him up with my coach. The next thing I knew he was playing with us and trying out for our team. I like team sports because you can get a lot of help if you ever get in a jam. It goes right along with having mentors and someone steering you in the right direction. Timothy and I stayed close for many years before he had got himself into some trouble.

I ask God to mend our relationship like it once was before. I pray blessings on his life and his children's lives. We are not children anymore. I miss talking to him and doing things with him. I don't miss the lifestyle I used to live. I want to reunite and be a big brother to my little brother again but in a different way. I want him to realize that Jesus Christ can change his life for the better. He doesn't have to throw his life away anymore. God forgives, and he loves us unconditionally. I want him to know that and truly believe in God. He has been through enough as it is. He needs to know about being obedient to God's word. He will change his life for good. When he does come home, I pray that he allows God to come into his heart and turn his life around. I pray he turns from his wicked ways and move on from sin.

I will never forget the times we had. Life goes on because I have moved on. I haven't seen him in seven to eight years. I sometimes wished that things hadn't happened the way they did. I realized that if I stayed back home, I wouldn't be where I'm at today. I know many people prayed for me. I'm glad they did. We need to pray for people every day because some people are one paycheck away from losing their home and car. Some people don't have enough food on their table. People are struggling all over the world.

I remember coming home from my basketball camps and games. Timothy asked me where I got my trophy. I wasn't into trophies anymore because I had so many kinds of rewards. At one point, I wanted to play lousy, so someone else could bring home the awards. By the time I was ten years old I had already won about twenty basketball tournament trophies. I played hard because I liked to run, jump, pass, shoot, and play defense. We would pass the ball back and forth in school games. I would do most of the shooting. I was a fundamentals type of player. I liked the simplicity of scoring fifteen points, five rebounds, and eight assists. I was good at most sports. I trained year-round. I did all I could to make the teams at tryouts. Some of the guys that my brother and I play with and against made it to the N.B.A. I was proud of them because they have deserved it. Some of them were from our hometown, and some of them were from very far away. I learned that no matter where you are from if you can ball, you have done something. You have made a name for yourself instantly. We battled for everything like school work and ball games.

My wife and I have a loving relationship. We know each other's likes and dislikes. We know how to push each other's buttons. When we disagree with one another, we sit down and try to meet one another in the middle. Most of the time we laugh a lot at each other's jokes. We go out to dinner. We love to travel. We love to be invited to different galas, churches and choir functions. I truly learned many things from my wife. We have personal time and date night together. We never mix business with pleasure. We don't make engagements with other people without consenting to one another. I love the healthy relationship we have. It's built on trust and honesty. God put us together for reasons we may never know, but I'm optimistic about our future together. I truly believe that communication is the key to a healthy relationship and friendship. She is my best friend. We know that every day is not a good day. When you truly love your significant other, you know exactly what they are going to do before they do it. Our souls are in tune with one another. We are soul mates.

On one of our cruises, we went to Key West, Florida. We went on a historical bus tour around the island. We saw colonial-style homes that were built in the 1900s. These types of houses are built with columns on them. The pillars were like the ones you see on the front of the White House. They also were made of wood. They had two shutters on each window. Most of the houses were pure ceramic white. Beautiful gardens surrounded them. Each house had large and small fountains with bird feeders. We went to Duval Street, and we saw all the restaurants and bars. I told my wife that we should into the store to buy some cold drinks and some Halls because she wasn't feeling well at the time. After we left the store, we did some walking around the island of our own. We walked about ten blocks, and we were in awe of the city because it was a joy to see some of the old things that were left behind.

We went to the President Harry Truman Presidential Library. It's called the "Little White House." It had lots of books, figurines, and statues. The walls were all white. The library had huge windows inside and looked like a small miniature White House. It was a Colonial style white house. Outside had white wooden vintage benches that were surrounded by flowers and bushes. We thought about all the things we did once we boarded the cruise ship. As we laid down and got some rest, we noticed the boat was moving around. We felt the waves, and I looked out the window. I heard the captain come over the intercom and say, "We are now headed to Cozumel, Mexico." I used the bathroom and laid back down. I looked at my wife, and she said, "Just lay down and close your eyes." The next thing I knew is I fell into a deep sleep. We didn't wake up until late in the night to get some dinner and snacks. She had awakened me at 10:15 p.m. We had some burgers and salad on the top deck. After that, we sat on the edge of the boat and just looked across the water. It was late at night, and you couldn't see anything but stars in the sky. We heard water chopping against the boat. I felt that cool breeze, and we decided that we were going on the beach chairs on the ship. I looked at her and noticed that we were closing our eyes. We meditated and took it all in as we were on international waters. It felt good, and we felt special as a couple. It was one of the first times in my life when everything not only felt good, it was right. We knew God had given us the freedom to take this vacation and enjoy it because it was well deserved.

The next morning, we were in Mexico docked. We showered and put on our clothes. We headed downstairs to leave the boat. It was scorching hot. I'm glad I had put on an orange pair of swimming trunks, a white shirt, and sandals. I had a baseball cap on as well. We went and got some breakfast at 10:00 a.m.

that morning. There was a whole lot of people leaving the boat in front of us and back of us. We were turning our heads because it was in upwards to 200 or 300 people just dispersing in many ways and we were all given time to return before 7:00 p.m. My wife and I first went on a little tour through the island first. Then we went inside one of their restaurants. We decided that we could go into a nearby water hole near the city where the boats docked. I got into the water, and it was cold. She looked at me and said, "You swim like an otter." We started laughing. I swam underneath the water and put on a show for her. She didn't swim with me.

We noticed two older white ladies there, and they asked us where we were from as we were leaving. We told them New York and one of the ladies said they had been there. The other one said she had never been there. We looked at each and said to ourselves, "We have never been to Cozumel neither." We said, "God bless you all," after having a brief conversation with them. We started walking back to the boat, and we stopped to shop for souvenirs. We got a couple of key chains and T-shirts. We returned to the ship. As we went back, we smelled food. I told my wife that someone was on the boat was grilling. Once we got back on the ship, I was right. They were grilling steaks, potatoes, desserts, drinks, and more. I knew that we were going to get something to eat and hang out on the deck all night. It was a perfect day. We were eating and listening to music all night as we were headed inland through the night back to Miami. It was a five-day trip, and it went by fast. We had lots of fun.

When we got to the deck after we had finished eating, my wife wasn't feeling well. I told her, "Let's go back to the room." She said, "I'm going to enjoy the trip sick or not." She started searching through her purse. She had found her Zicam. It is a cold-fighting remedy that is made with vitamin c and zinc. After she took the cold medicine, she felt much better. The day she had taken it went away. She said, "I feel better and we can do more activities on our last day." We looked at our itinerary and found that on the last night, there was an all-white farewell party for all the passengers on the boat. Later that night, we arrived on the deck. The music was playing, and everyone was dancing wearing all white. About an hour later out of nowhere, it started pouring down rain on us. We all ran inside to stay dry, and we went into the club. The host announced to go to the club to finish the white party. Half the people didn't show up because apparently, they got wet.

An hour later we went to our room at 12:30 a.m. While we were inside the club a man had the nerve to ask me if he could dance with my wife. I said no because the man was a stranger and he looked crazy in the face. He had a long ponytail and a mustache. I didn't know him from Adam. I'm my wife's protector, and prevention is everything when it comes to God, my wife, and family. We had to get up in the morning. We ordered some food. We ordered hot chocolate lava cake and burgers. There wasn't anything on the T.V. My wife and I went to sleep.

The next morning, we got up at about 6:00 a.m. My wife sat on the bed talking to me. I got up to use the bathroom and when I opened the bathroom door, we heard someone jiggling the knob to our cabin door. My wife said, "Who is it? We are not dressed." A lady's voice answered, "Housekeeping." Before we could tell them to wait a minute, the door was already opened. The housekeeping lady and two U.S. customs agents walked into our cabin. They asked me my name, and I told them, "Jerome Meriweather." I stood in the hallway handcuffed with a pair of boxer underwear on with no shirt and no shoes. They told me that I had abandoned a child. I told them, "I have never done such a thing. You got the wrong person." They said, "Let's go downstairs and get on the computer in the system to see what's going on." My wife and I asked them to allow me to get dressed, put on some clothes, and shoes. I told my wife to pack everything up and get it ready because they got the wrong person. I was going downstairs. It was embarrassing because some of the people my wife and I met were looking at me like what's going on. I went inside this small room and waited for three hours so they could run a check on my background. They asked me if I had kids and I told them, "Yes. I have a daughter that is a teenager in Kentucky. My son is grown. What's going on?" I was worried about my wife, and I knew that God would vindicate me because at 10 a.m. in Miami they released me. They said, "They don't want you. We have the wrong person."

I went back on the boat, and I will never forget my wife and I cried. We couldn't believe that this happened to us. We eventually caught the plane that day, but we had to be on standby because of what happened to us on the cruise ship. I was furious, and I knew that it was a false arrest. I knew that we weren't being treated right. I said to myself, "How can they do this? I must seek God about this matter. If it were anyone else, how would they have handled this situation? How did my wife feel as I was being detained?" I was hurt, and this taught me a lesson about life. Storms may come, and storms may go. Only God can correct your path. We can't do it until we decide to allow God to take over. I wasn't shocked considering all the things that keep on happening to us. It shouldn't be something that we needed to be accustomed to. My hope and faith are in God. I agree with God Almighty because the things that were done to Him before He was on the cross. He was beaten while being hit on His face and thorns pierced in His head. I haven't been through anything like that and never will because God is Lord all by Himself. He went through pain and suffering. I know without a shadow of a doubt that no man on earth could have paid the price for us like He did. That is why it's imperative for me to have a relationship with God in these three areas: Father, Son, and Holy Spirit. God was always talked about in the Old Testament. The Son of God, Jesus Christ was mentioned in the New Testament. When you get to Acts, the Holy Spirit was talked about.

You began to see changes happening in sinners' lives. I prayed all day and night. You must develop a prayer life. We all need to pray continuously every day and throughout the day. We need to function as a person and as a body in Christ. The pain and the emotions of it all started fading away. I never will forget the ordeal of what happened. God wants us to move to the next level. We can't have things that hold us hostage. Some things are geared for us to have problems and to be mistreated sometimes. The thing is we can't get caught up into the downward spiral it brings. I used to fight. I can't mentally, physically, or emotionally fight anymore. I can only fight spiritually. It's one thing when we know the word. It's another to stay silent and allow God to do His thing. I'm in the process of mastering that now. He must be in front of you always to have a great relationship with Him. You must move totally out of the way.

Some of us get right back in the place where he is trying to bless us. I hope you realize that if you don't get out of the way, your blessings will always be stagnated because He is telling you to move. Don't be scared to move. God speaks through us in so many ways. I had numerous close encounters with death on all sides in life. God heals us from all our wounds. I have been wounded and felt some way about many situations in my life. Once I realized that I could do all things through Christ who strengthens me, I felt more powerful even though I may not know the outcome in all situations. I can trust in God for directions and answers to life's problems. We may not have it all together. I'm convinced that God will take us on a new level. A level that we have never been on before.

After the arrest, my wife and I were home that entire year. We were soul searching for making some changes in our lives. My wife asked me about a workout membership. I asked, "Why do you want to go to work out?" She said, "We will stay in shape, and we can work out together." I didn't want to do it at first, and I thought it was going to be a waste of money. Today, we are still going to the gym at least twice a week. We get on the treadmill. We get on the stair master and the elliptical. I go hard at first when I get there. Once we have been there for an hour, I start slowing down. My wife gets on her exercise machines. I was glad we started working out because we look forward to doing things differently as far as our health is concerned. We went back to eating more salad and stayed away from fatty foods. We changed our diet. We also changed the people that we hang around with. We have kept our circle of friends small. People are not to be trusted because if they don't have the Lord in their lives nine times out of ten, they will probably cause you to stumble. You must keep a solid relationship with God and your spouse. You will be tested on all phases in your lives. Our lives have changed dramatically.

My relationship with my church family can be better. I know that everyone is different. I talk to some of the ministers and some of them I speak to from a distance. I can't help but to pray and ask God to bless our group of ministers. I thank God for them. You can have insight into different personal views. It's a part of life. We are all human. I realized that God had given us all gifts and talents. God determines what level of anointing we all have. The relationship with God is what we should be striving for. I hope that we don't get complacent. We don't do what others want us to do. We must consecrate ourselves and set ourselves apart. The work of the Lord is vast. In His vineyard are many levels of blessings. I always ask God to help me do His will. It's not easy and sometimes I have to think outside of the box. I always say, "Lord let Your will be done, not mine. Use me as you see fit. Use me Lord on all areas of ministries where you have called me to." Sometimes I am at church, and God gives me an assignment. I do the assignment that He gave me. Then I will help in many other ways. For example, I might do the security ministry that God has assigned me too. He may ask me in the next service to preach, read the scripture, pray, or to be on standby in case something happens. You are there to help other members of the church in whatever way possible.

God has blessed me with my job and now I'm a Fire Life Safety Director. My job offers free classes for building management 1, 2, and 3. God has given me all these opportunities. I know that I don't deserve anything that is going right in life. God gets all the credit because there are so many opportunities that have come my way. Do not take it for granted because God can give it, and God can take it away. God bless the child who has His own. I prayed for our group, and I will cherish every moment that I have with them no matter what happens. God will see us through. Are we perfect? No. God is. Do we make mistakes? Yes, God forgives us.

I learned how to be more flexible and how not to take everything so seriously. I think that when I first came on the scene, there were some things I didn't know about and didn't understand. But God allowed me to understand Him by and by. That was the difference between serving God and man. I was hurting, and I couldn't find anybody to talk to before I met my wife. The trust that I had for people was out the window because of my past hurts and pains. It was always about me being made out to be the bad guy. I knew I was a good person. I no longer wanted to prove that. I wanted God to guide me, and He guided me to my wife. Someone who I could trust and love. I could talk to her about anything.

I waited a long time before I was able to propose to my wife. I knew that God was working with me then because I was never allowing God to do nothing for me. I wanted to have all things done my way. I was asking for everything. Lord, I want my wife, a new car, and a new home. I want this and that. God spoke to me about the "Process." He knew that I needed to clean up a lot of things on my end. Self had to go, and friendships in ministry had to be established. I had to give up some old friends and old habits. I still had some long-distance relationships in California, Indiana, Ohio, and some other states. I knew that God had brought me here to change me. I'm glad he chose New York for me because this is the best city in the world. This is the land of milk and honey. But that's not all, New York is a place where if you make it here, you can make it anywhere. It has everything that a person can get: a good education, job, or business. When I first moved here, I thought that there was a church on every corner. I knew that this was the place for me when I was accepted into the family of ministers. Some of them when I first came have passed away. Some of them are still there.

I know that we all will see one another again by the grace of our Heavenly Father. I do know that the church is headed in the right direction. I'm grateful for that. I have been to hundreds of churches. A church can't just survive off tithes and offerings. There has to be the Holy Ghost that takes the church, along with the Bishop with the vision from God, to move the church in the direction that it needs to go. I know that it's not easy. I know that everyone is not on board with "Thus saith the Lord." Some of us are scared to take that next leap of faith just because we don't know what the end is going to be. I put my faith in God. I have no one else. I want to be loved, blessed by God, and His people. I know that I'm where I am supposed to be. Don't allow people to tell you any different.

Between 2006 and 2018, I had been involved with ministries all over the country for 12 years. Once I started with a ministry, I went above and beyond what was expected of me. God doesn't want you to be somewhere where you are not supposed to be. When my time came to an end, I moved on gracefully and did not look back. I reflected and tried to understand the purpose of the training I received. Some people are meant to be in your lives in ministries. There are some that will only be there for a season. I saw it many times. Some people that I meet maybe one or two years they are gone through death, a new beginning, or a new assignment. I asked the Lord to lead me and guide me into whatever His will is for my wife and me. I know it won't be easy. I know there will be obstacles. I know that God will be with us all the way.

The best relationships that I ever had was with Godly men and women. I knew that I was going to be in some trouble if I tried to serve two masters. It was so confusing to be making deals and bargaining with the enemy. I'm happy to be out of that scene where anything goes and people do what they want, not caring about who is around or who they hurt. Today, I'm serving the master, Jesus Christ, the only wise God of my understanding. I'm still on the battlefield. I'm still standing. My family and I stand on Jesus Christ.

Psalm 24:7-10 says, "Lift up your heads, O ye gates: and be ye lift up, ye everlasting doors: and the King of glory shall come in. Who is the King of glory? The Lord strong and mighty, the Lord mighty in battle. Lift up your heads, O ye gates: even lift them up, ye everlasting doors, and the King of glory shall come in. Who is the King of glory? The Lord of hosts, he is the King of glory. Selah."

Jesus Christ also said in John 12:32, "And if I be lifted up from the earth, I will draw all men unto me."

These scriptures helped me realize that once I continue to serve Jesus Christ, it's not only about me. I can help someone out in my wife's family, my family, and our friends that don't understand the word of God. I can help the men in her family, and she can help the women in my family and vice versa. We can help our friends and co-workers get closer to God. I never thought that I would be on that level. God will do it for you. Won't He do it? He did it for me, and He will do it for you if you continue to seek His face. We need to work harder at bringing people back into the church. Many people have strayed away from the church because of the lack of God being presented in the church. Some sin hasn't been dealt with properly or at all. There is a history of people acting like there is nothing wrong. They don't say anything, turn the cheek, and say nothing.

We can't continue to look ahead without looking at the fact that people are not happy with what we are doing in the church. Women are dressing seductively in the church. Men are into shining for themselves and not for the Lord. I hope that we get a hold of what the message of God is supposed to be. I know that there are some great pastors and bishops. I don't condone being self-centered because many people are looking up to you and they need your help. They want to talk to a messenger of God. They want you to help them. I will never forget that for Christ I live, for Christ I will die because I'm fully persuaded. God is 'training' me for my next level.

People speak about what is going on in the country today. We need to focus on education, social injustices, voting rights, and civil rights. I received the invitation on my cell phone to attend the minister's luncheon, and my mouth dropped. I thought, "Who sent this to me?" I respect the order of my church. I respect my Bishop Calvin Rice because he can preach and teach God's word with ease. I saw him be playful in the pulpit by joking around and being funny. I want to have a preaching style like that. I love him first as my pastor and my bishop for keeping order in the house of the Lord. One thing you can't forget is First Lady Rice. She has shown me a lot of love and respect. When I first came to our church, I was like a deer in headlights. They accepted me with open arms and didn't even know anything about me. For that, I'm grateful and very blessed to be apart of the ministry. Several months later, after the luncheon, I got a call that changed my life forever.

My Cat Syrus

Left to Right: Gary ,Robert,Christine,Tim,Kathy,Greg

Jerome's grandma Alma in the middle. Front row (left to right): Mitchell, Aunt pinky, Grandma Alma, Thomas. Back Row (left to right): Clarence, Judge, John, Joe, Fred, Winston.

(Left to Right): Jerome's older sisters: Geraldine and Christine

(Left to right): Christine, Ted, Geraldine

CHAPTER 22

Basketball Hall Of Fame

I got a call from a family member saying, "There is someone in Evansville starting a Basketball Hall of Fame roster, and he is trying to get donations to get a museum erected." I asked who and when I found out, I was shocked. His father coached me at Harwood Elementary back in 1980 and 1981. I got his phone number and called him. It was a sure thing. He asked, "Where is your brother?" I told him that he was away right now, but he is okay. I felt terrible trying to say to him that he was in jail. I couldn't bring myself to that because I wanted him to come with me to the ceremony. After calling Tim, I listened to him. He said, "Do you realize that you were one of the Evansville, Indiana basketball legends?" I felt like I was a long time ago. I felt like it was a bad taste in my mouth for years. I knew that my younger brother and I played. I asked, "What about my younger brother?" He said, "I'm going to induct him into the Basketball Hall of Fame as well."

I was so happy to hear that my brother and I would be inducted on August 11, 2018, in G.E.B.B. Hall of Fame. I knew in June of 2018, and I was anticipating it. Once I found out that my brother and I were being inducted into the Evansville Basketball Hall of Fame, I immediately started to thank God. I was so happy to be a part of something special. I called my older brothers and sisters. I told them what was going on. They were excited and was happy for us. I believe that everyone's question was, "Why did they wait so long to acknowledge us?" We realized that we had been out of High School for over 30 years. Why now? I thought, "Well my brother isn't going to be there. Why should I even go?" I was bothered by that.

We need to allow God to do what He needs to do and stop questioning everything. I'm learning how not to question everything that comes my way. Some things are questionable. But this ceremony and induction are valid. I looked back on all the years all my brothers and I were playing in the snow and rain. Even when it was too hot outside, we played basketball when we weren't in the hood. In other words, we played on other people's playgrounds and turf. We played our hearts out on the weekdays and weekends. We know so much about basketball that my brothers and I can be great coaches. We know defensive schemes like the 2-1-2 defense. We know the 1-2-2 defense. We know the trap defense, all kinds of zone defenses, man to man offenses and defenses, all the out of bounds plays, and the double stack offense. When you are the point guard, you bring the ball up the floor. You set a pick after passing the ball to your shooting guard so he can get open. If he doesn't have a shot, you reset back to the point guard. Set a pick for the small forward. If he doesn't have a shot, you reset it up to the power forward and center. Penetrate inside to draw fouls to get the opponent in foul trouble so you can take over the ball game and win the game for your team. Play as a team. We win as a team.

These were games early on in my career in Biddy basketball and A.A.U. I would score 40 to 50 points as when I was 13 or 14 years old. I started dribbling the ball. I was just that type to always have a ball in my hand. The texture I felt grabbed me, and I would pound it on the court and pavement. I even slept with my basketball. We were married for a while until God said, "No. I'm Your first love." I truly believe that God allowed me to play basketball to get to him. It was what I wanted to do. When I was in the car wreck with my brother-in-law, I had no choice but to live because I was interested in playing basketball before and after the incident. I had to work harder to get my body back in playing shape because of the accident. I had to learn how to walk and talk again. I was in bad shape until I decided I wanted to live again.

God will fight your battles. He will help you in all types of ways. He did it for me because I knew without a doubt, He blessed me with the anointing to do some great things for Him. The Lord will heal your broken heart. He will help you with pain and suffering. He will allow you to get yourself together so you can be of service in His ministries. He has shown me many things that made my head spin. I saw some things that made me think how this happened. I have been through my hell, but sometimes we set ourselves up for things that have nothing to do with God. I used basketball as a tool to further my endeavors in the sport. I didn't go as far as I would have liked to go, but I still was recognized for it years later. We never know who, how, or when you're going to be honored.

I knew that it was God who allowed this to happen. I had forgotten what I did for sports in my hometown. To be honored as one of the legends there is a blessing. Thank you, Lord. Not only that but I owe God. I appreciate all the coaches in Evansville Aces and Mini Aces. I played for many different teams and met different players. I played for the Indiana All-Stars and the McDonald's All-American teams. Many of the guys I played with played for several N.B.A. teams. What I love about the game is that the coaches took care of the players when they have done an excellent job on the court. They take them out to dinner. Certain functions went on that not too many other teammates may have known about. There were parties, and when some shoes came in, I would get two pairs instead of one. I had the first shoe called the "Top Ten Addidas" that came out in my school and community. I had a pair of blue and white shoes and a pair of red and white ones. The Executive Director of H.O.F. said to me, "Do you remember being the first player in the school to have those shoes?" I thought for a moment and said, "Yes."

There were many players from different teams in the area and my teammates asked, "Hey Jerome, where did you get those shoes from?" Then they were ordering those shoes left and right.

I had all kinds of shoes to play in. Once I had 30 pairs of basketball shoes. I had Adidas, Nike, Reebok, Converse, and Puma. I was very grateful to God. The best shoe I ever had was a regular pair of Nike shoes that I played the entire game and scored 40 points. My feet never hurt in them. Every other shoe that I had felt great once I put them on and they were the right size shoes.

I never understood the shoes because they were never tight or never too big. I thought that it was the material or the heels on the bottom of the shoe. I wore those Nike shoes out until it fell apart. The second good pair were Reeboks that were grey and blue. I still have them today. I have had them now for ten years. They never hurt my feet and are worn out. I call them my fishing and everyday shoes. I don't care what anyone says, I'm going to keep my special shoes. Someone can say, "Throw them away. They are old." I will say, "Mind your business. My feet are comfortable in them." A shoe tells a lot about a person's style, brand, and design. I knew that I was going to make it in college and pros.

Reminiscing about it, I had many opportunities. I was around the right people, and it seemed like all the things I did wasn't good enough. I begin to get down on myself. I asked God to help me as I was coming out of High School. I went to Junior College in Illinois. I knew that it was over because I was winding down my basketball career. I had fun, and I will never forget the people that I came across. Many of the people that I came across weren't Christians. I knew that some of them were Christians. One thing I never tried to do is push my agenda on someone else. I prayed for them. I knew that I was a sinner saved by God's grace and mercy. I played basketball because it was fun, and it allowed me to escape reality. I never really tried to make it a career until I got past high school. I said to God, "Whatever it is in Your will for me to do. I will do it." I owe the rest of my life to the Lord Jesus Christ.

Today I'm a minister at a great church. It is not easy serving the Lord. There will be people that call on you to do things like pray for them and counsel them. Once, a man called me to talk about his bad marriage that he didn't know what to do with. I have been involved in funerals and many other things. I learned that you must be patient. Allow God to help you navigate with some seasoned ministers, pastors, and bishops who can help you be prepared in season and out of season. There are many things in ministry that I don't understand.

I have been speaking to God on things like starting a basketball ministry in 20 to 40 churches in the New York area. There will be a start roster for "MINISTER JEROME MERIWEATHER BASKETBALL CAMP OR THE MINISTER JEROME MERIWEATHER BASKETBALL HALL OF FAME CAMP." I desire to start a feeder school who can recruit some Christian athletes from our churches and colleges. There are many things that we can do. It would be for girls and boys. God has given me a gift. I want to give back to the community and the kids. I hope that I will get the opportunity because I want to become a basketball coach some day.

I see coaches on T.V. coaching the players. I would often say to myself that I wish I could coach as they do. Coaching is a gift from God. You must be interested in people, and you must be a people person. I truly believe that my calling is in ministry. I truly believe that God called me to coach some young men the game of basketball and life skills from His church ministries. I talked to people about going to the next level. I want the right coaches and assistants (ex-NBA players or ex-college ballplayers) to run the organization from a Biblical perspective. The future of basketball for African Americans looks great because if they don't make it in sports, they need to be told the truth about having basketball as a springboard to getting a college degree so they could make it in another profession. They could make it in business administration from a college scholarship using the sport to advance them to a college degree. There are many ways to go, but the right way is Jesus Christ. Some of our young people are misrepresented by things like rap music, fashion, and clothing. They are not thinking about their future. They don't realize that there are not that many artists that make it in rap or fashion. There are many pitfalls, and the greatest inspiration from a pitfall is God. He will protect and provide for you. He will guide you into your profession.

Don't expect anyone to do it for you. I had to pay for my wedding, classes at New York Theological Seminary, my daughter's child support, and rent where I live. I had to pay for many things and always will. Some things I will never have to pay such as my salvation that God has given me. He will provide you with all that you need and more. He makes no mistakes. He will let you know who to deal with and who let go out of your life. Recently, I heard someone say, "Picture a rocket flying high into space. The higher the Rocket goes before it enters space, the more rocket boosters that will fall off the rocket on the way up." It's just like people in your life: they are there for a season. When you climb higher, they disappear out of your life. Some people are not going where God is taking you. Some people are in your life as an opportunist. It appears that they want to be with you, but all they are looking for is accolades and validation in ministries.

All I wanted to do was to serve and stay in my lane. God has blessed me with the gifts and anointing to show the world that He has put me in a God-fearing church with God-fearing people. We are not perfect. God has given us a new life and beginning. We stopped thinking that we can do it alone. We stopped fighting God. We stopped lying, cheating, and living anyway. Thank you, God, for saving my life. I see clearly now. God has changed our lives. Had we kept on doing our own thing, we wouldn't be here to tell. I don't deserve His blessings, but I see it His way. All the things that happened to me, I deserved because God gave us dominion over everything if we are doing His will. Everyone should know that God is the only way. Don't believe in any other religion because they create false gods that will lead you from the truth.

There is only one way to the father. That is Jesus Christ who is our petitioner to God. God allows Jesus Christ and the Holy Spirit to grant us our petitions while we are here on earth. I believe totally in Father, Son, and the Holy Spirit. The Old Testament has great meaning, and it will always be a serious part of the "Torah" or the law. I understand that the New Testament is about grace and mercy. People are starting to understand that there are God, Jesus Christ, and Acts. The Holy Spirit cannot be left out. I know that all my gifts and talents that God has blessed me with are from Him and Him only. I know He blessed my parents with gifts and talents that I have inherited. One of my dreams is to play the piano and organ like my mother did. I also want to be involved in many other things as I continue my journey with the Lord. I'm sure that God will direct my path into many other things, but for now, I'm content with what He has done in my life. I was not myself years ago, and I couldn't stop doing what I wanted to do until He released me from Satan.

I haven't forgotten where I came from because my parents taught me how to live for God. I believed that I had to walk into my destiny as I went through life. I tried to play ball. One thing I never really tried to do is please my parents because they allowed me, my brothers, and sisters to make mistakes as we went through our lives. They knew that we were going to make them. I tried to be the bright one. I realized that all I was doing was spinning my wheels. I was doing just as bad as my brothers were. There is nothing righteous about us. No matter how much I tried to impress people on the basketball court, I was still feeling empty inside.

I remember there was a pizza shop owner who sponsored us. He was a nice white man who respected us and our families. His business was in our community, and he made most of his money off black families. He didn't just help the families in the hood, he helped many other people. He used to invite us after games. 'Deke' was my nickname. He said, "Deke, you guys played a heck of a ball game. Come to my pizza shop. Get any size pizza that you want at any given time." I could come after a game or when there no games. I thought, "Who gave me that right of passage? Did God tell him that? Was I that good that he had given my teammates and me that much of a privilege to be able to get what we wanted?" I remember ordering two large pizzas. They were awesome because of the green peppers. I would go home and eat one of them. Then I would eat the other pizza the next night or a couple of days later. I thanked him for that because he didn't have to do that. The pizza shop owner never asked us for a dime. He came to the games, and his daughter was a cheerleader. When she graduated, he still was giving the athletes food and whatever else they needed. That's the kind of person he was. His wife and kids were some very nice people inside and out.

Another person was my first coach, Mr. Barclay. He was inspirational in my basketball skills and taught me the fundamentals of it. He taught me how to dribble the ball with my head up. If you feel the ball on your fingertips and palm, you still can control the ball. Don't look down. I practiced for months to be able to dribble the ball behind my back without looking around. He also taught me that family was very important. He told me about his brother getting into trouble and how much it affected him and his family. I prayed for him because he wasn't just my coach, he was my history teacher as well. I respected him.

He took me over his house to meet his family, and I was shocked at what I saw. We drove up to his home. It was a huge red trim and white house that had four bedrooms and two baths. It had a nice size picket fence. My jaw dropped when we went inside. I met his wife and kids. I knew that we were friends. He let me know where we stood as far as what he expected of me and what my role as a leader. Sometimes as a leader, we must work harder than most people and do more than your peers expect you to do. I know that many of us want to be recognized for what we do. Coach Barclay taught me how to continue to lead on and off the basketball court.

Coach Turpin taught me how to lead by example and be a leader in the classroom. He asked, "How are you doing in class and is there anything you don't know about? I can help you." He was another coach that was concerned about my destiny. Coach Paddock was my other coach, and he was another person who allowed me to be free on the basketball court and in life. They knew my ups and downs. They were always there for me no matter what the circumstances were. They looked me in my eyes and told me the truth just like my father did. Coach Paddock gave me a lot and helped me out a lot in so many areas in my life. He took me on trips that I will always cherish. I was like one of his kids, and they treated me like family. He had one son and two beautiful daughters around me all the time in the summer and winter during practice or family dinners. I was so happy to be a family friend. I owe a lot to them. He has contributed to me becoming a minister and becoming a basketball Hall of Fame Inductee. I want to thank all my teammates from all teams: Barry Paddock Jr., Benjamin Garland, Barry Cato, Kelly Cato, Darren Cato, Mike Davis, David Snaden, James Fellows, James Jordan, Jeff Thomas, Barry Johnson, Robert Calhoun, Evie Waddell, and Mark Freels.

I'd like to thank Coach Joseph Mullan who was my high school coach. He lives in Phoenix, Arizona with his wife. Thank you, Coach Mullan, for all you did for me and my brother Tim. There were times where we disagreed on some occasions. He was there when no one else believed in us. He stood by us and with us. Coach Richard Risemus was my coach in my freshman year at Memorial High School. Don Mattingly went to the same high school. I went there for one semester, and I smelled success. I saw first hand where people make the cut, or they move up or move out. Coach Risemus told me that I was going to start on the varsity team. I knew that was the biggest mistake I had ever made in my life. I knew that if I stayed at Memorial, I would have ended up at Notre Dame or another Ivy League school. It just wasn't who I was, so I went back to my original self. I was given an option to stay in the Catholic High school or go back to public school and be the Protestant young man that I am. I knew it was the right thing to do. I went back to my roots. I still wasn't going to be happy until I had to be back to where God wanted me to be. That is why I couldn't see myself going to a Catholic church and attending a Catholic high school or college. I went back my freshman year and finished my school year at Bosse High School because I knew that was where I belonged. God still blessed me for it. God was there the whole time making sure that I was where I belonged. I didn't feel right there because there was a certain type of aura that was there and as far as religion. I felt out of place because I wasn't a practicing Catholic. I didn't know anything about Catholic churches. Knowing what I know about the Catholic church now, I'm so glad I decided to go back to where I belonged because I would have made a religious mistake.

On the other hand, I would have probably had a better position in as far as me getting a better education and job. I realized that my faith in God had always been upfront and not placed somewhere else as far as my priorities were concerned. The thing that I didn't like is the secretive ways that they went about doing things. Many people would know about what was going on about sin. I was only 14 years old at the time, and I had enough sense to sit down with my parents to look at the truth for what it is. I thank the Lord for His direction. I thanked my parents for allowing me to see the "truth." God will move you past all the things that you didn't see coming. He guided me in the right direction because God honored me in the first place. I want to thank Memorial for having me on board for three months, and I thank them for accepting the fact that I had to go. God didn't want me there to play basketball. That's why they recruited me in the first place.

Other than the perks, players do not need to cheat themselves when it comes to being recruited out of grade school in team sports. I would advise them to look at the big picture first. Look at their faith in God first and foremost. Everything comes with a price to pay. You must live with the decision you have made. I did. I hope that in life God will come first because if he doesn't, you need to check your motives. I look at athletes today, and they sign big contracts. Some of them are just good players and serve God. Some of them their money is their god, and they fall after they retire. I heard a story where this basketball player played 14 years in the N.B.A. and made over 100 million over his career. Another player had made over 150 million in a 17-year career. Both are now broke and just surviving until they are old enough to receive their N.B.A. pensions. I pray for them because had they trusted the Lord; they would not be in this position today. They wouldn't be dealing with bad investments and bad agents telling them to do things that cost them their wealth so they can benefit from their contracts.

I heard so many stories about things that have happened to people. I prayed to the Lord for His covering over any business decisions or contract decisions that are coming my way. When I start feeling that God is tugging on my heart about something, immediately I tell my wife. We sit down and talk about it. I waste no time in making sure we benefit as a couple. I will always be in tune with what the Holy Spirit is saying to me in our lives. We must act upon what it is He is conveying to us. Sometimes He speeds up the process. For instance, I now have a full load of school and many other things I'm presently doing. At first, I thought it was going to be a bit much. It turns out we are winning.

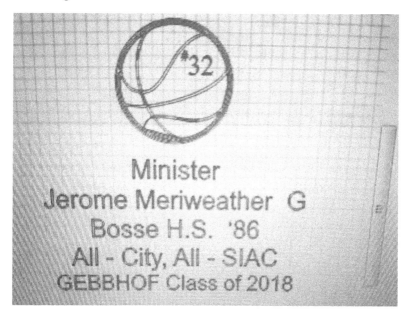

Greater Evansville Basketball Hall Of Fame for Jerome's induction on June 2018

Jerome Meriweather playing at Bosse High School in 1984.

CHAPTER 23

Grandson

My grandson was born on July 27, 2018. When my son sent me a picture of him, I was so blessed. My wife and I were at the New York Yankees game. I decided to go on Facebook LIVE to express how I truly felt. I knew that God did it again. He has blessed my wife and me so much every year. We have some great expectations from the Lord. We want to thank Him for our blessings. My grandson looks just like me but a lighter complexion of me. He is a very handsome, healthy, and strong. Due to my work schedule, I hadn't seen him yet. I will fly to Evansville to see him as soon as I possibly can. He is what I expected as far as what I have seen so far. My son told me he is growing fast.

I told my son when I come, we have to take family pictures together. You never know what tomorrow may bring. It is just the times we are living in. My son told me some things that he wants to do. He said that he wanted to move back to Indianapolis. I told him that I don't blame him because I knew that I had outgrown Evansville and that he can always come back to visit. He said yeah. But I know my son wants to make a move because I know that he doesn't like it there anymore. I told him that I started wanting to move away because I had lost my parents. It seemed like it was a bad thing and it was. I had to figure things out. It took time. But I decided to leave long before I made a move. I knew God was preparing me but what I didn't know was I was going to end up living in New York City. I'm glad that I live here now because of the good things that God promised are happening to me now. I respect the power of God, and His direction is far greater than what I expected. I don't miss some things I use to do when I was there. I don't miss some people places and things. I don't miss hanging out all night. I miss my family, a few friends, and some church friends.

When I was in Evansville, I was living a double life. You can't go into His sanctuary half high or lit and say, "All you have to do is serve the Lord." It is more to it than that. I had to move away because I wasn't happy there anymore. I had run out of options, and now I see my son facing the same thing. It is my job as his dad to tell him to pray and ask God for direction for himself and his family. I know that he will be alright because now God has brought our two sons together with me so we can continue his legacy.

Psalm 78:4 (ESV) says, "We will not hide them from their children, but tell to the coming generation the glorious deeds of the Lord, and his might, and the wonders that he has done."

Psalm 102:18 (ESV) says, "Let this be recorded for a generation to come, so that a people yet to be created may praise the Lord."

Daniel 4:3 (ESV) says, "How great are his signs, how mighty his wonders! His kingdom is an everlasting kingdom, and his dominion endures from generation to generation."

Exodus 34:6-7 (ESV) says, "The Lord passed before him and proclaimed," The Lord, the Lord, a God merciful and gracious, slow to anger, and abounding in steadfast love and faithfulness, keeping steadfast love of thousands, forgiving iniquity and transgression and sin, but who will by no means clear the guilty, visiting the iniquity of the fathers on the children and the children's children, to the third and the fourth generation."

I truly know that God has left me with a legacy. He now has blessed my son and grandson to carry the torch long after I'm gone to Heaven to be with the Lord. I understand that He will protect them and give them the decrees and the covenant. My job is to explain to them that they must go this way and any other way isn't an option. God is number one in my life. Therefore, He must be number one in their lives. No matter how bad things get, they have to know not to allow anyone to cause them to denounce God out of their lives. We must stand on His promises and not be afraid because He will protect us on earth and in death. Death had no "sting" on Him. Death will have no "sting" on me or you.

Joel 2:28 (ESV) says, "and it shall come to pass afterward, that I will pour out my spirit on all flesh; your sons and daughters shall prophesy, your old men shall dream dreams, and your young men shall see visions."

I want my sons and daughters to do what the Lord commands. I want them to realize what God says in the Bible and get the full interpretation. I want them to live by it, teach by it, and preach by it. I want them to tell people about God, save souls, and save lives by the word of God. There are great rewards in the beginning and end. I want God to say at the end of their lives, "Well done thy good and faithful servant."

I can't get over how beautiful my grandkids are. They are healthy, and they are doing great in school. I love my granddaughters even though I'm miles away from them. They are always in my heart. I think about them every day. I want them to do well in school. I will be there for them in whatever capacity that a grandfather can, no matter what the issue or circumstance. I send them Christmas gifts every year, and I see them when I go to Indiana. Time on earth is short. I want them to know that when we see one another, we can take family photos, talk about issues, or things that are bothering them. I don't want them to hold anything back from my wife and me.

We have been through tough times and weathered many storms. Sometimes when your money gets funny, you don't have things you need. You must improvise, eat what you have, and do what you must do to get through the pain of illness or the loss of a loved one. We have to let our legacies know that this too shall pass, God is in control, and not to give up. It took me some time to heal from my old wounds, and it will take others time to heal as well. I fought my way back to Jesus Christ. Many people don't get the chance to fight their way back to God. My grandchildren need to be taught that God will provide their needs according to His riches and glory. It's not about you and me. It's about Jesus Christ and what He is directing them to. My grandkids need to understand that right now they need to be kids and do what is expected of them by their parents. They need to do their school work, keep it simple, enjoy their parents, and their time at home. To my grandchildren, don't step out of your blessings from God and your family for nothing. He said, "Be ye Holy for I am Holy."

I went to see my granddaughters last year, and they were so happy to see me. I was happy to see them. I hugged them like it was my last hug that I would give them. I immediately prayed to God for them to be protected, nurtured, and loved by their parents. I also prayed that if things didn't go right in their lives, if they wanted to start over away from something, or if they needed a new beginning they could come to my wife and me and spend time with us in New York. I hoped that no matter what they are going through, the matter would be addressed before it gets out of hand.

When I visited, my youngest granddaughter didn't want to let me go. She held me so tight that she didn't want me to leave. I tried to give her back to my son, but she still hung on to my shirt. That was a sign from God that she not only loves me, but she knows that God is in me. That was a powerful scene.

My brother was messed up over that. It affected him to see my grandbaby hug me like that. Jesus Christ has His hand in that. I was shocked because it was the first time that I laid eyes on my grandbaby. My wife and I looked at each other and were very shocked that she did that. We were so happy to be in their lives. I reached into my wallet and gave them a few dollars. We left there just thinking about all the fun we had and the love that my wife and I received from our grandchildren. Seeing all of them together was very special.

I want to take pictures with my son, daughter, and all my grandchildren. I hope to have that done as soon as possible. I want to see them all together in one setting and to see how they all get along. I want to take them to meet all their aunts, uncles, cousins, and everybody in my family. I don't live there anymore, so it's kind of hard for them to get to know everybody. I want to sit down one day and tell them about their grandparents and their great grandparents. There will come a day when that will happen. I can't wait to see if some of the things like character traits and attitudes that I see in myself will be in them. My son and grandson automatically have my character traits because I see them already. I want them to have Jesus Christ in their lives and I want all my kids to serve God. I don't care how they feel or what they think. Don't dispute what God can do for you in your life. I know that I can't push that on them. At least I can give them the road map to God. I want us to sit down and eat dinner to have this conversation. Even if we are going fishing, golfing, or at home, we can start the conversation at breakfast in the morning. It doesn't matter. You must catch them while they are young. If they get away from you while they are young, they may never believe that there is God. I truly believe that my son will carry the torch when I do leave this earth.

I know that if I'm alive that my son will tell my grandson about Jesus Christ. I asked God to allow my generation of sons and daughters to continue to serve God without a shadow of doubt. That is very important. There are lots of youth at my church. I want my grandson to be involved in church at an early age. I want God to allow him to carry the mantle where I will be able to teach him and move out of the way and be comfortable with my son and grandson leading people to Jesus Christ. I will give them my blessing because my dad gave me his blessing from the Lord before he passed away. I thank God, Rev. Judge L. Meriweather and Anna L. Meriweather for giving me the opportunities that I have today. It is a generational change in ministries because my parents did outreach and missionary ministry for years. They did it on an international level and domestically. For me to carry that mantle is a blessing from God. I want to hand it down to responsible family members who know the importance of serving God. One day, I will tell my sons that when God blesses you in return pay it forward to bless someone else. I want my daughters to do the same. I want them to know the word of God and to be able to expound on His word without hesitation or doubt. Don't let anyone make you feel like you don't know what you are talking about because of their belief system.

I came to realize and know if all else fails, I will not walk away from my God who has been in my life since I was born. He knew that I was going to be a minister before I did. He knew that I was going to do many great things. He knew that when the torch was passed to me that I was going to one day pass it to the ones who need a Saviour. I knew that I needed God early in my life because He knew that sin was upon me. I didn't stand a chance because it seemed like every thought as a youngster was about doing wrong and being contrary. It felt good to be able to get away with some of that stuff. It will catch up to you. It was time to give it all up, and I did. I wanted a better life. I moved away from Evansville, Indiana which will always be my home. God has blessed me with a new home. I said yes to His calling on my life. I take no credit for what God has done in me and for me. I look back on my 50 years of life here on earth, and all the things that I have been through and I see where I'm at now.

I cry because it wasn't me. He has done many things to turn my life around. He has taken many desires and urges. He has washed me in His blood and washed me white as snow. I have no regrets, no bad feelings, or no worries. I prioritize my ministry, my wife, my family, my finances, my home, and everything. God must be in every decision that my wife and I make from this point on. What a great way to serve God when you have good moral character and judgment. You can't make people happy, and I realize that. The only wise God can do that for them. I can't because you can preach until 'cows come home'. People don't want to change until they get ready. There is always some dispute when it comes to Jesus. I waivered before because of my unbelief.

I had to know for myself who Jesus was and is. After my parents passed away, I had to do some soul searching for myself. I questioned God, and I said to myself that the only way to find out is through reading His word. I still had some doubts. Finally, I said, "Lord, show me who you are? Reveal to me what you want from me?" He will show you who He is. I was very impressed that He showed me. No man can show me. What He has done for me, no man can do for me. Today, He has done more for me than what I have done for myself. That is so powerful. People need to wake up and know that we serve a God of blessings and a God of love. I praise the Lord no matter what I'm going through. It's a lifestyle and the only way for my family. I had a smile on my face ever since I knew that God had given me my grandson and my daughter back all in 2018. I am at peace now with God because of His mercy. I will honor Him and His plan forever. If you would have told me that I would be getting all these blessings from God all in one year, I would have told you that it is impossible. But we know that He makes the impossible possible.

I want to thank my son's fiancé for blessing me with grandchildren. I have never talked to her face to face too much because I haven't had the chance. I know that my son loves her, and he did tell me that he wants to marry her. He has my blessing if they continue to serve the Lord. They seem to be happy with one another. I know how it is when you are first starting out, and you don't have all you need. Your money is a little funny. They are trying to make ends meet, and occasionally, I have to help out. That is what I'm here for. I want them to make it and not struggle like I did. I truly believe that every parent wants their children to have it better than they did. That's how I feel about all of them. I want them to be successful in God, spiritually, financially, health wise, and in all areas that God has for them.

I'm a firm believer in what God has for all the young generation. They are our future. When you have made an impact on someone's life, it is a beautiful thing. The thing is to continue making an impact on other people's lives for the Lord. It will never go unnoticed because it is designed to build God's Kingdom. Just like now, "My Baby Boy" is four months old today. I got to get to Evansville to do my baby dedication for him and his entire family. I want their names to be in the Lamb's Book of Life. I want to hear their names called after the trumpet sounds. I know that God is powerful, and He will do more for them than I can do. On everything, I want to hear all our names called on the day of Jesus Christ's second coming.

It can happen at any time because of the way the world is and all the sin. The violence and sin are so out of control; it is unbelievable. People are murdering one another. People are hurting each other and unforgiving. Sexual sin is at an all-time high. Drugs are so easy to get, and our children are at risk. I pray to God for my babies. I want them to say "No." I want them to recognize the danger and move away from it immediately. I want them to have Christian friends and friends that when they see something, they say something. They are not afraid to stand up for themselves and others. I realize that things are going on inside and outside the church. You have got to call it as you see it. There is a code of ethics to abide by but once those ethics are broken, you must address the situation accordingly. I have witnessed wrongdoing in ministry before. You are just as bad as the person who commits the crime when you don't say anything, and you knew about it.

That is why I learn how to do what's right, so my wife and I can not only have a successful marriage, but to have the Lord move us in the direction so we can continue to be successful in our jobs. God comes first in my household. We have a limited amount of friends. I'm not too friendly with people I don't know. It is not worth it to be involved with people who don't have our best interests. If you don't talk to me, that's okay. If we are serving the same God and you don't speak to me then who are you serving? I speak no matter what, and I love you no matter what. God commands me to love you. I love God and hatred doesn't live in me. I want my grandson to know when he is old enough to understand the difference between loving people God's way instead of loving them his way. I know it is a long way off, but he will come to know that God will use him for His glory. I charge God to him right now to direct his path and claim the rights to my son and grandson.

"Lord, you have the covenant and decree on their lives. Lord, use them for generations to come and allow them to continue to serve you. Bless them in all that they do and protect them from danger. Show them in your visions and dreams what you want them to do. Lord, bless their homes and their children's children for generations. Give them your riches, Oh God. Separate them from their enemies. Carve out a huge plot of land for them, Oh Lord, so they can dwell there. I pray that they have festivities to serve you and their families have churches on the land that you blessed them with. May the land be rich with soil so they can tilt it and spring forth crops. Bless others with their land and not to use up all the land for future reasons such as being to lay to rest or to leave it barren for future reasons for the family."

(Grandson) Jerome Darnell lll

Jerome Jr. (Son) and (Grandson) Jerome Darnell lll

CHAPTER 24

New York Seminary

I started N.Y.T.S. on September 6, 2018. I enrolled in the fall semester, and it has been one of my greatest accomplishments. I enrolled in 2014 but didn't finish or go all the way. I got hurt on the job during 2014 and had a slight setback. Now that I'm back, God has commissioned me to go all the way until I finish the Certificate Program. From there I plan to enroll in C.N.R. and get my Ministry and Communication Degree. Then I will go back to N.Y.T.S. and go into the Master of Divinity Program. Afterward, I will go to the Doctorate Degree Program from there and finish unto God of completion of His assignment for me.

I have dreams and goals, but more importantly, Jesus Christ is all I have. We will always have because no one or nobody will stand in the gap for us but Christ. He has me focused on Him.

He has given me an assignment at my church. It may feel like I'm protecting people and the congregation. God has spoken to me that there is a great reward in protecting His flock. You must protect them all the way, not when you feel like it. He also allows me to protect people from my job. I protect my home, my wife, my Bishop and everybody in our class. I want to protect my children and grandchildren, but I ask the Great Lord God Almighty to cover them daily and to wrap His arms around them and keep them safe.

On the first day of my class, I was happy sitting in the classroom with other students. It is a small class of only eight people. I like my professors. They are teaching us "Old Testament," and the other class is "Biblical Exegesis." The classes are on Tuesday and Thursday nights. There are three men and five women in the class. I learned something new in the class: it was in the "ANTIOCH" Church that we were first called Christians.

I'm very glad to be around them because they bring a lot of knowledge to the table when it comes to learning from one another. I get a kick out of that. They are very smart and intelligent with who God is. I learned something in class, and that is when you are watching people speak and talk about God, you must, first of all, see God in them. I saw God speak through them. One day we had an assignment where we all had to pick a prophet out of all the major and minor Prophets. I picked Jeremiah the Weeping Prophet. I stood up and went over the time limit. They said, "You were long-winded, and we felt like it was a sermon instead of an assignment talking about Jeremiah being a weeping prophet. But that's okay. When I got to my seat to sit down, and I thought about it, they were right because it was supposed to be a presentation.

One of the students said something to me. She whispered, "You are an orator." The professor said, "What did you say?" She repeated it and said I was an orator. I just took it as a compliment because I went all into Jeremiah's history. He was preaching for 40 years, and nobody was listening to him except his scribes. It must have been painful for him to be in Jerusalem at that time where people were sinning and not caring about what he was saying. He had to have had a close relationship with God to have gone that long without getting people to stop sinning. Just like today, people have false gods. Back then they had gods that were murdering and killing children. It affected him. Prophets back then had a meaningful task. They were ordered to do more and be subjected to more scrutiny if they didn't follow through with their calling.

I get off work, and I go straight to class. Sometimes I get off at 5:30 p.m. and I catch the train to get to class. I switch to two different trains. Sometimes I am tired, and other times I can't wait to get there. Once I get there, the Holy Spirit is glowing in the room. I see angels hovering in the room. I often wonder if my classmates see them. It's almost scary because I don't want to freak them out because there are certain things that God will allow me to see. There are spiritual gifts. I know that God has opened the door to blessings that we don't know about yet. I heard some of the students in my class say that they want to further their education well after these certification classes are over.

I plan to go to Rosa Parks College because I like the civil rights and injustices that God has called me to deal with. Rosa Parks stood up and said no when asked to go to the back of the bus. She moved me because she wasn't scared. I knew that the civil rights movement was going to be on my radar. I recently went to the luncheon and met two civil rights icons. I know that God will put you with people, develop you, and train you into what needs to be said and done. It's one thing to know your calling, it's another thing to know how to operate in your gifts and talents. When God calls you out in front and moves you up, it's time to stand up and rise. Just say, "Here I am Lord. What must I do for you Father?" When he anoints you there is no turning back. There is nothing no one can say or do at that point. You don't need anyone to validate you when God calls you where you need to be and what your assignment is.

Do God's will, not your will nor anybody else's will. Let His will be done in your life. I had been to several bible colleges in the past in different states, and I have never been to one like this one. This is hands-on, and I had to buy my books. When I started class this semester, I had no books, so I sat in class for almost three weeks without them. I just ordered and waited for them to come in. I still went to class because I had already paid for them. There was a commitment that I had made before God that I would complete this certificate program. I want it more than I ever did now. I believe that the effort is made in the class and finishing, but the vision is made with God starting and completing what I started. I am learning all that I can with every fiber of my being in season and out of season. I understand the office and the legacy that God has given me to take it seriously and move forward searching for what He wants me to do.

I know that many of us don't know our calling because some of us allowed folks to tell us what to do. Pray and ask God to show you. Ask Him always to order your steps. I prayed for God to order my steps in seminary and at the church to see if He wants me to move on. I said, "Dear Lord God order my beginning and my ending of my life. I belong to You, and I need You to tell me where you want me." If you are out of order with Him, He will let you know. You may have to start all over just right where you are. He might do you as He did me which is moving you on down the road to something better. If you had told me that God was going to pull me out of a drug program and allow me to become a licensed minister, I would have told you you're dreaming and crazy.

1 Corinthians 1:27- 31 says, "But God hath chosen the foolish things of the world to confound the wise; and God hath chosen the weak things of the world to confound the things which are mighty; And base things of the world, and things which are despised, hath God chosen, yea, and things which are not, to bring to nought things that are: That no flesh should glory in his presence. But of him are ye in Christ Jesus, who of God is made unto us wisdom, and righteousness, and sanctification, and redemption: That, according as it is written, He that glorieth, let him glory in the Lord."

When I read these scriptures, I knew I wasn't any good. I also knew that we are some very fickle people. We are hard-headed and driven by secrecy, deceit, and foul at the same time. I knew I was going to hell in a handbasket. I knew what I was without Jesus Christ. I wasn't concerned the least bit about someone else's downfall because I knew I had to fix me first. It took a while, but once He fixes your problem, there is still some stuff that you can see about yourself that needs to be taken care of. I did not want to rely on my family for anything: money, advice, or phone calls. I had been down that road before. What I ask God to do for me, He did it. God allowed me to trust in Him for all of my needs. He did it without me doing a thing but thanking Him daily and doing what I'm supposed to do.

He also has me watching my level of comfort. When you relax and fall back into the idle time, be careful. I do not take many vacations and go to places because someone asks me to go. We have to question doing what people want us to do. It's okay to take vacations every once and awhile, but do not mix God's business with pleasure. The two have to be separated from the other. For example, when I was living in Los Angeles, California, I went into an acting school. God spoke to me, "I brought you here to go to Bible College. I didn't bring you here to become an actor."

I was so glad that He reminded me of what my purpose was when I was living in California because I wanted to get involved in some things that had nothing to do with ministry. For one thing, I wasn't ready to get into that kind of field. I was just a few months into the California Seminary. I had an awesome time when I was there. I graduated and that was one of my greatest accomplishments. The difference between the New York Seminary and the California Seminary is the New York

Seminary produces authors and theologians. The California Seminary are more hands-on when it comes to missionaries and outreach ministries. We traveled a lot when I was in the California Ministry. They both teach and preach the Father, Son, and the Holy Spirit. The professors are different as far as their teaching and preaching styles. This provides a diverse way of doing things and thinking. I like change and differences in opinion.

Another thing is the students that were going to the California Seminary were from Mexico or Asia. The students enrolled in the classes at the New York Seminary are from West India, Jamaica, or Haiti. I welcomed all nationalities because I know that God loves us all. There is no doubt in my mind that I went to both schools because God ordained me to go to those seminaries. I have learned so much about people from all parts of the world. Because of Jesus Christ and the relationship that I have with Him, I have friends from all over the world. They are from different countries like Africa, the Philippines, the Bahamas, Haiti, and many other places. I say, "Lord thank you for expanding my territory. Thank you, Lord, for calvary and your long-suffering because I know that I couldn't have done it."

I paid $350.00 for half the semester, and I was enjoying my classes. I saw all the authors who wrote the books that we had to buy for our classes. I immediately understood that this was the place I wanted to continue to be because I wanted to become a writer/author. Then fate happened to me, and I had to put classes off until now. I had to pay $740.00 per semester and start thinking that when I was in my sin, I would pay more for all the sins I was doing. I was thinking why not pay for my classes and my books altogether. It totaled up to about 800.00 once I ordered my books for classes.

One other thing was the California Seminary worked out of workbooks instead of authors and biblical geography. In California, I had more African American students that were in my class than African American faculty and professors. One thing I learned about people is they view God differently than what other races do. They don't feel the same about Jesus Christ as people of the church do. They have differences in opinions and different ways of thinking. I respect all that. One needs to know the truth about God.

Some people believe that there are many ways to the Father. Some people believe that He is just a doorknob. Some people are agnostic, atheist, and don't believe in heaven or hell. They think we are an existing matter or creatures. I think it is dangerous for a person to believe what they want to believe because you leave the door open for heresy. You leave yourself open and vulnerable to the opinions and commentaries of others. Therefore, keep in mind that God's word is the truth. Don't get it twisted because God will straighten you out. Live by the word. God is watching you because He knows all about you.

Believers and non-believers must be prepared on Judgement Day when we stand before God. Your opinion doesn't count when it comes to Him. Some people have been in church for 30 and 40 years. They have sat in the same pew with no change in their heart, mind, and soul for God. They still hate the bishop, the pastor, and everything that is of God. They hide behind church functions and dysfunctional relationships in the church. Something is always wrong when it comes to making decisions and if they're not a part of the plan, they won't participate in anything that God orchestrates. They get jealous of your calling and try to tell you to do something that God didn't tell you to do. Pray for them. Don't push them away. Climb the mountain top with love and peace. God has your back and has no ill will towards them. Don't get distracted because you will lose your blessings from God. Stay focused and march towards the goal as Apostle Paul did.

Go at the pace that God has set. I was in class one time, and I was preparing to take a test. I wasn't ready because every quiz that I took I failed. I just wanted to see how much I knew on my own. The first quiz I got 60% on it. The next five quizzes I got 40% to 50 % on them. We had a final test on all of them combined. Because I studied for the final, I scored 80% on all of them combined. You see it was God who helped me with it. That is a testimony that I share with people. Sometimes to succeed you must fail. Some people didn't pass it. I was trying to show them what to do. I know that everybody doesn't learn the same way. What I did was I looked over the things I already knew, and I chose to pay more attention to the things I didn't know. That is how I passed the test. The more I studied, the more I was familiar with the curriculum. I was always into education and learning since I was a little boy. I liked seeing what kind of classes that was hard. I learned my strengths and weaknesses in what I knew and what I didn't know. I realized that I was good at reading, history, science, and okay in math. But I didn't let it get me down. I only needed a tutor for Geometry in college years ago. I told myself to concentrate on my shortcomings first. I just wanted to learn and be an example by asking the Lord to show me what I needed to do to grow and be successful.

In Seminary, you must have the same but a different type of approach. When I took a test, I told the Lord, "I know a lot about your word. I want not just to pass the test; I want to know the dates and times of every event that took place." I wanted to know the when, where, and why? I wanted to know when He came on the scene and what the people worshiping on the dates, whether it was in B.C. or B.C.E. or A.D. I wanted to learn how to apply God's Word and 'apply' it in school and my life.

It feels good to know a lot about Jesus Christ, but I don't know everything about Him. That is why I stay thirsty and hungry for God because He is not through with me yet. As I continue to go to school, I will grow, learn more, get an education, and hands-on experience to become a Pastor someday. I hope that He will take me where He wants me to go. I hope that I follow Him and the bishop whom He has assigned me too. I realize that there is more to life than seminaries.

God has been speaking to me about taking a trip one day over to Israel. I don't know when my wife and I are going. We may go by ourselves or with a group. I want to go to some places where Jesus Christ traveled, taught, healed the sick, and grew up. I want to be in His presence over there. I want to put that on our 'bucket list'.

I need God all the time and every hour and every day. "Every second and every minute, I need thee. Oh, I need thee." It took me a long time to get to where God had me where He wanted me. I kept hearing stand firm on the word of God, and He will take you where you need to go. He will do what nobody can do for you. I have never been more pleased to serve God with my wife because every Sunday we wake up and say, "Lord, thank you." We get dressed and go to church. We serve Him every day: Saturday through Friday. It's our lifestyle. It's right and productive for us and our marriage.

When you want something bad enough, you will be willing to fight for what is right. I fought because I believed in God and I still believe in God even now more than ever. I will pay for many other classes in the future as I continue to go higher in education and learning. It's not easy, and it's not something you take lightly.

We live in a world where people are just caught up into everything but God. There have been several cases in the past years where several men who were the breadwinners in their families kill their families and then kill themselves or go to prison for the rest of their lives. It's very sad to see something like that. No one deserves to be treated like that. I hope that men and women get along and take their children to church, stay there for the rest of their lives, and serve the Lord instead of doing their own thing. When I did that, I stayed in trouble. I remained confused, and I lied. When I ran out of gas, I ran back to God. I stay drug-free and doing what is right is where I stand. I hope in the future that all seminaries will get more time to teach the people the right way.

God can do what He wants to in anyone's life. It is not easy serving the Lord. Don't give up on yourself, your children, or your family. We all need one another. I know that God has given me no options but to do one thing and that is to serve Him. I told my friends don't ever forget where you come from. I don't care how much you have financially. I don't care how many suits, cars, houses, or friends you have. It's all God's blessings. Allow your spouse, kids, and family to enjoy the fruits of God that He has given you. I realize that God gives, and He can and will take it away in any shape form or fashion. The other semesters at the New York Seminary starts in the spring. I'm looking forward to growing with God. I don't want to rush the semester because I think that the Lord is doing some changing in me that needs to be discovered. I don't want to think that I'm above or beyond anyone. I have seen people make that mistake and miss what He is doing in their lives.

I was sitting in class one day, and I sat by someone who has a lot of knowledge in Jesus Christ and wisdom but lacked the understanding in Jesus Christ. As a student I know without a doubt to have all three is very important. I was like that because I knew that knowledge is power, wisdom sets you apart, but if you don't understand how to fight with God's word, you'll fight in the flesh. Instead of fighting with your tongue, you'll fight with your fist. It's not good. I can disagree with you but don't have an ax to grind.

Just because you know something, it's good to keep your mouth shut sometimes and listen. I find myself doing it quite often. Somethings in the classroom, house, or job don't need to be said. There is a time and place for everything. I had to tone it down and ask God to fix my tongue. God doesn't want you to be mute or dumb. He wants us to do things in decency and order. I knew that one day I was going to get it together. I have come a long way. I desire to continue in God's word by preaching and teaching it wherever He wants me too. I want to continue in my education on Biblical Studies in whatever type of capacity: in school, college, or hands-on. As Christians, we make things difficult on ourselves by trying to figure out God daily. We need to study His word forever because I find out new insights and new meanings to what He is speaking to us. He doesn't always speak the same language. He speaks to us and through us differently. He uses people to talk to us. Just like in the Bible He used animals to speak to us, He can use many things, people, and objects to speak through and to us.

I have been blown away on my journey. I want to go all the way to see what the end is going to be. Just like the song says, "To see what end is going to be." I love church hymns, songs, and dances. It's our culture, and it's always progressing to be more creative.

God must be first in advancing the church. People always want to look at what's wrong in the church and seminary. We need to focus on the ones who paved the way. Then look at the leaders and take God's word to a new level. Keep the vision and move it forward. Let God's vision be your vision. Don't let your vision be God's vision. It won't work. Trust me. No matter how bad you want to be a pastor, teacher, bishop, evangelist, or prophet from the five-fold ministry, focus on God's vision. Many people have come to the ranks and stepped down because they weren't where God called them. They put themselves there, and they were told to go where someone else told them to go. Listening to someone else calling you from God is dangerous. You never grow that way. You stay stagnant, and you never can get what God has called you to do.

I know my calling. It is to proclaim the word of God to those who are poor, the sick, and have life-controlling problems like drugs, alcohol, prostitution, liars, thieves, murderers. Know your calling and quit trying to fix someone else. Fix yourself and apply God's Word through application. Then help others heal and through prayer and supplication. I saw my mother knelt next to her bed every night. I will never forget that. Thanks, MOM!!

I plan to finish New York Seminary in 2020 and then go on to further my God-given education for a Bachelor's Degree in Ministry in Letters, Writing, and Communication. It will take some time to finish what God has called me to do. I'm happy and grateful for what God has done in my life so far. I hope that other people can get to know God and His Loving ways. He knows what we can handle.

God wants you right where you are at. You don't have to have it all together. I never had it together. I was lost without a cause. I was doing any and everything I wasn't supposed to do. I felt hopeless and out of touch with reality. I never thought I couldn't get it right. Truthfully, I didn't care anymore about my life, myself, or others. There were times where I didn't see my family for days because I was deep down in my sin. I was ashamed and noncaring. I was let down countless times. I blamed God and others until God said, "What part did you play in it?" Then I begin to soul search my heart and other areas of my life. It takes working on yourself. It doesn't happen overnight. Trusting people is still a big issue with me. We tend to hurt people by the things we say. It bothers me when people keep secrets about things that they know will hurt the very people that they love. The best way to handle all situations is from a biblical perspective because you are keeping it real and the person doesn't feel alienated. It's wrong to see things only your way as a leader. We all need to be versatile, open-minded, and a good listener.

God wants us to master with Him and not ourselves. We rule with the word of God not with our loudmouths and forced attitudes. I have done these things before, and I still see it to this day. It is uncalled for in the church because some preachers think that it is okay to curse while they are preaching God's word. It is wrong, and it is not what the message is about. We need to be more careful in God's house. It is not good for the congregation nor the hearers because they are everywhere.

I was in my Fire Life Safety Director Class one morning, and my friend from my class and I were talking about ministers. He lived in New Jersey and said something terrible about ministers because he knew some that were in and out of church. He said he isn't a minister anymore. He had a foul mouth, and he just wasn't right. He didn't go into all the details, but I thought, "I'm a minister." I told him that not all ministers are the same, which is true. We must be cautious about the way we live our lives. The word of God teaches us how to live. It's only two ways to live: godly or ungodly.

I love going to my other classes through my union from my job. I'm presently taking Fire Life Safety Director classes because I'm embarking on a new career. I saw in the job program that it was open, and I called to see if they had an opening for me and they did. Once they said, "All we need is a copy of your high school diploma," I said, "Thank you, Lord." I have learned so much about buildings and what is in them: alarm systems, command centers, office buildings, lighting, building management, horns, bells, standpipes, etc. I know that these certifications will suit me well in the future for all types of Group A and B buildings, churches, non-emergency, and active shooter for all kinds of fire prevention endeavors. I hope that once I look back on my life, I can own a building or two like some churches and office buildings. I signed up for the course, and I started showing up.

Giving God thanks is very important to me. I would never be where I'm at today without Him giving me the chance to get my life in order. It has been a remarkable journey on my way up to serving God. It's not one thing with God. He blesses you with many talents and gifts you thought you never had. There are countless blessings.

I wanted to get a better paying job, benefits, and pension through my union. I want to get into building management as well. I must wait because I must do eleven weeks of computer training first then proceed to other classes which are free because of my union. My union dues are only $60 a month. Those classes would cost way more if I were to pay for them out of pocket. I never knew that there was on the job training programs like this. A package was sent to my home from my job with a union card. I was shocked at the brochure and what they offered is a gold mine of trades and classes that are free if you work for the company. God Is Great!!

I told my wife, "I'm all in honey. This is what I need. A new career and all the things that God wants for us." We both agreed. We kept on serving and aim to please God. No matter what, we give God honor and praise every day all day long. It is our requirement. I always say these words: "As for me and my house, we will serve the Lord."

CHAPTER 25

Fire Safety Director

I remember when I registered for the Fire Life Safety Director class. It was a day of liberation for me. I signed up for this class on September 22, 2018. I saw that the class was for 11 weeks. I told myself, "I can do this." I called my union and asked them a few questions about who was running the class like what kind of person he was. I like to ask questions before I start something new.

I was offered the class back in April of 2018 when I was cleared from my doctor to go back to work. I'm glad I did because it is a career change. The way I went about getting it was so awesome, and I was just so blessed by God that day. The day I went back to work I had gotten an Accessoride cab that day because I was still receiving that benefit because of my back surgery even though I was healed enough to go back to work.

A friend of mine told me about a security job in Bronx, New York. I had to go to the unemployment office to apply for it. I went there that morning, and I filled out the application. I sat there for about 15 minutes, and the receptionist was taking so long that I had to go because my driver had called me to pick me up. I told her what was going on and I waited outside. When my driver pulled up, I opened the door, he mentioned my name, and I was like great. He proceeded to drive away. I thought that the job wasn't meant for me. I hoped that he would drive by the security firm that I wanted to work for. He drove on the highway and I asked, "Where are we?" He said, "We are on the Queen's Highway. There was too much traffic, and I want to get off." I asked him to let me out of the car, and I got out after paying him. I later learned that I got the job and was so happy because I filled out the application and was there for two hours.

I found out that the union is one of the best unions in New York City. They have a free school after you are on the job for six months to a year. I signed up for the fire safety director class. I anticipated the class because I kept on hearing that for security this is the way to go. Having both a security license and fire guard license can get you into a building on the site that the building owner wants you to work at.

I was so happy to find this information out because New York City has thousands of old and new buildings that need an FLSD. I remember when I first got my fire guard license for basic fire watches and fire wardens. It is a requirement to have a license when you work in large office buildings. I studied for the test, and I failed it the first time because I didn't know anything about the job. I went back a month later and retook it. I learned so much about fire extinguishers, alarms, all the protocols, and everything. I study all the time now because I'm a few weeks from finishing my class. I have learned a lot of different terminologies and technical things that need to be addressed when the job requires during testing, etc.

I studied for eight weeks before I got my first test scores and I was happy. It was on the FLSD manual. I did great on that. I got 80% on the test and on the non-emergency test, I got a 72%. I'm waiting for the final test which is the active shooter final exam. I hope to get a higher test score on this one. There were a couple of people who didn't think that they were going to make it tested better than they did. I wanted to get as much information as I could. I want to transfer my security job into this field and then take the city test. There are three parts to it, and all I want to do is get all of them. I gave it to the Lord in prayer, and He will pass the test for me. All I have to do is my part, and I will continue to do that. The song that comes to my mind is, "He has made me glad, Oh He has made me glad, for I will rejoice for He has made me glad." I see all the beautiful people in my class from all walks of life.

I have three women and twelve men in my class now. Twenty-three people started off. I saw people leaving every week. I prayed for them, and I saw some unhappy faces on Saturday morning. I saw some people who were not godly and without hope. I wanted to be a part of something great. I will be finishing up soon. If I had to do it all over again, I would be there for some of the people. I saw people struggling financially and spiritually. They are broken and hurting while sitting in class masking. The writing is on the wall. I hope that they find God and get their lives in order. I don't care what job you have; you still need Jesus Christ to direct your life. I thank Him for blessing us for the position we have. Every Saturday I go; I see angels in my classroom protecting us all.

God has blessed me ever since I went back to work. I'm supporting my daughter and wife and I pay my bills with this job. I do many things that I thank the Lord for this job. I pay my tithes with this job. I provide food and clothing with this job. I have great benefits such as 401k, dental, health, and life insurance. I'm very grateful, and I'm peaceful. I love working and being able to provide for myself. It feels good to have to never ask anyone for anything. The only one that I asked anything from is God. He comes through all the time for my wife, me, and our cat, Syrus. I buy cat food for him, and I love him. He looks at my wife and me and runs through the house when we get off from work. I let him outside, watch him and play with him.

I set the family time with my wife after that I go to my prayer closet. Then I get into my fire life safety director's homework and studies. I look over the pages that the instructor gave us for the previous class. There are a lot of pages inside this huge big book. When I first went over it, I persisted in reading and doing more reading. I found out the importance of fire prevention. Some people don't check their fire alarms that often. I didn't do it that often. We think, oh no this can't happen to me? Yes, it can because it happens somewhere in America every day. Look at the California fires where all those people lost their lives, homes, and household furnishings. They must remember that they can replace those things. You can't replace a life. It is so important to pray for them because it can happen to anyone. Things will happen to us, and we think that we are the only ones that things happen to. It can happen to anybody. If you don't serve God, you are not protected.

To keep your protection and the guardian angels around you, keep reading the word. The Holy Spirit will be there to guide you in the right direction. Don't let 'doubting Thomas' come into your mind because the enemy loves to use people to put all sorts of things in your head. "Why did this happen? Whose fault is this? The fire department could have gotten there sooner. How could they?" When there is an inferno, I pray for the families that are affected by the loss of life. I pray that they find peace from God. I pray that their families receive comfort and love. I hope that they are okay. I studied my homework, and I found out that people can lose their lives in a fire in a matter of seconds. It is devastating and very hot in a fire. I don't think that people realize the importance of closing a door in a fire and leaving it closed. If you leave the door closed, it reduces the spread of a fire. If you open the door, it spreads the fire rapidly.

Don't ever touch a doorknob behind a fire door. You will find your whole hand melting. Most people think that in a fire that the victims burn to death. That's not always true. They lose their lives through smoke inhalation. That's when the smoke burns your lungs, and it also suffocates you so you can't breathe. It is very sad when there are preventative measures for these things. Our children, families, church members, friends, and co-workers need to be taught about the dangers of many kinds of fires and prevention measures.

Many people go through life without CPR training. I am CPR certified. If there are lives that need to be saved in a fire, this training will help. I remember when I was partying all night long, I came home to boil some hot dogs. The water boiled out, and I had awakened to a smoke-filled kitchen. There were people in the home at the time. I did some things that God has corrected me in my life, and I will never do it again. I was careless, lost, and just a bone head. Today, I wouldn't take the chance to do anything anymore.

The emergency and non-emergency, I'm done with that for now in my class. The active shooter is something that I don't fully understand. I understand gun laws and the right to bear arms. Why is it so hard to keep firearms out of the hands of a mentally ill person? I hope that they come up with more strict gun laws because these incidents are happening all over the world and in America. They always say you don't know when it will happen. Shootings can happen on the job, church, office buildings, parties, club, schools, etc. The prevention is to keep your eyes open for everything from suspicious packages and what a person wears and drive.

I never thought that I would be working in the fire safety field. It should be no surprise to me. I had a cousin who was a fireman that had fallen asleep and died from smoke inhalation years ago. My other cousin who I admire is a firefighter right now and has been on now for 26 years. I know that these types of jobs are in our blood because we are servants to our communities. I watched both growing up as a kid and saw some qualities in these two men that I didn't see in myself. I liked their mental toughness and their attitudes growing up.

My job right now is I go to several different buildings throughout the week. There are office high rise buildings. There are buildings where there are tenants from the apartments. It is like a mix use dwelling and a place where you see several different types of federal, state, and local government buildings. I look at their buildings. They all need FSD's in them for fire prevention and fire wardens. There is one fire warden per floor, and his job is to tell me where the fire is on each floor. The FSD is at the command center calling the fire warden to see where the fire is while evacuating the tenants and or residents out of the building.

I hope that the training that is being done now will always be done to improve or reduce the chances for no one to get hurt. I hope that all the fire drills are conducted properly. I hope that all fire pumps and all other devices are being changed and revamped as well. I'm very grateful for my instructor. He is the only instructor that I have that teaches this class in a way where it is supposed to be taught hands on. He jokes with us sometimes. I know that God will bless you with someone that knows his craft and someone who will help you possibly get a better position than what you have now. I like the job I have now, but I need to be in a better position to help my family. It pays okay but I know I can do better. You can't buy a home on $15.00 an hour. The prices of everything are going up, and I need better wages just like the next person. I want to be able to help my kids and my grandchildren. I desire to leave them an inheritance.

I thank the Lord and my wife for all that they have done for me. I didn't think that I could do this until I got this job and visiting many different buildings during the week. My schedule allows me to visit at least two to three different buildings during the week because of my job assignments. I saw so many buildings that are in violation and are not clean. They need new appliances and new things to be done. It's bad when a building owner doesn't do his part then he relies on you and the building manager to get things done. That will never work because he needs to be informed on both ends of what's going on in the building. He needs reports of what is going on daily, especially if it's a natural disaster and or fire in the building.

It is best to give the information away than to keep it. Pass the baton to the younger generation so they can learn how to grow. Pass the baton so they can take care of their families through God, the church and their jobs. Pass it so they can get their education and continue to pay it forward. I need to be free from the old man and the new man that I am today is a testament to what God can do if you let Him into your life completely.

I refuse to be that man that is a user and abuser. I'm so glad that God has broken me from my demise. It's amazing to see how many people refuse God's help only to realize that it is too late for some of us to turn back the hands of time. If I could just take some of the things back that I did, my life would be more of what I want. I don't think that I would be where I'm at today. We can't do it alone. The Lord must help us with our selfish ambitions, and our ability to reason is not what is helping us. I found myself always asking questions about something or a situation. It's okay at times, but sometimes there is no need for questions. Just do what you are told, continue to move forward, and learn from your mistakes in life. He let me know that I was on track with this job because the job branches off into HRA police as well. I praise God from Whom all our blessings flow.

I knew that God told me that it was time to upgrade my lifestyle. I had to get my thoughts and my mind right. I was thinking about taking a series of tests. I thought about my future and had to make my mind up. Do I want to go back to school to get a degree? Do I want to get a job and get a pension for a lifetime? I thought about my ministries and self-worth. I know that I'm worth a lot more than I thought. Today, I'm grateful for the things that God has done for me. I want more than I have now. I stay hungry for the Lord. I want God to show me how to go to higher heights. I want to be better in 2019 than I was in 2018. I know that God has given me great ambition. I want to stay by the Lord's side.

I had seen so many men and women go through stuff, and I said to myself, "I don't want to go through all the things that some of those people went through." I saw people growing up that struggled all their lives. Some were at the welfare office and stayed on it for years. I work there now, and I see that every day. I saw a guy with his girlfriend and two kids. I heard them talking and interacting. The girlfriend said to him, "You are not the kid's father how can you get on welfare with us." I didn't assume what they were talking about. It is sad what I see there every day. People are getting their benefits. Food stamps and Medicaid is where I work now. In all the buildings I work in now and every week they have required Fire Life Safety Directors. I want God to bless these people but some of them need the benefits, and some of them don't want to do better.

I tried to talk to some of my co-workers and tell them about the program. I wanted them to advance their career. I know that some of them are comfortable right where they are. I was never comfortable with just having a little when I know that the God, I serve owns the cattle on a thousand hills. I have thought about my wife, my family, friends, and me. All I keep saying to God is, "Open the door for my family and me to first go into the Lamb's Book of Life and into Heaven. Second, I desire to leave my family with generational wealth. I want to continue to serve His legacy the right way. Third, I want to help others get there." God's way is the best and only way to success and happiness. I will use my certifications that I will receive to further my job skills and continue to use the union to get more classes.

I have been up all night studying and learning more than I expected. I found myself falling asleep studying God's word and studying for all the active shooter courses now. I learned in the book that I have been studying that you must have a positive attitude about approaching someone like that. You must have evacuation procedures in order to get everyone out of the building. You also must plant a thick non-penetrating piece of metal desk type furniture in front of you if you can't get out of the building. Never confront the active shooter. Always stay out of harm's way of a crazy lunatic like that. I pray for all the things that are happening in the world today. These classes have been beneficial for me, and I hope that nothing like this happens. The way things are going now, I wouldn't be surprised about anything that happens anymore.

When we lose things in our lives, God can bless us. Losing a loved one and losing material things, God can bless us. Although I'm in the security field and I'm getting ready to transition into a fire director, I will not miss doing security anymore because I stand up all day and I barely get breaks. My ankles hurt sometimes. I move around, and I stand in one place for 20 minutes. I started walking around to relieve the tension in my legs. One day I will say I'm losing security. I will say thank you. I'm moving away from the field slowly but surely. This is a big step for me. You must stay on your 'A' game.

Move forward and dream. Don't stop making progress in your life. Try to do something in your life that you think you can't do. You might discover like I did that you have hidden gifts and talents that need to be manifested and cultivated. Perhaps you need a touch from God. Maybe God will send somebody to you for confirmation. You can also stumble upon a hidden gift that can do for you and your family no one saw coming. God works in mysterious ways. Don't ever dismiss the act of possibility and probability. Things happening in our lives can make us or break us. I want to share what God has done for me. God will always be there, and He will show us all who He is in due time. There are things that He has done for me that I'm in awe of daily.

On December 8, 2018, I graduated from the Fire Safety Certificate of Fitness three-part test. The next course is the city test and the on-site commercial building prep course in school. That whole week I wasn't feeling well because I had a bad cold. I was going back and forth to work and school. I thought, "When will it all end so I can take a break?" I just kept on pressing through my discomfort. I looked to the Lord for continuing forward. I remember waking up at night blowing my nose and using the bathroom. I had a hard time going back to sleep. I told my wife, "I'm not feeling well honey." She said, "You are going to be okay. Just pray and ask God to give you strength."

I got more out of this one week of sickness on how to persevere in times of feeling lousy inside. I felt like someone hit me in the head with a brick with this head cold and headaches to go along with it. I was at work on my post thinking about my wife, cat, final exams, classes, and the trials we had been through. The spring semester was coming up. I thought about the classes like Church History and Preaching 101. I was thinking about will be my professors for these classes. I said to myself that I want a challenge like the challenges I had for the Old Testament and Biblical Exegesis. I like the differences that I see in the professors. I liked both because one offered more of a practical approach to the classes and the other offered a Biblical approach. One was like a life experience type of professor, and the other one was more challenging us with how we feel about ourselves as far as to how we think about God. I learned a lot from both. The other professor was challenging us academically and grading us on our knowledge about God and how God has given us His power to go for His ministries because it's all about Him. We learned about being slaves to sin and slaves to righteousness. It is all great to know where you stand with the Lord.

I pray for all my classmates as we continue to further our education. My FLSD class is finished now. I studied for the city test that I took on February 8, 2019. I took the non-emergency test on February 17, 2019. I took them back to back so I could get the licenses to become an FLSD commercial building director. I must take an on-site test with a fire department inspector present. I must show him what I learned in the class. For instance, if he asks me to take him to the fire command center, I must know where it is located. I must take him where it is and tell him its functions and purposes.

I know many things about the FLS Director's job. I want to know more than I do now: the fire brigades, fire wardens, fire pumps, the two-headed hoses, all the alarms, pull stations, and all that good stuff. I thank Jesus Christ for the job and the readiness. I thank him for being prepared for the test and studying as much as I could. I study at least three to four days a week and I will be doing it for quite a while until I get at least 70% to 80% of the standard booklet which has about 400 to 500 pages in it. I will never forget this part of my life because I was going hard in 2018. I had two classes on Tuesday and Thursday night. My FLSD class was on Saturday morning. My accredited ministry classes were three months, and my FLSD class was 11 weekends back to back. Plus, I'm working and give attention to my church on Sunday, among many other things I have going on.

I told my Union Rep that I wanted to take Building Management 1,2,3 and use those certifications for on the job. I want to maximize my potential. I signed up for the computer class with my union as well. I started that class on January 5, 2019. I'm doing it because many computer training changes are going on with the computer now. I want to learn new things and get a refresher course on computers. I know that it will be beneficial to my wife and me.

God brought my wife and me through it all. It was a learning experience for sure. There were many things that I still need to work on. There are many challenges, levels of gratitude, and honoring God in the process of it all. It was a test. Do I think I can do better? Sure, I can. I know that I have a long way to go. I do believe that I'm ready and built for the next level God is taking me to. I trust the Lord all the way. I fought all my life and kept getting knocked down. God gave me the strength to get back up even when I threw in the towel. Somehow, I got back up on my feet and dusted myself off. I wanted to finish this race. I'm determined to win this race by not looking at my problems. You win the race by seeking God daily and allowing His will to be done not yours. I put all of my troubles and misfortunes in His hands.

CHAPTER 26

Merry Christmas

There were twelve days until Christmas, and I was glad that God gave me another Christmas. Some people see it as a pagan holiday. I see it as another blessed day that the Lord has given us in remembering and observing him as God and God all by himself. I remember being a little snotty nose kid and it being cold outside. The Christmas tree had nothing under it. I looked up a couple of days later, it had a present or two under the tree. Then a week before Christmas, the tree had 100 gifts under it. It's not how it used to be because my parents, many of my relatives, and some of my friends have passed. God is still present and real. He is powerful still despite all that is going on in this world. Even if I didn't have a Christmas tree, I would still honor God on December 25th.

I will honor God every day for the rest of my life. I hope that the New Year that is coming has new blessings from God, refreshed financial situation, a new home, and better health. I want my wife and me to embark on new job careers, a deeper level relationship with God, and new friendships with people. I hope that when the spring semester at NYTS starts, God will give me the opportunity to start the Masters Degree Program of Divinity. I went many years searching for answers and trying to make sense of what God was trying to get me to see and do. I have finally come to a place in my life where I have found love, joy, peace, and self-control. I have a tremendous amount of confidence now. I had some good times in my life. I just wasn't happy until I re-established my life with the Lord. I remember those days when it wasn't so good. I remember sometimes on different years and occasions when Christmas wasn't Christmas, which means I had a bad spirit that I couldn't shake because of my family life. Some of it was just pure ignorance then some of my situations were so sad because of the nature of who I had become. I didn't care anymore during that time if I lived or died until I met Jesus Christ. He saved my life from tragedy and self-destruction.

God has transformed me to the point that I have no reason to do the things I used to do because of life changing blessings I have experienced. I have no more struggles with anger management. The ability to let God have his way in my life, I no longer fight with words. I fight with the word of God. I want to keep a kind and tender loving righteous heart. I want God to use me as a messenger to spread His love and word. The only way is through the Holy Spirit to guide me towards victory in Jesus Christ.

Many doors have opened for us through our church. My wife and I, through our Evangelism Ministry, are going to the nursing home. We praise and worship God with the elderly. We sing several songs and hymns with them then we hold hands and do corporate prayer. I was so happy to be a part of this Ministry because I knew God wanted me there. God opened doors for my wife and me to participate. We have been going strong for the Lord ever since. I looked everywhere and tried to see what God was saying to me when I first joined the church. I didn't join something because everybody else did. God had spoken to me because I knew He didn't want me to be out of line with what He is doing in my life. Now I'm the security minister at my church and oversee the Security Team in what needs to be done on a daily and weekly basis for church functions. We help with gospel concerts, plays, and different functions. We are watchmen for God to protect the head clergy of our church: mainly the bishop and executive minister. My hope is that we tighten the screws on the security team.

We need to have things in place in our homes and jobs as well because we are in some dark times in America. God speaks to me about the things that are coming to us. We need to get it together because this next election will be a defining moment in American history. The economy and political landscape are constantly changing which impacts us all. Things are more expensive now. What can we do when we are faced with obstacles? What can we do when we are struggling? Ask God for His guidance and worship Him more. I guarantee you He will bless you. Don't doubt God. Praise Him every second, minute, and hour. Give Him your attention in prayer every morning, noon, evening, and night. Fast with adoration. Anoint yourself to give Him praise and honor.

Christmas is about commemorating the 'birth' of Jesus Christ observed on December 25th as a religious and cultural celebration among billions around the world. People think that Christmas is about having fun, feasting, and decorating the tree and Santa comes to deliver the presents to the children. It's about how Jesus came into the world to save us from sin, and that is the best gift of all.

"JESUS CHRIST BIRTH"

1. Isaiah prophesies that a pure young woman will give birth to God's Son (Isaiah 7:14)
2. Isaiah's prophecy is fulfilled (Matthew 1:18-23)
3. Isaiah prophesies that Jesus Christ will come as a baby; Jesus is described by several names (Isaiah 9:6)
4. Micah prophesies that Jesus would be born in Bethlehem (Micah 5:2)
5. The scribes knew that Bethlehem was the prophesied birthplace of the Messiah (Matthew 2:4-6)
6. A virgin named Mary will be the mother of Jesus Christ (Luke 1: 26-31)
7. Jesus is born (Luke 2:4-7)
8. A new star appeared in Israel (Matthew 2:2)

Jesus Christ was born King of the Jews. The Bible says that we have seen His star in the east and have come to worship Him. Unto us, a child is born; unto us, a son is given. As Jesus Christ is a child in His human nature, He is born, begotten of the Holy Spirit. He was born of the Virgin Mary. Certainly, a child, as any other man that ever lived upon the face of the earth. Jesus Christ is God's Son. He is not born, but given and begotten of His Father before all the worlds. Begotten is defined as not made; being of the same substance with the Father. The doctrine of the eternal affiliation of Christ is to be received as an undoubted truth. Our holy affiliation of Christ is to be received as an undoubted truth of our holy religion. You can perceive that the distinction is a suggestive one and conveys much good truth to us. This is a summary of the Biblical account of the birth of Jesus. You can read more in-depth Bible verses from the scripture above and use the articles and videos to understand the meaning of this world-changing event in the bible.

Almost 2000 years ago a young woman from the town of Nazareth named Mary was visited by an angel named Gabriel. Gabriel told the Jewish woman that she would have a son named Jesus and that He would be the Son of God. At this time Mary was engaged to her soon to be husband Joseph. When she told Joseph, he was hurt and confused because he did not believe Mary. The Angel Gabriel came to Joseph and told him that Mary would be pregnant from the Lord. Her child will save people from their sins. Mary and Joseph had to travel to Bethlehem because of an order from the Roman Emperor that a census, or record, of all people be taken in their hometown.

After traveling pregnant on a donkey for several days, Mary and Joseph arrived in Bethlehem and told there no places to stay. The inns were full. Seeing that Mary was due at any moment, the owner of an inn told Joseph that they could stay in his stable. Mary and Joseph settled down on the hay in a stable with animals sleeping. Mary went into labor, and Jesus was born in a stable. The only place for the sleeping baby to rest was most likely in the animal's trough, known as the manger.

During this time the angel appeared to shepherds who were watching their flocks in the fields near Bethlehem. The angel told the good news of the Savior and Messiah, Jesus Christ. The shepherds immediately went to find baby Jesus, which the angels told them they would find sleeping in the manger. After some time, the wise men, also known as magi, saw the brilliant star in that sky that rested over where Jesus was born. The wise men traveled from a far eastern country to find the new king. During the wise men's trip, Herod the king of Judah met with the wise men and told them to come back and let him know where the baby king was so that he could worship Him as well. The wise men continued to Bethlehem and found Jesus right where the star pointed. They knelt and worshiped the Savior and gave Him gifts of gold, frankincense, and myrrh. Then they traveled back home a different way knowing that King Herod did not intend to worship Jesus but that he planned to kill baby Jesus.

In the New Testament, the massacre of the innocents is the incident in the nativity narrative of the gospel of Matthew in which Herod the Great, King of Judea, orders the execution of all male children two years old and under in the vicinity of Bethlehem. Most biographers of Herod and the majority of biblical scholars dismiss Matthew's story as an invention. The Church has claimed that the children murdered in Jesus's stead as the first Christian martyrs, and their feast - Holy Innocents Day - is celebrated on December 28th.

When Herod realized that the magi had tricked him, he was furious. Matthew says he was in fulfillment of the words of the Prophet Jeremiah. "A voice is heard weeping in Ramah, weeping and great mourning, Rachel weeping for her children and refusing to be comforted because they are no more" (Jeremiah 31:15). The massacre fails to kill infant Jesus because His father was warned by an angel. They escaped with Him and His mother to Egypt and waited there for Herod's death and a safe return to the land of Israel.

I read this story repeatedly. I find it interesting that Jesus Christ was so powerful as an infant, because His birth changed the entire landscape of that nation. It tells me that He was hiding out as an infant and a kid. I hope people can see all the things that Jesus went through for me to honor and glorify Him. The true story about Jesus should be told daily. The truth should be told about His birth and why scholars don't believe He was born on December 25. Many scholars believe that Jesus's birthday was on March 25 between 6 BC and 4 BC. Historical evidence is too incomplete to allow a definitive date. The date is estimated through two different approaches. One by one analyzing references to known historical events mentioned in the nativity accounts in the Gospels of Luke and Matthew. The second by working backward from the estimation of the start of the ministry of Jesus.

I'm so glad Jesus was born and came to save us from our sins. I had been very sad when I heard as I was reading that all the princes were murdered because of the evil King Herod. Herod didn't want baby Jesus to rule his nation, and He rules the whole world now. I love Christmas in terms of meaning, and I know many children believe that Santa is on his sleigh. I was lied too about all that Jesus Christ represented. I wasn't confused. I was skeptical at times. When I got older, I just processed the information and came to a conclusion: Jesus Christ is the Gift. Monetary gifts are okay, but God sent His only son down here to die for our sins. I didn't understand it at first. Now I do because he makes it so plain and clear to us. I hope that we as Christians will honor Jesus for who he is and for what he has already done. We will never be going through what we are going through now if we will read more of His word and execute what He is saying to us. This world would be a better place.

I have a burning desire to travel where all these things had taken place some day. I know that my wife and I will be shocked to see where all these events had taken place. I want to go all over Israel and Egypt. All the artifacts, tools, and settings that had been done before I can get a mental picture of what Jesus went through at the time of His birth. I will be there soon someday. I hope we can go to Israel by 2020. That will be on our to-do list.

I went out the other day and saw some Christmas cards. I was looking at many other things in the store. It dawned on me to get some cards too. I was never into buying Christmas cards and things like that until one day my oldest sister Christine called me. She said, "What is your address?" I was shocked because she had never asked me that. I knew it was God that had her ask me that question because I wasn't into sending out cards at Christmas time. I have done it in the past but not in the last few years. I thank God for her calling me that day because I was going through something all that week. I love my sister, not for the card, but I love her because I know that God laid it on her heart to send my wife and me a Christmas card. It was the thought that counts. When I looked in the mail and saw her name, and I just laughed. I know my sister loves me. That to me is awesome.

I hope that many other people have a blessed Christmas Eve and Christmas. I know that there are not a lot of people who are happy because they don't have the money to buy what they need for their loved ones. They don't have enough money to buy food. Go to someone's house to eat or go to the churches to eat before Christmas. Go fellowship with the pastor and the congregation. God will supply all your needs according to His riches and glory. I remember times when I didn't have all that I needed, and I struggled from time to time even when I was starting out. I moved out of my parent's house, and even years after I moved out, I struggled from time to time with money, food, drugs, or alcohol. I want to know that I don't struggle with these things any more by the grace of God.

In your struggles, God is there waiting for you to get your life together because I was the guy who every time it was a holiday, I had to be drunk or high. I realized that it's not worth it. It makes no sense when you are not yourself. People are laughing at you and mocking what you did. My family members said, "There he is, let us walk on the other side just in case he tries something." I wanted peace and God gave it to me. Many family and friends got drunk and high. We didn't need each anymore. I'm so glad I moved away because now that God has changed my life.

I have no regrets of what God has done for me because I'm free from bondage. I have strength and good health by the mercy and grace of God. I miss my family because I don't travel back home anymore. I will someday, but for now, God has allowed me to grow up and give all of me to Him. I gave a good portion of my life to the world. I have no time for foolishness. I hope that these young kids understand that partying can ruin their lives. It will also make you lazy, and you are not going to want to do anything for yourself. You need an education like a high school diploma, a college degree, Master's degree, and Doctorate to make it. God will bless you, and He will provide for you what you can't provide for yourselves. He made way for me, and this Christmas is one of the best for me because I truly know Jesus Christ. He is the gift that I never had. He is my Father, my Brother, everything I never had, my strength, my friend, and my all in all. I had many situations, and he told me what to do and how to do it. He gave me options and sometimes no options at all. He told me this is the way and you must deal with what you have created. He spoke to me one day, "Are you done doing things your way yet?" I said, "Yes." He said, "No you're not." It wasn't until I threw in the towel that He is able to pick me up, set me on my feet, and put me on His solid ground. It was a foundation that stuck with me until this day. When He has makes you a child of God, you start thinking and acting like him.

Most importantly, I had a relationship with him. I cry when the Holy Spirit comes upon me. I was in Bible study class with the other ministers. We were talking about how people can sit in church and show no emotions to God I was struck because I looked back and reflected on all the things I had been through. God brought me out of my mess, and He still brings us up out of messes. I love my Heavenly Father, and I'm forever taken back. I will never forget what He has done for my family, my church family, my friends and me. We all should be worshiping Him no matter what our situations are.

Once I stood in a long line for my grandkids. I was at the church down the street close to where I live. They were giving out free Christmas gifts, and I thought about the gift of Jesus Christ as I stood in line. There were approximately 300 to 400 people were standing in line. I saw many gifts and food given away. I saw little girls standing in the parking lot singing Christmas songs. It was a beautiful scene. They were singing amazing grace and Christmas carols. I saw in my community how outreach ministry is supposed to be done. They were passing out ministry tracts. I was there from 10:00 a.m. to 1:00 p.m. It was freezing, and it was brisk. People were complaining that they should have opened the doors so we all could get inside and stay warm." Many people there didn't belong to the church. They were there like I was getting the gifts and thanking God that there are churches that still help in giving not only food but gifts. I know without a doubt that God is always into blessing ministries.

I will never forget when God gave me all I wanted for Christmas, and I felt so good receiving the gifts I ended up playing and having fun with all that God blessed me with until I realized the identity of Santa. I just stopped playing with all my toys, games and understood who the real Santa is when I was 16. I had gotten a brand new two-speed kickback bicycle. I had all I could handle, and I felt powerful. I knew it was God. I wasn't my gifts as much after that encounter with the Lord. I felt like God was telling me that He is Christmas and He wanted me to know for myself instead of relying on my parents or someone telling or explaining the truth to me. I never had my parents telling me anything about Santa and Jesus Christ. I was just into whatever was going on for that in that moment. My life changed after that because I no longer expected anything for Christmas because I knew who the true Gift.

I still get gifts, and I celebrate Jesus Christ every day. He deserves a tribute all the time. I remember my mother cooking all that good food for the family. I miss all those things. Christmas is by far my best holiday of all because of Jesus Christ's birthday. Many people prefer the 4th of July over Christmas. There is no comparison when you are talking about fireworks vs. baby Jesus. I have enjoyed all the holidays and have been to some awesome gatherings.

I needed a friend, and that was Jesus Christ. When I was sick, He was there. When I needed a lawyer, He was there. When I didn't have any money, He was there when I was broke as a joke, he showed up and put money in my pocket. When people were using me and talking about me, He hid me from my demise.

I went to school with nothing at times, and all I had was school books. I went to lunch and didn't have a dime. One girl said to me, "You want to go out to lunch with me?" I said, "I don't have any money." I will never forget it. She said, "That's okay I got you." We went to McDonald's, and I ate a few burgers, fries, and drinks. I thanked her, and she said that's okay. She wasn't even my girlfriend. I knew of her, and I just wasn't interested. She ended up being so successful in her life. I wasn't shocked about the outcome of her life. She was a good role model for me. She was nothing like the other people I would end up hanging around. She offered me a Christmas gift one week before we let out of school back in 1984 before the Christmas and New Year's break. This was the best Christmas that I can remember that I ever had as a teenager.

I hope that people understand that God is willing to help you with your needs and your wants. Can you give Him what He is asking of you? Give Him your time, love, money, and obedience. Give all of yourself to Him, not some or part of you. Your whole life is His. It took me a while to figure that out. I wasn't ready. I had to work my way into doing what he asked of me. Don't be scared and don't walk away from His presence. What most people don't understand is that even when you don't feel you need him because you have everything, praise God anyway.

When the name Jesus is being mentioned it hits me hard. I think about when He was on the cross and the images of Him carrying His cross. I was so excited about Him doing whatever He wanted to do. If God was in control of Jesus's life, He did everything and more. The Bible says that all the things Jesus did you couldn't record it all. I'm so happy to be a minister of the gospel currently. People take a lot of things for granted. I see people going all over the city protesting about everything but Jesus Christ. I see people who want to do whatever that is convenient for them and not for others. It's a shame when you see people killing their children, little kids dying in fires, and all that kind of stuff two weeks before Christmas. Not all people are happy for those things I just mentioned. I see people who are sick in the hospital on Christmas Day. Go to the hospitals and nursing homes to pray for these people whether you know them or not. I go to jails and detention centers before Christmas to provide hope to the young men and women who are incarcerated in the system with no one in the family to come to visit them at all. Stop by a friend's house and see how they are doing. Ask them if they need anything.

"Lord, Jesus Christ, I need thee. Oh, I need thee every hour. I need thee. Lord, please stand by my wife and I side when we are weak and when we are strong. Lord take us on new levels in You and allow us to move forward to please You in your ministries. We need your love and direction. Lord, thank you for giving us your covenant. We praise and honor you, Lord, always and forever. Lord, it's not about going to church every Sunday. Lord God, it's about our relationship with you. Please help us get closer to you without compromising your ministries to no one. Lord, we honor and adore You. What you have done in our lives has been what we have expected. We will continue to serve you and your church. I want to thank you. I love Thanksgiving and Black Friday. Christmas is the day that most people love. I will honor you, oh God, forever."

I hope all of you who have access to gifts to bless unfortunate people. I hope you drop a bag of groceries off to someone in need. I hope you pay it forward because God loves a cheerful giver. I will never forget the times when I borrowed money from people and paid it back knowing that I had to turn around and do it again someday. I lost all hope in myself and others until I decided that Jesus Christ is number one in my heart, my soul, and my body. He has all the answers to your problems and all the situations. I stopped feeling sorry for myself. I will never turn my back on people like they have turned their back on me. I was left for dead at times, and I will always forgive people because of what the Lord has taught me. We must keep them in prayer and keep it moving.

Brooklyn, NY by the Metro Tech buildings in 2018

CHAPTER 27

Happy Birthday

My wife and I had a blessed day on my birthday, December 28, 2018. We went shopping on Long Island. I was so happy to go to work that day and met my wife at the mall. The whole week was a normal leading up to my birthday. She'd already given me a gift from Bath and Body Works and a card. We walked around, got some groceries, went home and enjoyed some dinner and movies. I didn't want to go out for dinner on my birthday. I just wanted to be with my wife and my cat.

I was so glad to get home that night because we were planning on changing our home around. While we were out, we went shopping for a comforter set and pillows. After we got home, my wife took off the old bedding that we had and started to put on the new comforter set. I said, "Baby, we are starting off the New

Year the right way." We looked forward to 2019 and bringing in the New Year at church.

I was very glad to have turned 51 years old because truthfully, I didn't think that at the rate, I was going I was going to make it. God saw fit that I would make it and get my family and friends back in my life. I remember some birthdays I was high and drunk. Nothing else mattered. Today, everything matters to me. I remember times when I didn't care about anyone else or anything else. God has shown me things that I couldn't understand. I just wanted to do my own thing all the time. I didn't want to listen to anybody or even be apart of the crowd anymore. I'm a sinner, God still loves me, and He will always be there for me because He forgives us of our mistakes. No one is perfect. Just get on your knees, pray, and ask God forgiveness. He will direct your path to righteousness. I never dreamed that He would do things for me and would take a wretched old man like me that was so stubborn and non-caring. I hid my feelings in cocaine, alcohol, cigarettes, and weed.

I knew out of my 51 years that at least 20 years was thrown into the wastebasket because of me. We must take responsibility for our actions. I knew that I had made a big mistake when I was in my early 20's. I was a mess spiritually, emotionally, and psychologically. I wanted more than what I was giving myself. People wanted me dead. It seemed like the more drugs I took, the greater the urge to kill myself. I realized that my thinking had to change because there was a problem with my thoughts. "I will never make it. I don't care because no one else cares." I started feeling guilty because of my addictions. I heard stories of how someone died or how someone went to jail and how they ended up crazy for doing ten years. I also heard that people lives were changed, and God blessed them to be clean of drugs, alcohol, and all other addictions. It was always a stigma with people on drugs. One thing that is a lie is that they can never be trusted. Well, I thank God. I'm trustworthy. I don't open easily to people, but I will give a person good advice about the route they are taking.

The last ten birthdays were spent in different states and cities in America. They were some of the best birthdays I had ever had because those were the years that I was reintroduced to Jesus Christ, in ways I never imagined. Live life to the fullest. Don't have any regrets as you are thinking about the end of your life while you are eating dinner with your loved ones.

I went to bed the other night, and it dawned on me that I was 51. Some people are thinking, "Hey what another lousy birthday," because some of us are approaching 60, 70, and 80. "I don't want to die this way," or, "I want to die that way. I don't want to suffer." Allow God to be in control. He will give you hope and prosperity to live on to the fullest until you meet him in paradise. I hope that I can see my grandchildren's children. I asked the Lord to give me and my family long life and prosperity. I desire to see my family sometimes on my birthday. I want things to be done God's way for the rest of my life. I know that my way is not God's way and it is not going to be the right way. I know how to move out of the way and let God have His way. It took me a long time to realize that, but now I know when it is time to let go and let God have His way.

I have been accustomed to parties all my life because of growing up in a huge family. You get used to setting up for events: cleaning, mopping floors or decorating the house or wherever the event is being held. The greatest place to have a birthday party is at church. I have experienced it before when I was in the teens. I had a birthday party at church. It was probably the best birthday party that I have ever had. The reason was my God, my parents, and family were there. I was a junior in high school during this time, and I was full of myself.

I was 17 years old still in high school. I thought I knew everything. I felt like I was untouchable. God let me know differently. Reality set in because it was the first time that I knew that I had an addiction to something. I was going through the motions. I started one bad habit after another one. I was doing things that I couldn't tell my parents or my friends. Every family back then kept secrets about something.

I once heard an old lady at my dad's church say, "Yes. He is sleeping with two other ladies in the church." I was ear hustling. I wondered who they were talking about. I hoped it wasn't someone I knew. I found out it was one of the pastors in the city who was doing that. My father knew him, and I knew that it wasn't right. Every time I saw him, I couldn't speak to him. I would try to avoid him at all cost. My father explained things to me. Sin is powerful, and some people will always follow what they think is right. Some people want to do wrong. Some men have the fear of the Lord upon them. It just amazes me that a man or woman of God can sit in church and know that they are having extramarital affairs. They are still preaching, teaching, and going around in the church like nothing is wrong until someone says something to them is absurd. It not only happened when I was a young man, but I have heard many other stories. I pray to God that it doesn't happen to my wife and me. It's tricky nowadays.

I have been to certain parties where you don't want to be a part of. I was at a Christmas party one time where the hosts of the party were a married couple. I had gotten in line, got my plate, and was getting ready to stack my plate high. This lady whom I had never met before said to me, "I have met you somewhere before haven't I?" I looked at her, and she looked at me. I told her, "Lady. I have never met you. I don't know you." I got the rest of my food, and it got worse. I sat down to the table and started to eat. The host got right in front of my face while sitting on the footrest eating. People were looking at her like what is she doing. I was intimidated by her actions because it was so unexpected. "I'm at your house, and I feel very uneasy." When God has done a new thing in your life, He will let you know what is appropriate and what is not right. I ended up easing my way out of their home. I didn't even let her know I was gone. I told her husband, "Nice meeting you and God bless you." That was a strange night, and when I got home, it was a relief.

I tried to stay away from any kinds of parties because it is always someone at the party that is drunk, high, or arguing about something. Through my experiences, if it didn't happen before the party, it was always the after party. When the holidays come, I brace myself sometimes and don't go anywhere.

My wife was born May 11, 1967, at Fordham hospital in the Bronx, NY. As a kid, her birthday consisted of cake, ice cream, food, and family. Sometimes her birthdays were at Coney Island which is an amusement park in Brooklyn. It is also a major tourist attraction in New York City. One day her mother took her to the aquarium for her birthday. They got inside of a submarine made for amusement parks that maybe about 50 people can fit inside of it. The submarine has huge windows so you can see the fish swimming around in the tank. The park worker closed the door and the tank began to sink to the bottom. They saw big and small fish floating past the windows. My wife started to panic and told her mom, "I want to get out." She was claustrophobic and only four years old at the time. Her mother told her that everything was going to be alright. She hugged her mother and closed her eyes until the tank came back to the surface. After she got older, her birthdays consisted of going out to places with her sister, their friends, and family. When she got a better paying job with benefits, she was able to go on vacation on her birthday. She went on cruises with her friends. She has been to the Dominican Republic, Cancun, Mexico, Montego Bay, Jamaica, Miami, and Florida.

There were times when her friends would get a homemade cake from a lady that bakes a short strawberry cake. It was all white with strawberries on top. When you had a slice of that cake, it melted in your mouth. The sugar was at a balance: not too sweet and not too bland. The icing taste like whipped cream. My wife said that she was always having fun on her birthdays. She wasn't going to church regularly. When she did attend church, she went to Calvary Baptist Church on Willis Ave in the

Bronx. It was a small church with maybe 50 people in it. She got to know the pastor better because it was a small church.

They had holiday events, bible study, and all kinds of different things. They had a group of mission's trips that they would go on. They had about 20 clergy members at this church. This church had a Youth Ministry, Mission Ministries, Outreach Ministries, and Food Pantry Ministries. They passed out tracts to allow someone to get to know Jesus Christ through a story or a life experience. I told her that God changed her life because she grew up Catholic. She was about 12 years old when her mother took her and her sister to Baptist and Catholic churches. When her mother got sick and passed away, my wife started going back to a Baptist church.

I have nothing against denominations. It's easy to criticize folks about how they ought to be. I have been someone to help people navigate to where they need to be. It's okay the ask the bishop, pastor, ministers, and clergy what is of God and what's not. I do know that God answers prayer to us freely. Salvation is free and God has all the salvation that anyone needs. I was a slave to sin and now I'm a slave to righteousness. My wife's birthday was so nice earlier in the year. I had gotten her a nice ring, a card, and we went out to dinner. My sweetheart likes a variety of things. I know without a doubt first and foremost she loves Jesus Christ. I was very impressed when I met her. I saw where she grew up and where she came from. God will bless you with someone of the opposite sides of the track. She grew up in the city and I grew up in the country. I knew she was the one for me. Her birthday in 2018 was awesome because when God is totally in your relationship, you can't go wrong.

It seemed like everywhere we go we have success together. I was with her, and we went to our favorite BBQ's spot. She got her favorite chicken wings. I got my steak and fries or chicken and fries. We sat there and talked about the blessings of God. We talked about how much we would like to grow old together and still be in love, be friends, and work as a team. It amazes me where I can see some things and God see all things. I feel like shouting for joy.

My wife and I believe that you are supposed to serve God daily in whatever type of capacity that the Lord has shown you. It starts with the word of God then the home because home is where God and your heart is. It tells me where your relationship with God is. God ought to be in you so people can see Him on you on the job and wherever you go. It is like God's stamp is on you and His seal of approval. He will not approve of everything either. I wanted to do some things around the holidays like take a mini-vacation. God said, "No you can't do that right now." In 2019, we are due for a major vacation for at least seven days. Since we have been married going on four years now, this the best relationship that I had ever had with a woman besides my mother and my grandmother.

I remember besides my mother's and my grandmother's birthdays as a kid. They were always cooking something out of the house in those days. Nowadays everybody wants to go out to eat dinner. How things have changed... My mother would make homemade chicken and dumplings. My grandma would have a pot of stew on with the bouillon cubes, onions, and carrots in the winter time. I miss those birthdays where cakes were homemade. The store-bought cakes are like fifty to one hundred dollars or more. The cakes my mother and grandma made were Bettye Crocker and just plain homemade cakes. They were a dollar a box, and you brought the frosting. I used to go to the store for my parents many times. They would give me a long list of things to do.

I met many people along the way since my parents have passed on. I have never met anyone like them. My father always had me pay attention to detail. He would always tell me to think outside the box. I knew that my destiny was going to change because I was feeling an empty void for something. I would eat breakfast. I wasn't full, and I had eaten a lot. I would go out for lunch and felt the same way. Then I would eat dinner and some snacks at night. My eating habits were ongoing. I still was empty until I allowed Jesus Christ to fill me up with His Glory. Now sometimes I don't have to eat anything to be full of His mercy, grace, and love. To be full of His power is enough with the Holy Spirit. God took me places where most people would not even go. He can do that for you. On my journey, I have seen God transform thousands of people's lives. When we don't deserve it, He will bless you and others.

I will never forget one of my birthdays that I was in my late 20s. I had a party at a friend's house, and we were playing all sorts of music. We were drinking, and around several women. I tried to impress them. It seemed like the more I tried to impress them the more I got drunk. We drank, ate, and smoked everything. We went to bed around 5:00 a.m., but before I got to bed, I decided that I wanted to take a shower. When I was in the shower, I was so drunk. I turned on the water and grabbed the soap. I had hair on my head during this time. I wasn't paying attention, and I grabbed a bottle of what I thought was shampoo. I squeezed the bottle, but it was diaper rash cream. I was so angry at myself, and I just washed the rest of it out of my head. I was a mess.

There were times when God blessed me with everything, and I threw it all away. When a person doesn't have God in their lives, they are waiting on disaster because they don't have anything to hold on to. There is no one to catch them when they fall. What are they getting back up for? They will only do the same things over again. They continue doing the same old dumb stuff and never fessing up to what the real problem is you. God took me from that lifestyle to show me that I too can live without having all these problems. He showed me how to do it. He simply told me that it's over. "You are done, and it's my turn now." I said okay.

I remember one of my ball games where I had gotten fouled on a fast-break layup. I had missed the shot from being fouled. If I had made the shot while being fouled, I would have a 3-point play. I was on the foul line getting ready to shoot a free throw. As I was getting set to shoot from the foul line, I placed one foot in front of the other side by side. My left foot was slightly behind my right foot. Why? Because most of my weight was on my right side because I'm right-handed. When you are shooting free throws, the ball tends to rotate where you want it to go, which is in the basket. Every time I would do that, the ball would go in the hoop 90 percent of the time. I kept on practicing and worked on the technique.

I had one foot on God and one foot in the world. When the ball would go in the basket it was God. When I would miss the shot, it was the world calling me back. I did that for so long until I quit playing basketball altogether and decided where both of my feet should be which was not on the foul line anymore. God had blessed me with all those great times. I tried to forget my past. I'm clean and sober from all the birthdays that were a bust because I chose to do what I wanted. Today, I'm free from all manner of diseases and all substances. It's easy to play advocate, the hypocrite, and the person that goes around to say you can't or shouldn't be doing this or that. Don't be like that. Meet the people right where they are. Pray for them and ask God to help them through their struggles. Be a support system for them. Ask God to heal them, you, and both of your families. Sometimes it is best to say nothing and just be there for them.

I have a heart for people that have been through what I have been through. I had been through a lot and have overcome many things by the grace of God. There is nothing left in the tank when it comes to going backward or relapsing. I'm tired of suffering and not being able to have a life that God has purposed me for. I look back and see all the family and friends who have gone on. May God bless you and your family. I have been taught by the best and will always be grateful for the knowledge that has been passed down from them.

God doesn't make mistakes, and He always has room for people like me who has made many mistakes. He will make changes in your life that will last forever. I have done wrong, and I paid for it. I hadn't paid the full price because I know that if I had, I wouldn't be here. I know that God wants me to do a better job in other areas of my life and I'm asking Him to push me more in the direction that I need to go. I want better for myself. I feel the need to do better. I pray that my wife, my children and my birthdays will be a blessing to others. Many of us need God, and we need Him now.

I sent a birthday and Christmas card to my daughter. I also sent my son and his wife a gift card and cash. The kids got Christmas gifts, and I explained to them the greatest gift is God. I had put a Bible inside of the box so my son can read it to his family. This act was the best thing that I had ever done for my family. Sometimes it takes a tract or a bible passage to get inside someone's head to allow God to move in on their lives. He uses us to help stir up the Holy Spirit. I always sent my kids birthday cards and a few dollars. They are always happy about that.

I want to say Happy birthday. I wish all the best for today and in the future. I hope your birthday is just the beginning of a year full of happiness! May all your birthdays be filled with happy memories and wonderful moments. To my wife, I'm grateful for your love and your friendship. I wish you love, hope, everlasting joy, and happiness. Thank you for being my best friend. I am so proud to be your husband. William Barclay quoted that the two greatest days in a person's life is the day we are born and the day we discover why. We all have a purpose in life. God gives us a purpose, and it is our job to walk in it. God gave us the gift of life; it is up to us to be like Jesus. Love everyone, even your enemies. Even if you don't get along with someone and they are mean to you, pray for them that they change their evil ways. It's a struggle to do these things because we are not Jesus Christ and we are not perfect. Conflicts will always come our way. The more we celebrate the birthday of Jesus Christ and praise Him, the more our lives will be celebrated.

The greatest gift that we can give a person is unconditional love and acceptance. Just like on birthdays, cakes and pies are special. Every birthday celebration ends with something sweet, a cake, and people to remember. It's all about the memories. Every year on your birthday, you get a chance to start new. Every birthday and day are a gift and blessing from God. Let us celebrate the occasion with sweet words. Life is all about balance. There are certain times of the year, such as birthdays, anniversaries, and holidays, that are meant to be enjoyed without guilt. Every day is the Lord's day. Go to the source of how we honor and praise God. We worship Him in spirit and truth. I want men to know one thing about women. I can speak of the experience of being married to my wife and witnessing through the years from the old ladies at my church. Anytime women come together with a collective intention, it's a powerful thing. Whether they are in the kitchen preparing a meal, making a quilt, reading a book, or planning a birthday party the blessings of God always show up.

The things that bother me today is the fact that we don't invest enough time or money into our friendships. While expecting to have more friends in the future, it makes no sense to have friendships just based on God alone without going places together and only seeing one another every Sunday at church. I joined the evangelism ministry because we do go out to dinner and for a ball game or two. I believe in fellowship ministry. I can also say that the greatest gifts you can give your children are the roots of responsibility and the wings of independence. To me, a gift consists not in what is done or given, but in the intention of the giver or doer. If you look over the years, the styles, clothes, hair, education, production, songs, and lifestyles have changed. When we wake up every day, it's a new birthday. It's a new chance to be great again and make great decisions.

There is only one thing I wished for during every birthday candle I blown out or every penny I throw over my shoulder in a wishing well: the wisdom of God. The Lord is getting my attention on all sides of my life. Whether it was good or bad, He let me know that it was Him the whole time in control of my life and the lives of my family's lives. I hope that people understand that God is all things. I heard my Bishop say he has grown fond of having respect for bees because they must pollinate. Without them doing their job, the whole ecosystem is thrown out of whack. We won't have any food, and our water systems would be bad as well. He is right because without God we will have no life.

In 2017, my wife's cousin invited my wife and me to their birthday celebration at a well-known country club in upstate New York. We paid for a hotel for this occasion. My wife and I were getting ready for the time of our lives. We got ready to catch the New Jersey Transit. We called the Uber to the hotel and after we had gotten to the New Jersey Transit. It took us 45 minutes from Queens to get to the NJT. I told my wife, "Let's go to the hotel now." We called a car to come to our destination. It only took us 25 minutes to get us there. We checked in and met the family in the lobby before we went upstairs to our room. We bought some food from the cafe and took it up with us. We ate and relaxed until two hours before we had to get ready for the event. It was a black and white birthday affair. I had a black box tie and tuxedo with a white shirt. I had on patent leather black shoes. My wife had a black leather dress with black sparkling shoes and white stockings. One of my wife's family members was assigned to pick us up at 8 o'clock because we didn't know where we were going or all the people that we were going to be around.

We arrived at the event and seated at the assigned table. We started eating snacks: bites of finger foods and pastries. We were there earlier because my wife's cousin had to drop off some food, decorations and finalizing everything. Over the short distance from the hill, I saw an 18-hole golf course, and I knew that we were at an exclusive country club. I talked to one of the managers, and he told me that there had been quite a few celebrities that had been at the country club. I wasn't interested in that. I was feeling the place out. I had never been to this place before.

We were there with all these people, and we were saying hello to people we didn't even know. It was weird. My wife knew the D.J., and she told me that he won many awards for disc jockeying. He was a longtime family friend. We greeted her cousin, the birthday girl. We hugged her and said happy birthday to her. Her cousin was wearing an ice blue evening gown with a long cape connected to it which was the same color as her dress. We sat down to eat the main course. As we were eating, we saw people dancing, drinking champagne, and dancing to old school R&B music.

Then it was time for the birthday girl to come to the middle of the dance floor. She gave presents to all her family members and friends that had birthdays in May. After she gave the gifts, she danced by herself in the middle of the floor while we sang happy birthday to her then her husband joined her and danced. Afterward, everyone else danced the night away. I just wanted to enjoy our time.

I met hundreds of people that night. I can't remember everyone that I met that night except one of my wife's friend's boyfriend. He was so eager to sit and talk with me. We talked all through the event and had good clean fun. Her cousin passed out gifts left and right to people and everyone was so blessed. She was even giving away food and gifts to people who didn't even know her. I was impressed to have seen her do that because most people wouldn't give people all that they had left over but she did. She said that she didn't want to take the food home. It made her day to see people happy. I was impressed because whenever she would have a cookout in the summer, she would try to give us a whole bunch of food to take home. I told my wife that I don't want all that. We ended up taking it anyway. As we were leaving the party, we all pitched into cleaning up and helped the country club staff. We finished cleaning up in an hour. Sometimes you forget how appreciated you are when you lend a helping hand.

CHAPTER 28

Happy New Year

My wife and I worked all day. We couldn't wait to get off work to meet each other. I was at work just thinking about my wife. It was raining practically all day long. I was standing around, and most of the clients were at home that day. We finally got off work and met each other at the grocery store. We were very happy to see each other. We took the groceries home and relaxed until it was time to go to church. I woke my wife at about 9:30 pm on New Year's Eve night. We were tired, but we still went to church.

We called an Uber. My wife and I were standing in the rain for at least 15 minutes waiting on this guy because he was lost. I noticed that he was from another country and I was skeptical because he didn't sound like he knew where he was going. I talked to him on my wife's phone until he found us.

When we finally made it to the church, it was packed, and God was there. It was so spectacular and Holy Spirit was busy that night. I saw a smile on everyone's face. We sang, danced, prayed, and worshipped God. The praise dancers were wearing blue and silver. They danced and praised God through the aisle in front of the pews. Bishop preached about not letting money change you. He shared how Solomon had all the money and was tired of his sin. He realized that he needed God and not his money. He asked God for wisdom. The moral of the story is don't let things get in the way of what God has purposed for you.

No matter what I have, it's all the Lord's. Don't let money rule your purpose in life. God has a purpose for all of us. Be the messenger for God. I was so happy that our evangelism team went to see elderly people. It taught me how to be considerate to people less fortunate. These people could be my grandpa, and it could very well be me in 20 or 30 years. We shake their hands, smile and talk to them. We know the reason for being there, and that is to uplift Jesus Christ's name upon high. This group is awesome, and we took a photo that I will always cherish. We serve God with unshakable power. We serve God with all power in His hands. We serve a God that is the bright and morning star.

THE SEVEN NAMES OF GOD IN CHRISTIANITY:

1. Jehovah Jireh-The Lord will provide (Genesis 22:13-14)
2. Jehovah Rapha-The Lord that healeth (Exodus 15:26)
3. Jehovah Nissi-The Lord our Banner (Exodus 17:8-15)

4. Jehovah Shalom-The Lord our Peace (Judges 6:24)
5. Jehovah Ra-ah -The Lord is the way
6. My Shepherd (Psalm 23:1).
7. Almighty God.

2019 is going to be even better for Christians more than ever. We are going to see a great impact of God. It will never be the same ever again. I will always cherish the Lord because of His conviction in my heart. For that, I will never be the same.

I met my wife in 2013. I had been in New York City a couple of times before I met her but never went to see the ball drop. I came to pick her up, and she had to put layers of clothes on because it was very cold out. I kept telling her, "Let's stay warm and keep walking." We walked ten blocks to get as close as we could to see the ball drop. Finally, we got as close as we could to see the ball drop on 45th St. We passed five metal detectors before we got there. I was so happy to be down there for the first time in my life with my wife. We were tired of being down there because we had nowhere to sit. We were standing up for three hours. It was about 11:30 p.m. We were anxious for the ball to drop. We only had a half hour left. Minutes turned into seconds and before we knew it, our screen downtown showed 20 seconds, and everyone was counting "10,9,8,7,6,5,4,3,2,1." "HAPPY NEW YEAR!" Then the Song by Frank Sinatra started. "Start spreading the news. I'm leaving today. I wanted to be apart of NEW YORK, NEW YORK." We kissed the same time the confetti started floating down. I knew that New York was my new home. This is a city that never sleeps. In the middle of the night, you can get a suit, clothing, shoes, food, ice cream cone, a bag of groceries, and a Bible.

People are envious of someone else's home, car, clothing, husband, and wife. God is going to bless you with whom He has for you and what He has for you. Just wait on the Lord and allow Him to do His work. He does want you to do your part because we all need to work, take care of ourselves, and our families. Just imagine if we did the same things every day constantly. We all would be bored. I know that God has great things for us. He has shown me things I would never ever imagine. If anyone would have told me that I would be living the rest of my life in New York City, I would have told you that you're crazy. If anyone would have told me that I would be attending New York Seminary, I would have told you that I wasn't qualified. I realized today that God qualifies you. I know that if I weren't at the right place, at the right time where that preacher saw me with my brother just high as a kite, eating at a soup kitchen, I would never be a minister. God is always changing us for His greater good, not for our greater good and what we can get from him. We are not to become profits, but prophets, bishops, and ministers of the gospel. We are the messengers for God. We can spread the word to believers and non-believers of how great our God is and how he can become your Saviour. Give your life to Jesus Christ and get Baptized in the holy water. You will be washed clean.

Pray without ceasing and give your life totally back to Him. I'm close to my entire family. To my church family, I want to say thank you for accepting me into your lives because I know it's God when you allow someone new to come on the scene and be a part of God's plan. I was welcomed with open arms. Thank you, Lord, for putting me in the right church at the right time because you truly have restored my life completely. I may not have all that I need. But the truth is I have all I want, and that is God the Father, Jesus Christ the Son of Man, and Holy Ghost, along with my blessed family. No more womanizing. No more cheating on anything at all. No more fighting. I will fight you with God's word. I have learned that is so powerful. I love people including my enemies. I will encourage you to love your enemies.

Conclusion

This book is for people who need help finding their purpose in life. You have read about my life and the struggles I have been through from childhood to an adult: the good, bad, and ugly. I hope this book blessed your life. I have given you some real-life experiences. The most important message is to give your life to Jesus Christ and get baptized. I once heard someone say that every time, he looked out the window, he saw people walking and that is the reason he became a minister. He said many people are lost and dying in the world. People need to be ministered to. Ministers need to be the example of Jesus Christ so people can see Jesus Christ in us. We need to stop judging folks because we are in the position to judge. Just meet the people right where they are at. Don't allow others to validate you. Allow the validation of God's word to show others how it is supposed to be done by living the word of God. The Lord will vindicate you when you feel like others have done you wrong. When we make mistakes, let's learn from all our mistakes and problems. I don't care who you are and where you are from, none of us are perfect. We all need to be retrained in some capacity. Many people are running from the church today because of how we act as Christians. All of us can do better in church, homes, work, and many other places. God is on your side and He loves you. He will bless you from the four corners of the earth. He wants you to give your entire life to him. He is a jealous God.

Some of us have been in the ministry for days, months, and years. Some have backslid, while some people are sitting in the pews every Sunday not reading or learning anything about God. Some people want to be in the way and have no reason for being there except for causing trouble. I attend church because I know that my God is real. My Jesus heals, saves, blesses, and delivers. He is a doctor and lawyer. He blesses my wife and me daily. He got me my job, my cat Syrus, my home, my family, and friends. He has done things for me that is just speechless.

Words can't explain how He blessed my life. When He blesses me, it's a shock because it comes so naturally. I got some paperwork reinstated that I prayed for a long time. Blessings were coming back to back. God does answer prayers. Can I tell you something? God had answered all my prayers even when it in times where I had doubt. Suddenly, tears were rolling down my face. Whatever you ask for in the name of Jesus, He will bless us in ways that will blow your mind. I learned how not to be impatient. I'm still learning about God, and I will forever be a son of God. "Abba Father, let your will be done in my life for the rest of my life." God is not finished with me. I'm still on a long journey. I'm still attending seminary, and I plan on going all the way to finish my Masters to Doctorate degrees. These scriptures are how I feel today.

THE GREAT COMMISSION

Now the eleven disciples went to Galilee, to the mountain to which Jesus had directed them. And when they saw him, they worshiped him, but some doubted. And Jesus came and said to them, all authority in heaven and on earth has been given to me. Go therefore and make disciples of all nations, baptizing them in the name of the father and of the son and of the holy spirit, teaching them to obey everything I have commanded you and surely I am with you always, to the very end of the age (Matthew 28:16-20).

God bless the readers. I hope this has been a blessing to you. This book can be read for all ages. Amen.

About the Author

Minister Jerome Meriweather was born in Evansville, Indiana on December 28, 1967, to Rev. Judge and Anna Louise (Slaughter) Meriweather. He has five brothers: Tim, Greg, Gary, Robert, and Judge Jr. He has four sisters: Doris (Deceased), Kathy, Geraldine, and Christine. He graduated High School in 1986. In 2009, he was a graduate of David Wilkerson Ministries in Southern California.

Minister Jerome Meriweather is an author, coach, and a clergyman of the Queens Federation of Churches. He is happily married to Ramona. He has two children and three grandchildren. He was player thirty-two and inducted into the EBB Hall of Fame as well as the Greater Evansville Basketball Hall of Fame on August 11, 2018. He's a minister at NJWC and presently attending NYTS and currently living in New York City.

Index

A

accident, 21, 23, 307
acupuncture, 303
addict, 89
addictions, 65, 285
Adolescence, 15
Adulthood, 42
Africa, 150, 407
airport, 174, 326
angels, 333, 436–37
anger, 286, 390
animals, 39–40, 437
anointing, 81, 361, 379
Arizona, 196, 203–4, 293
Atlanta ministry, 235
attractions, 312

B

Bahamas, 317, 325–26
basketball, 35, 38, 46, 373–74, 378
beach, 177–78, 312–13, 325
believers, 408, 467
Bethlehem, 435–37
bible, 41, 65, 86, 130, 264, 287, 299, 436, 467
Bible College, 169, 183
birthday party, 460
birthdays, 53, 72, 453, 460, 463
birth defects, 331
bishops, 218, 287, 363, 377, 414, 434, 465, 467
bless, 58, 82–83, 110, 148, 360–61, 394, 398–99, 416, 424, 427–28, 434, 454, 456, 467, 470
blood, 24, 424
breakfast, 57, 116, 135, 153–54, 161, 176, 185, 191, 204, 217, 239, 264, 319, 323, 325
bride, 315
buildings, 416, 419, 424–25, 427
bus, 4, 118, 121–23, 140, 188, 193, 404
business, 18, 63, 127–28, 169, 246, 380
bus station, 121, 174, 188, 233

C

California, 184, 195, 201–4, 349
Camp Pendleton, 207
Catholic churches, 250, 383, 454
ceremony, 134, 226

cheating, 74, 250
Christians, 95, 97, 162, 206, 223, 268, 332, 413, 466, 470
Christmas, 53, 132, 433, 435, 440, 445
church, 1–3, 61, 114–15, 239, 288–89, 297, 309, 314, 330, 336, 408, 411, 415, 445–46, 453
churches, 75–76, 138–40, 175, 206, 246, 258, 268, 287–88, 307, 313–16, 333, 362–63, 365, 413, 451–52
church functions, 434
city, 6, 78, 125, 185, 320, 336, 354, 356
classes, 47, 54, 179, 201, 213, 283, 291, 403, 408, 417–18, 427, 429
club, 52, 90, 357
coach, 33, 50, 53, 375, 378, 382–83, 472
college, 37, 49–52, 59–60, 143, 149, 308, 376, 383, 413
commandment, 268
confirmation, 428
crosses, 126, 175–76, 246, 268, 276
cruises, 317–18, 322–23, 354
curse, 102, 279, 415

D

darkness, 145, 287
daughter, 103, 106–7, 338, 348, 394
death, 77, 210, 307, 364
demons, 159, 274
destination, 158, 285, 317, 319
devices, 323, 424
disciples, 232, 259, 471
doctor appointments, 331

donations, 126, 148, 246, 313
dreams, 7, 41, 285
drinking, 55, 83, 90, 287
drugs, 49, 51–52, 74, 167, 179, 269, 414, 450
DUI, 101

E

education, 35, 49, 51, 252, 308, 366, 403, 441, 461
enemies, 104, 274, 332, 399, 422, 460
engagements, 354
evangelize, 336
Evansville, 2, 5, 11, 20, 40, 44, 50, 52, 60, 74, 77, 99, 188–89, 262, 267

F

facilities, 22, 64, 158
faithfulness, 390
farm, 39–41
father, 1, 3–4, 12, 21, 28, 36, 39, 67, 71–72, 76, 299–300, 305, 345, 348, 382
fellowship, 314, 440
flight, 313, 317, 325–26
Florida, 169–70, 173–74, 189, 312, 322, 354, 453
foreign relations, 254
forgiveness, 97, 257
freedom, 284, 355
fundraising, 210–11, 217
funerals, 96–97

G

gifts, 29, 68, 81, 83, 227, 361, 379, 404, 439, 448, 460–61, 463

girlfriend, 9, 47, 50–52, 54, 56, 73–74, 143, 145, 286, 292, 296, 312, 315

glory, 332, 364–65, 456

God, 26–33, 76–92, 214–25, 239–43, 252–60, 289–93, 295–301, 304–8, 329–39, 389–98, 401–6, 408–15, 431–36, 454–61, 465–71

gold, 205, 348, 350, 365, 417

graduation, 134, 149, 152, 213, 217

grass, 126, 128, 154

groceries, 318, 448, 464, 467

H

heal, 111, 210, 285–86, 392

healing process, 331

health, 91, 254, 330–31, 361, 397

heart, 23, 44, 98, 140, 190, 346, 373, 446

heart disease, 269

home, 27, 42, 45, 47, 51–54, 56, 59, 154–55, 210–11, 326–27, 329, 332, 394–95, 448, 464

homelessness, 250

hometown, 353, 436

honeymoon, 314, 317–18, 325

hospitals, 25, 28

hotel, 313, 320, 325, 461

house, 7, 9, 16–17, 38, 40, 125, 127–28, 154, 158, 251, 254, 256, 351, 354, 451

Houston, 209, 271–73, 275, 279

I

interview, 163, 168

J

Jacksonville, 172, 174, 177, 180, 184, 186–87, 198
Jesus, 6–7, 97, 164, 253, 258, 294, 396, 435–39, 460, 471
Jesus Christ Atlanta Ministries, 245
Jesus Christ Ministries Arizona, 204
Jesus Christ Ministries/Atlanta, 231
Jesus Christ Ministries/California, 191
Jesus Christ Ministries/Dallas, 261
Jesus Christ Ministries/Houston, 271
Jesus Christ Ministries/Missouri, 132
Jesus Christ Ministries/New York City, 245
Jesus Christ Ministries/Ohio, 120
jokes, 36, 353
journey, 18, 121, 129, 299, 336
joy, 27, 354, 455
jumping, 323

K

Kentucky, 13, 18, 39
kindness, 204, 286

Kingdom, 327, 335
knees, 147, 265, 449
knowledge, 80, 210, 330, 402, 412, 429, 458

L

liars, 181, 414
life skills, 285
liver damage, 269
lobby, 462
Lord, 126, 167, 181, 188, 220, 225, 235, 256, 282, 284, 326, 350, 361, 375, 390
love, 11–12, 23, 28–30, 112, 116, 171, 173, 286, 346, 349, 351, 353–54, 393, 396, 398
loving, 30, 341
luxury, 3

M

Manhattan, 250, 277, 281
manipulation, 333
marriage, 299, 411
mentors, 50, 173
mercy, 23, 379
mess, 208, 457
messengers, 246, 467
Miami, 312–13, 317, 319, 325–26, 453
Minister, 1–2, 21, 63–65, 149–51, 189–91, 217–19, 223, 261, 287, 297, 305–7, 441–43, 453–55, 467, 469
ministry classes, 163, 166

Missouri, 133–34, 136, 248
money, 42, 49, 72, 90, 109, 185, 215, 243, 254, 277, 279, 380, 406, 440, 444
    mother, 6, 28, 75–76, 92, 94, 351, 435, 453–54
    murderers, 181, 414

N

newspapers, 17–18, 330
non-believers, 408, 467
nursing homes, 126

O

offerings, 243, 363
Ohio, 134
Ohio River, 161
Oklahoma, 184
opposition, 266, 336
organization, 215
orientation, 110

P

parents, 1–2, 15, 38, 41, 45, 51–52, 75, 97, 101, 248, 333, 341, 384, 392, 394
    party, 34, 47–48, 50, 108, 200, 452, 463
    pastors, 82, 203, 206, 218, 223, 287, 297, 377, 414, 440, 454
    peace, 204, 287, 409
    persecutions, 26

perseverance, 26
person, 27, 220, 252, 307, 320, 346, 363, 382, 398, 408, 458
personal problems, 173
players, 51, 375, 384
plenty, 215, 320, 330
power, 11, 42, 44, 82, 112, 150, 285, 299, 333–34, 374, 429, 456, 465
pray, 73, 85, 88, 135, 257, 265, 292, 297, 343, 352, 359, 361, 445, 449, 458
prayer life, 359
preach, 82, 206, 336, 361, 366, 395
presence, 86, 410, 444
presentation, 403
price, 40, 48, 359, 384
prisons, 254–55, 411
property, 125, 153, 155, 333
prophets, 414, 467
prosperity, 450
pulpit, 243, 300

Q

quit, 144, 293, 414

R

recovery, 21, 24, 26
regulations, 62, 110
rejoice, 288, 420
relatives, 69, 256

relief, 192, 452
responsibility, 449
road trip, 135
rocket, 212, 378

S

sanctification, 405
scriptures, 127, 130, 223, 266, 274, 361, 436
secrets, 162, 275, 451
semester, 183, 401
seminaries, 410, 412–13
sermon, 306, 402
sex, 32, 65, 109, 113, 250
sex abuse, 287
shelter, 8
shoes, 15, 265, 467
shopping, 251, 325, 448
sinning, 90, 403
sisters, 2, 6, 28, 50, 52, 68, 101, 191, 193, 229, 334, 370, 380, 453–54, 472
sleep, 57, 72, 86, 160, 232–33, 235, 264, 355, 357, 429
staff, 153, 162, 183, 200
stipend, 162, 232, 273
strength, 23, 73, 290, 431
students, 130, 134, 137, 146, 156, 158, 162, 207, 210, 222–23, 226, 265–67, 285, 403, 407
surgery, 303, 326, 329–30
surroundings, 118

T

teachers, 146, 150, 414
Texas, 3, 209, 259, 265, 271, 274, 280
tickets, 212, 327
time, 3–4, 11, 17–18, 30, 34, 73, 100, 139–40, 149–50, 170–71, 177–78, 319–20, 323–26, 345, 351
tribulations, 159
truck, 13, 17–19, 154, 185
trust, 12, 27, 78, 152, 227, 284, 346, 349, 360, 406
truth, 11, 27, 82, 267, 293, 348, 378–79, 382, 384, 408

V

vacations, 109, 254, 313, 322, 324, 355, 455
vehicles, 17, 43, 141, 182, 185
verses, 127
vision, 298, 363, 404, 414
voice, 143, 209, 262, 289, 350, 438

W

walls, 40, 276
water, 185, 205, 238, 251, 291, 312, 320–21
wealth, 254, 385
wedding, 311, 314–15, 318
wife, 248, 314, 316, 319–20, 322, 325–26, 356–57, 360, 388, 391–92, 395, 431–32, 448, 453–54, 460–62
wisdom, 210, 330, 405, 412

word of God, 87, 97, 130, 144, 162, 254, 258, 264, 272, 285, 415

work, 42, 62–63, 90, 103–4, 112–13, 205, 293–94, 326, 330–31, 335, 360, 417–19, 421, 464, 467

work orders, 127, 237–38

world, 70, 210, 215, 223, 228, 254, 286, 299, 332–33, 350, 353, 405, 407, 411, 435–36

worship, 76, 220

CPSIA information can be obtained
at www.ICGtesting.com
Printed in the USA
LVHW081933271219
641843LV00014BA/199/P